STRIKE
FROM THE SEA

The Royal Navy & US Navy at War in the Middle East

STRIKE
FROM THE SEA

The Royal Navy & US Navy at War in the Middle East

IAIN BALLANTYNE

Pen & Sword

For all those who gave their lives...
and the survivors too.

First published in Great Britain in 2004 by
Pen & Sword Maritime
an imprint of
Pen & Sword Books Ltd
47 Church Street
Barnsley
South Yorkshire
S70 2AS

ISBN 1-84415-059-3

A CIP catalogue record for this book is
available from the British Library

Printed and bound in Singapore by
Kyodo Printing Co (Singapore) Pte Ltd

For a complete list of Pen & Sword titles please contact
PEN & SWORD BOOKS LIMITED
47 Church Street, Barnsley, South Yorkshire, S70 2AS, England
E-mail: enquiries@pen-and-sword.co.uk
Website: www.pen-and-sword.co.uk

CONTENTS

GLOSSARY

AA - Anti-Aircraft

ADAWS - Action Data Automation Weapon System

AEW - Airborne Early Warning

AMRAAM - Advanced Medium Range Anti-Air Missile

ARG - Amphibious Ready Group

ASM - Anti-Shipping Missile

ASRM - Assault Squadron Royal Marines

ASW - Anti-Submarine Warfare

ATF - Amphibious Task Force

AWAC - Airborne Warning and Control

BBC - British Broadcasting Corporation

BP - British Petroleum

BW - Biological Weapons

CAG - Carrier Air Group

CBG - Carrier Battle Group

Cdo - Commando (equivalent to an Army infantry battalion)

CENTCOM - Central Command

CIA - Central Intelligence Agency

CIC - Combat Information Center

CIWS - Close-In Weapon System

CNO - Chief of Naval Operations (also Chief Naval Officer)

CO - Commanding Officer

COI - Contact of Interest

COMATG - Commander Amphibious Task Group

COMUKMARFOR - Commander UK Maritime Forces

COMUKTG - Commander UK Task Group

COSAG - Combined Steam and Gas

CPO - Chief Petty Officer

CTOL - Conventional Take-Off and Landing

CW - Chemical Weapons

DAL - Defence Analysts Limited

DoD - Department of Defense

ECM - Electronic Counter-Measures

ESM - Electronic Support-Measures

FA2 - Sea Harrier, Fighter-Attack Mk2

FBI - Federal Bureau of Investigation

FOB - Forward Operating Base

FOST - Flag Officer Sea Training

GQ - General Quarters

GR7 - Harrier, Ground-attack Reconnaissance Mk7

GROM - Grupa Reagowania Operacyjno Mobilnego (which can be translated from Polish as Operational Mobile Response Group)

HARM - High-speed Anti-Radiation Missile

HMAS - Her Majesty's Australian Ship

HMNZS - Her Majesty's New Zealand Ship

HMS - Her Majesty's Ship

HQ - Headquarters

ID - Identity

IFF -Identification Friend or Foe

IRA - Irish Republican Army

JAGMAN - Judge Advocate General Manual

JHU - Joint Helicopter Unit

JMC - Joint Maritime Course

LCT - Landing Craft Tank

LST - Landing Ship Tank

MCJO - Maritime Contribution to Joint Operations

MCM - Mine Counter-Measures

MCMV - Mine Counter-Measures Vessel

MEB - Marine Expeditionary Brigade

MEF - Marine Expeditionary Force

MEU - Marine Expeditionary Unit

MIDEASTFOR - Middle East Force

MIF - Multi-national Interception Force (or Maritime Interdiction Force)

MIOPS - Maritime Interdiction Operations

MoD - Ministry of Defence

MP - Member of Parliament

NAS - Naval Air Squadron

NATO - North Atlantic Treaty Organisation

NBC - Nuclear Biological and Chemical

NCO - Non-Commissioned Officer

NGS - Naval Gunfire Support

NORAD - North American Aerospace Defense Command

OVL - Operations in the Vicinity of Libya

PA - Public Address system

PM - Prime Minister

RAF - Royal Air Force

RAN - Royal Australian Navy

RAS - Replenishment at Sea

RDF - Rapid Deployment Force

RFA - Royal Fleet Auxiliary
RM - Royal Marines
RN - Royal Navy
ROE - Rules of Engagement
RPG - Rocket-Propelled Grenade
RPV - Remotely-Piloted Vehicle
SAG - Surface Action Group
SAM - Surface to Air Missile
SBS - Special Boat Service
SDR - Strategic Defence Review
SEALS - Sea Air and Land
SHAR - Sea Harrier
SLOC - Sea Lines of Communication
SNFL (or STANAVFORLANT) - Standing Naval Force Atlantic
SNFM (or STANAVFORMED) - Standing Naval Force Mediterranean
SRBOC - Super-Rapid Blooming Offboard Chaff
TERCOM - Terrain Contour Matching
TLAM - Tomahawk Land Attack Missile
TOC - Tactical Operations Center
TOW -Tube-launched Optically-tracked Wire-guided
TWA - Trans World Airlines
UAE - United Arab Emirates
UK - United Kingdom
UKMCC - United Kingdom Maritime Component Commander
UN - United Nations
UNSCOM - United Nations Special Commission
USA - United States of America
USAF - United States Air Force
USCENTAF - US Central Command Air Force (s)
USMC - United States Marine Corps
USN - United States Navy
USNHC - United States Naval Historical Center
USNS - United States Naval Ship
USS - United States Ship
USSR - Union of Soviet Socialists Republics
VLS - Vertical-Launch Silo
WMD - Weapons of Mass Destruction
WTC - World Trade Center

ACKNOWLEDGEMENTS

Without the generous help of a large number of people it would not have been possible for me to write this book.

Those listed below offered advice and inspiration, allowed me to interview them about their experiences in the Gulf, provided some other form of direct material help or otherwise illuminated my path. I wish to express my wholehearted thanks to all of them and apologize to anyone my roll of honour accidentally overlooks.

When it comes to serving members of the Royal Navy and Royal Marines, I either interviewed them specifically for this book, or for articles that were published in 2003 by *WARSHIPS IFR*, the naval affairs magazine that I edit. I also gained access to the testimony of serving members of the Royal Navy and Royal Marines while writing the script for the Royal Navy internal corporate communications video 'Operation TELIC: Fighting and Winning'. Serving members of the Royal Navy and Royal Marines who contributed via any one of the above means were[1]: Admiral Sir Alan West (Chief of the Naval Staff and First Sea Lord), Admiral Sir Jonathon Band (Commander-in-Chief Fleet), Rear Admiral Adrian Johns (Assistant Chief of the Naval Staff), Rear Admiral James Rapp (Flag Officer Sea Training), Rear Admiral David Snelson (Commander UK Maritime Forces), Major General James Dutton (Commandant General Royal Marines), Commodore Alan Massey, Commodore Jamie Miller, Colonel Mike Ellis, Captain David Lye, Colonel Gordon Messenger, Lieutenant Colonel David Summerfield, Commander Chris Alcock, Surgeon Commander David Campbell, Commander Andrew McKendrick, Commander Jon Pentreath, Commander Iain Richmond, Commander Richard Thomas, Lieutenant Commander James Newton, Lieutenant Commander Andrew Swain, Captain Birty Cross, Captain Dave Abbott, Lieutenant Victoria Arden, Lieutenant Rolf Kurth, Lieutenant Stuart Yates, Chief Petty Officer Ian Calvert, Chief Petty Officer David Randall, Chief Petty Officer Gary Richardson, Chief Petty Officer Kev Shore, Colour Sergeant Nev Nixon, Petty Officer Gary Davies, Leading Chef Savory, Leading Operator Maintainer Clare Farrar.

The incumbent Director of Corporate Communications (Navy), Commodore Tony Rix, helped facilitate access to serving members of the Royal Navy, with his PA, Nikki Lightly, providing me with some invaluable assistance in gaining permission to use quotes taken from the 'Fighting and Winning' video. The indefatigable Des Good, Managing Director of Grosvenor Television, very kindly allowed me to adapt transcripts of interviews filmed for 'Fighting and Winning'. Lorraine Coulton, the Royal Navy's senior press officer in the south-west of England, and her colleague Nikki Dunwell furnished essential access to events, ships and submarines.

Other serving members of the British and American naval forces who took part in the 2003 Iraq War made their contribution either via press releases, published on official web sites or distributed via e-mail, or were quoted in pool copy provided during hostilities. Particularly worthy of note are the contributing writers and photographers of the US fleet's Navy News service and the US DoD's excellent American Forces Press Service. Newspaper pool copy reports on the Iraq War that proved invaluable were taken from the UK's *Daily Mail, Daily Mirror, Daily*

Telegraph, Evening Herald, Plymouth, *The News,* Portsmouth and *The Western Morning News.*

Lucy Halsall, of British Forces Cyprus, covered the British task force's exercises in the eastern Mediterranean and also visited the USS *Theodore Roosevelt,* just prior to hostilities. The material she produced enriched not only the coverage provided by *WARSHIPS IFR,* but also this book.

When it came to those conflicts and crises that pre-dated the Iraq War, in addition to drawing on my own interviews with participants at the time, between 1990 and 2002, I was able to consult (and often quote) a number of friends and acquaintances, some of whom I first encountered in my earlier life, as a newspaper reporter. A number of them have since contributed to *WARSHIPS IFR* magazine or my previous books.

Captain Chris Craig RN (Retd), who commanded the British naval task group in the 1991 Gulf War as a temporary Commodore, selflessly gave his time, recollections and reflections, as did Captain Doug Littlejohns RN (Retd), Commander 'Sharkey' MacCartan-Ward RN (Retd) and Commodore Toby Elliott RN (Retd). Captains Craig and Littlejohns, together with Commodore Elliott, very kindly allowed me to use images from their excellent private photographic collections.

Similarly, on the other side the Atlantic, Keith Jacobs USN (Retd) and Commander Mike Scherr USN (Retd), also earned my gratitude for their invaluable contributions.

One must not forget Dr Jeremy Stocker who was, in a previous incarnation, a warfare officer in a Gulf patrol warship.

Other friends and colleagues on both sides of the Atlantic who deserve a mention for contributions great and small are: Mike Barlow, Bob Drayton, Derek Fox, Neil Hall, Mrityunjoy Mazumdar, Charles Strathdee, Guy Toremans and Anthony Tucker-Jones.

Important contributions have come from a loyal band of photographers: Nigel Andrews, Ray Bean, Tony Carney, Jonathan Eastland and Mike Welsford. Nigel, Tony and Jonathan have, over the years, accompanied me on various trips to cover naval activities in the Middle East.

My priceless mentors in all matters naval, including the US Navy and Royal Navy in the Gulf post-Second World War, have been Peter Hore - a former Head of Defence Studies in the Royal Navy - and Syd Goodman, who not only opened up his private archives but also willingly gave images from his renowned Goodman Collection.

Pen & Sword Books publishing manager Henry Wilson, who suggested writing this book within days of Baghdad falling, deserves special tribute for patience and understanding.

Last, but by no means least, thanks are due to my good friend and stalwart Dennis Andrews, who not only helped with research and proofread some of the early draughts of various chapters, but also created two excellent maps.

NOTES
1) Ranks used in the main body text of the book may differ from those listed here. The former are those held at the time of the 2003 Iraq War, or during earlier events, rather than the ranks held at the time of writing or at the conclusion of a contributor's military career.

INTRODUCTION

In addition to providing a chronicle, and allowing those who were there to speak, this book seeks to explain in simple terms the reasons behind the deployment of British and American navies 'East of Suez' in the post-Second World War period.

It is a broad canvas, and it will be clear that naval forces - aircraft carriers in particular - have been decisive throughout the decades, especially as the Gulf region is often politically, and frequently culturally, hostile to the presence of large numbers of Western troops on the ground.

The British and American fleets have been at the forefront of upholding the rule of international law with respect to Weapons of Mass Destruction programmes, in the vanguard of liberating two oppressed nations from a brutal dictatorship (Kuwait and Iraq) as well as leading the way in safeguarding the flow of vital oil supplies to the world economy, when threatened by the Ayatollahs in the 1980s and Saddam Hussein between 1990 and 2003. The roots of the Iraq War, the Gulf War and the Tanker War reach back to the confrontations between the Anglo-American axis and other strongmen of the Middle East - Iran's Mossadegh, Egypt's Nasser, Iraq's Qasim and Libya's Gaddafi - who quite rightly sought freedom from Western interference, but too often miscalculated and, with the exception of Mossadegh, chose to pursue their aims via terrorism and the bullying of brother Arab states. They have been included here because they were the precursors of Saddam and also Osama bin Laden. Like some of the men who inspired them, the Iraqi dictator and the Al-Qaeda leader sent their agents of destruction to strike on the high seas, with British and American fleets often in the firing line.

Aside from being an investigation of the roots of conflict, this book also represents the culmination of a personal odyssey.

As a journalist working for an evening newspaper and, lately, as the editor of an international naval affairs magazine, a good deal of my time since the summer of 1990 has been spent writing about the confrontation between the West and Iraq.

The carrier USS Dwight D. Eisenhower (background) and frigate HMS Cumberland in the northern Gulf, late 1990s. US Navy.

Material for this book has therefore been gathered aboard a US Navy super-carrier off Libya...during the UN sea embargo on Iraq in the autumn of 1990...in warships during the Royal Navy's final combat exercises at sea prior to hostilities in early 1991 ...in the minefields off Kuwait at the end of the conflict... aboard a British carrier waging the forgotten war of enforcing a No Fly Zone over southern Iraq in 1999 ...in Oman, in 2001, as cruise missiles winged their way to destroy terrorist training camps in Afghanistan. Although I make no pretence of ever having been a war correspondent, in 1991 I did at least see the evil of which Saddam's regime was capable, during short periods ashore in the immediate aftermath of his army being ejected from Kuwait. Entering war-torn Kuwait was a profoundly disturbing experience, as I witnessed widespread destruction and the remains of some of its victims first hand. Returning to Kuwait just over a year later, and mingling with the ghosts of Saddam's slaughtered army in the desert, while the Beast of Baghdad continued his reign of terror (and pursuit of Weapons of Mass Destruction) just across the border, was equally character forming. Heavy work commitments in the UK relegated me to watching the Iraq War of 2003 unfold live on television; in itself profoundly disturbing. Often, despite being 4,000 miles away, I knew more about what was happening in the war than the marines and sailors actually doing the fighting.

In the aftermath of the conflict, I was privileged enough to fly aboard HMS *Ocean*, which I had previously visited the day before she left for war, as the

With the Coalition campaign to destroy the Saddam regime underway, the guided-missile cruiser USS Cape St. George, in the eastern Mediterranean, launches a Tomahawk Land Attack Missile (TLAM) against a target deep in Iraq. US Navy.

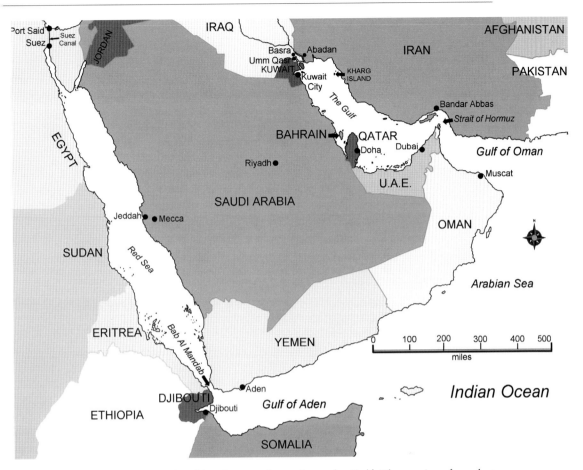

helicopter carrier completed her journey home from the Gulf. The stories of combat that I heard were astonishing, not least because the ship suffered only one death in action. A visit to the nuclear-powered attack submarine HMS *Turbulent* allowed me to gain an equally fascinating insight into how she fought her war.

Working as scriptwriter for two videos on the Iraq War, for the Royal Navy and Royal Marines, has given me further insight into what really happened and how the participants felt. One thing that comes through is that the much-vaunted special relationship between the USA and Britain endures, and often finds its finest expression in the tight working partnership under fire between the US Navy and Royal Navy (despite some sticky moments). Colleagues in the USA generously helped me stitch together the story of the American fleet 'East of Suez', but the US Navy itself has developed an awesome publicity machine - via the power of the World Wide Web - that allowed me to keep track of the Iraq War as it developed, on a day-by-day basis, while also furnishing access to analysis of past and present events.

Those who assisted me, both in the UK and the USA, on this journey receive their proper thanks in the acknowledgements. While this book may be unique, at the time of writing, in examining the history of conflict in the Gulf from the point of view of

13

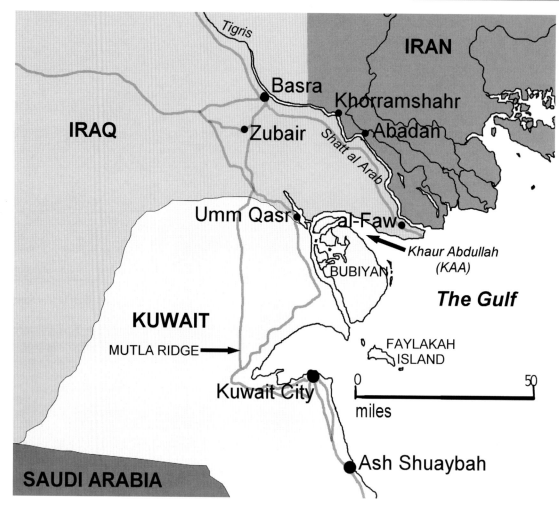

two navies, it will not be the last, as the story of the British and American fleets in the region is still being written. It is to be hoped that readers will, at the very least, go away impressed by the endurance and bravery of the Royal Navy and US Navy between the late 1940s and 2003.

PROLOGUE

IF NOT GADDAFI, THEN WHO?

Aboard the 'Mighty Ike'...Somewhere off Libya, May 1990.

Two hours flying time to the east of Sicily, the 95,413 tons nuclear-powered aircraft carrier USS *Dwight D. Eisenhower* turned into the wind for her next launch cycle. The horizon appeared to shift rather than the ship - the world revolving on the axis of the *Eisenhower*'s five-acre flight deck.

On the catapults, Tomcats and Hornets crouched low to the deck, suddenly exploding in flame and fury, as they launched into an azure sky above a twinkling Mediterranean Sea. Waves of heat rippled off blast deflectors, sucking the air out of the lungs of the flight deck crew who had prepared the aircraft for their missions. The flight deck appeared to be swirling chaos, as jet after jet was brought forward for launch, or moved around to be fuelled and armed, each one narrowly missing the other. In fact, it was all as carefully choreographed as any ballet, for, in the high

The carrier USS Dwight D. Eisenhower *makes an impressive sight at high speed in the Mediterranean, summer 1990.* US Navy.

An F-18 Hornet strike-fighter is shepherded by flight deck crew aboard the USS Dwight D. Eisenhower, as she steams off Libya in the summer of 1990. Iain Ballantyne.

pressure environment of an aircraft carrier during flying operations, even the slightest error could result in death for the worker bees crawling over and under the aircraft; being sucked into jet air intakes; decapitated by aircraft propellers or helicopter rotor blades; blasted overboard by a roaring engine; fried alive by an afterburner; or even sliced in two by a snapping cable. The crash, bang, wallop of the jets slamming back onto deck as they returned signalled maximum stress for the arrester wires. Every landing was a perfectly controlled crash, tailhooks snaring the third of four wires stretched across the back of the flight deck. Each jet piled on power the moment its wheels touched the deck, just in case the wire had not hooked and it needed to go around again.

High above the thunder of the flight deck, looking on from his captain's chair on the bridge of the carrier, sat Captain 'J.J.' Dantone, a veteran of combat missions over Vietnam more than twenty years earlier, who was also a hardened Cold War warrior. 'There is no way you could ever describe the Ike as a nimble thing,' he observed, with evident pride in the sheer awe his ship's physical presence inspired.

> *But, even when we're doing our top speed of 30 knots we can usually bring her to a halt in 4,000 yards.* [1]

The biggest warships ever built, the Nimitz class vessels, of which the *Eisenhower* was the second to be commissioned in 1977, were the symbol of a superpower's recovery following the demoralizing experience of the war in Vietnam. Capable of carrying around eighty aircraft, the Nimitz class has remained to this day the spearhead of American power, the USA's 'Big Stick' with which to threaten potential enemies with a dreadful punishment.

The *Eisenhower's* position off Libya in May 1990 was no accident, for the Mediterranean-based 6th Fleet carrier was keeping an eye on a rogue state that was an acknowledged sponsor of global terrorism. In 1986, Libya had suffered the pain of being struck with the USA's 'Big Stick' when a series of air raids were launched in response to terrorist acts thought to have been helped by, if not all carried out by, her agents. Among the outrages that had increased tension was the hijacking of a TWA airliner and attacks at Rome and Vienna airports. Back in the 1980s there was also the freedom of the seas to be enforced. The Libyans had claimed the Gulf of Sidra was their domain alone, despite the fact that the US Navy regularly deployed its forces there for exercises. The Libyans' illegal extension of territorial waters beyond the twelve-mile limit had been emboldened by the apparent ease with which they had 'chased' the Royal Navy from the Mediterranean. In the spring of 1979, Libyan dictator Moammar Gaddafi had attended the ceremony to mark the final withdrawal of the Royal Navy from Malta, hailing it as a triumph over Western imperialism. To Gaddafi, the Americans seemed equally timid. But, while the Carter administration had backed down in the face of Libyan hubris, cancelling the US Navy's 1980 exercise in the Gulf of Sidra, in 1981 the new Republican President Ronald Reagan was having none of that. The resurgent, no-nonsense stance of the American navy off Libya was a sign of how it would respond to other aggressions in the Middle East.

On 19 August F-14 Tomcat fighters launched by the USS *Nimitz* shot down two Libyan SU-22 Fitter fighters some sixty miles from the North African coast, when it appeared they were intent on contesting the US Navy's right to be in international waters. The Libyan jets had made a head-on pass, firing missiles that missed - but the aim of the F-14s' Sidewinders was true. Tension remained high over the next five years and the Libyans dared anyone to cross their so-called 'Line of Death' into the Gulf of Sidra, all the while seeking to erode the American will to confront them by other means.

Violence was still thriving, but under other names - low-intensity conflict, undeclared war, unconventional warfare, war without fronts...[2]

In addition to sponsoring terrorist attacks, in 1984 the Libyans were suspected of sowing chaos in shipping lanes. The US Navy and Royal Navy led a mine sweeping effort in the Red Sea, prompted by the discovery of mines that were probably laid by a Libyan merchant ship seen acting suspiciously in the area. The British recovered a mine that was of Soviet-origin and had been manufactured no later than 1981. [3]

At the beginning of 1986 the US Navy initiated a series of moves called Operations in the Vicinity of Libya (OVL), that were ultimately to involve three carriers - the USS *Coral Sea*, USS *Saratoga* and USS *America* - and evolve into a series of skirmishes. On 24 March 1986, missiles were fired at 6th Fleet aircraft that had entered airspace above the Gulf of Sidra, but none found their target. The Surface-to-Air Missile (SAM) site that had launched the missiles was later destroyed by air strikes carried out by US Navy A-6 Intruder bombers. The next Libyan move was to send out Mig-25 Foxbats to make provocative passes over US Navy warships, and these aircraft were chased off. The cruiser USS *Ticonderoga* had crossed the 'Line of Death' around noon the same day and the 6th Fleet's Commanding Officer, Vice Admiral Frank B. Kelso, decided that any air or naval units that departed Libya and headed towards his ships or aircraft would be considered hostile and attacked.[4] An Intruder used Harpoon missiles to destroy a Libyan patrol boat when it appeared to be making an attack run. The Libyans next sent a Nanuchka missile craft out, but it retreated, heavily damaged by a cluster bomb from an Intruder. On the morning of 25 March another Libyan Nanuchka made an aggressive run towards US warships in international waters and was sunk by a couple of A-6s employing Harpoon missiles and cluster bombs. Satisfied that the limits of its territorial waters had been demonstrated to Libya, the 6th Fleet backed off on 27 March.

However, on 3 April four American civilians were killed when a bomb exploded on a TWA airliner. Two days later a blast in a West Berlin disco killed one US serviceman and a German woman, with another seventy-three US services personnel among more than 200 injured. The Libyans, who had openly rejoiced in the results of the 3 April attack, were suspected of both bombings.

The American response was OVL-V, also known as Operation El Dorado Canyon. Launched on 15 April, US Air Force F-111 bombers flew from British airbases, joining carrier-borne aircraft in attacking targets in and around Benghazi and Tripoli. At least 100 Libyans were killed and also some foreign nationals, thanks to munitions going astray and hitting embassies in the diplomatic quarter of Tripoli. The Libyan dictator was almost killed when an American bomb landed outside his residence and thereafter he became more circumspect about his links to terrorist activities. In 1990, though Libya was suspected of being behind the Pan Am Flight 103 bombing of late 1988, nothing could be proved, so, although the *Dwight D. Eisenhower* loitered off the Gulf of Sidra with plenty of deadly intent, her jets carried practice bombs, not the real thing. Their destination was the island of Sardinia, to sharpen their skills on a NATO bombing range as part of Exercise Dragon Hammer '90.

The Berlin Wall had fallen six months earlier and, in the upper levels of the military in the various nations that made up the defence alliance, there was a growing realization that, without the old enemy, a new one would have to be found. But, who? Global terrorism, as represented by Gaddafi, posed a serious threat, but it was disparate and nebulous. The strike on Libya had been an effective, if ultimately temporary, deterrent to many terror groups wishing to strike America and its friends.

America's navy was alone in its muscular approach, as had been proved during the raids on Libya and its aggressive stance in the Gulf, where Iran was regarded as the main threat to security. While intervention was seen as working in the Gulf and in the case of Libya, the US Marines had come off badly during their peacekeeping mission to the Lebanon in the early 1980s. A suicide attack by an Islamic fanatic, driving a truck containing around 2,000lbs of explosives into the main US military barracks in Beirut, killed 220 marines.

The venerable assault ship HMS Intrepid in Augusta Bay, May 1990. Iain Ballantyne.

It was the harbinger of a new warfare that would reap its bitter harvest in New York and Washington DC nearly two decades later. With that new asymmetric danger yet to crystalize into something that was a direct threat, grand exercises held on a regional basis certainly kept everyone sharp for conventional warfare, whomever that might be against. Dragon Hammer '90 brought together the armed forces of NATO's southern sector, plus a few with a special interest in the Mediterranean. The main event of the exercise was a massive 'invasion' of Sardinia, which was representing the threatening homeland of a putative foe. Fifty naval vessels and in excess of 30,000 soldiers, sailors and airmen were involved.

Dragon Hammer had been held annually since 1987, with a thinly disguised scenario involving Soviet-led aggression previously providing the training framework. But in 1990, the action was 'unscripted' to allow a wider variety of training routines, reflecting the uncertainty about exactly who the NATO forces might be fighting. In Augusta Bay, Sicily, the veteran British assault ship HMS *Intrepid* prepared to make her way north for the 'invasion'. She was at anchor alongside several other amphibious ships from the NATO nations, including the American assault carrier USS *Saipan*.

The *Intrepid* was on her last legs and the Royal Marines that she traditionally carried into action were unsure of what their future was after her decommissioning in a few months' time. This might seem a surprising notion in the early years of the twenty-first century, with the Royal Navy's primary mission being expeditionary warfare that revolves in large part around putting the Royal Marines ashore to fight. But, back at the end of the Cold War, the Falklands conflict of 1982, in which *Intrepid* and sister ship *Fearless* had been so vital as launch platforms for the Royal Marines and British Army in their victorious campaign to evict Argentinian occupiers, was seen as a one-off. It was regarded as a mere diversion from the real business of confronting the Warsaw Pact in central Europe. In that scenario the Royal Marines had a subsidiary role as infantry on NATO's exposed Norwegian northern flank, and the likelihood of any true amphibious warfare was slim, if not non-existent.

With Russia and Eastern Europe imploding, even that role was disappearing, to be replaced by deep uncertainty. It was already clear by the early summer of 1990 that the British government was eager to cash in a 'peace-dividend' and discard ships, aircraft, tanks and even whole military units that it felt UK Plc no longer needed. Consequently, a review of defence spending priorities had been launched. 'It is expensive for Britain to maintain its amphibious capability, but that is a political decision,' observed the Commanding Officer of 40 Commando, Colonel Adrian Wray, who was embarked with his marines in HMS *Intrepid*.

> *The Royal Marines cannot conduct amphibious operations without assault ships like HMS* Intrepid, *that is for certain.*[5]

There were rumours that the Royal Navy might give up the Royal Marines to the Army, which would merge them with its paratroopers. With thirty years on the clock, it was increasingly expensive to keep *Intrepid* and *Fearless* going. The latter was just nearing the end of an expensive refit at Devonport Dockyard, in Plymouth, and *Intrepid* was set to go into mothballs. One new British amphibious ship present off Sicily was the Royal Fleet Auxiliary *Sir Galahad*, a Landing Ship Logistics built in the late 1980s to replace a predecessor that had been destroyed by Argentinian bombs. There was a requirement for a helicopter carrier to be built as the flagship of future amphibious task groups, but this looked unlikely to be fulfilled.

In the meantime the creaky, old, steam-powered *Intrepid* soldiered on and, as she

A Royal Marine sniper waits to go ashore during a mock invasion of a Sardinian beach, during Dragon Hammer '90. Iain Ballantyne.

prepared to conduct her assault on Sardinia's beaches, the ship's Commanding Officer, Captain Richard Bridges, reflected on the uncertain world the fall of the Berlin Wall had created:

> *The huge tank battle on the German plain that everyone has been preparing for is less likely to happen now. But there could be trouble in other parts of the world. Amphibious forces can be used for letting someone know your intentions without giving ground. They can drop anchor in international waters, sending a signal to a potential aggressor, which can have the desired effect without a shot being fired. The meaning of such a military signal is obvious - provided the political will to back it up is there.*[6]

In fact, trouble was to erupt little more than two months later, with a chain of events that would lead to massive tank battles after all, not in Germany, but rather in the deserts of Kuwait and southern Iraq. It would be a severe test of political will and both the Royal Navy and US Navy would be the primary instruments of power used by political masters to signal intent.

Aboard the *Eisenhower*, the commander of the US Navy's 6th Fleet, Rear Admiral Thomas Lynch, had recognized that the new threat would come from the south. He noted:

> *While tension may have dropped off in Europe, there are still dangers in this part of the world.*[7]

In the early hours of 2 August, three divisions of Iraqi dictator Saddam Hussein's Republican Guard swept into the sheikhdom of Kuwait, easily overcoming its armed forces and appeared to threaten an invasion of Saudi Arabia. The *Eisenhower* was in the vanguard of America's response to this aggression, as she was soon steaming towards Egypt, to make a passage through the Suez Canal. The older, conventionally-powered carrier, USS *Independence*, was carving her way across the Indian Ocean, while already in the Gulf was the US Navy's Middle East Task Force of around half-a-dozen warships and the command and control vessel USS *La Salle*. The Royal Navy Type 42 air-defence destroyer HMS *York* was in the Gulf, while the Broadsword class frigate HMS *Battleaxe* and Leander class frigate HMS *Jupiter* were both on stand-down from the Gulf, the former at Singapore while the latter was at Mombasa. Under the guise of the Armilla Patrol, which had been established a decade earlier to safeguard UK merchant ships against aggression from both Iran and Iraq during their disastrous war, the Royal Navy still managed to exert a presence 'East of Suez'. Although in 1990 the British fleet was very much the junior partner of the US Navy, the last time Iraq had made moves to occupy Kuwait, in 1961, it had been the White Ensign that reigned supreme over the Gulf.

However, that crisis itself had been shaped by a confrontation that found the Royal Navy and the US Navy eyeball-to-eyeball with each other in the eastern Mediterranean, rather than shoulder-to-shoulder in the face of adversity. At the heart of the crisis that split the two allies was the canal that enabled the *Eisenhower* to be among the first naval units to apply pressure to Saddam in August 1990.

CHAPTER ONE

...THE HARDER THEY FALL

In the winter of 1956, as the Suez Crisis reached its peak, the US Navy and Royal Navy found themselves engaged in a dangerous game of chicken. British and American warships came close to colliding as they jostled for space, while US Navy helicopters carried out dangerous acts of provocation, including hovering over the flight deck of the carrier HMS *Eagle*. A sailor in a nearby Royal Fleet Auxiliary ship, who had looked on in astonishment, later remarked:

> I watched signal lamps flashing at it but it did not move away until a petty officer rushed to a multiple Bofors gun and swung the barrels directly on to the helicopter which was only a few feet above it...[1]

The American helicopter backed off but the same RFA sailor later saw a reckless US warship sail through the middle of a British naval formation carrying out the tricky task of refuelling on the move. Such tactics could be expected in relation to shadowing Soviet warships, but the Americans, who had so recently been comrades-in-arms against the communists in Korea? There was, in fact, a 'general convergence of US naval power worldwide on Suez'[2], with fleet dispositions as far away as the Pacific adjusted to free-up warships and amphibious warfare vessels, so they could head for the waters of the Middle East.

As British warships commenced combat operations against Egypt, the Commanding Officer of the US Navy's 6th Fleet, Admiral Charles Brown, received a signal from the Chief of Naval Operations, Admiral Arleigh Burke, advising him, as if he needed telling, that the situation was tense and that he should '...prepare for imminent hostilities...' Admiral Brown sent a slightly sarcastic signal back:

> Am prepared for imminent hostilities, but whose side are we on?

Not to be out done, the CNO sent an equally pithy response, which advised that US Navy ships should keep clear of the French and British operating areas, something

The aircraft carrier HMS Ark Royal *passes through the Suez Canal in 1965, en route to the Far East. Nine years earlier Britain had gone to war to try and retain control of the Canal.* Jonathan Eastland/AJAX News & Feature Service.

they clearly did not do. The CNO finished his response by advising Admiral Brown to:

> *...take no guff from anybody.*

As these signals flashed back and forth between the Mediterranean and the USA, a US Navy spokesman in Washington DC declined to acknowledge that anything other than 'routine training exercises' was underway. When asked to give the 6th Fleet's current position, he would only say that it was 'somewhere in the eastern Mediterranean'.

In reality, of course, the US Navy was keeping a tight watch on the Anglo-French invasion fleet and was clearly meant to make its presence felt and show the US government's strong disapproval of the action. To further add to the confusion, the Soviets threatened to use force in the Middle East to 'restore peace', but it was difficult to see how they could intervene decisively in the Mediterranean at that time as their naval forces were not powerful enough.

This strange sequence of events came about because the Egyptians, under the leadership of Gamal Abdel Nasser, an army colonel who had been a key player in a 1952 military coup that deposed the pro-Western King Farouk, had seized control of the Suez Canal through which much of Britain's trade, including oil from the Gulf, flowed. The canal was also the chief route via which troops were transported to police the remnants of the Empire. British Prime Minister Anthony Eden was intent on ordering the canal to be taken back by feat of arms, against advice from many in his own country, and contrary to the United Nations, which wished the affair to be settled through diplomacy.

A bankrupt Egypt had sold forty-five per cent of shares in the Suez Canal Company to Britain in 1875, for four million pounds, and British troops had occupied the Canal Zone from 1882 until June 1956.

However, a terrorist campaign had been waged against the 80,000 British troops in the Canal Zone since 1952, with the Fedayeen (freedom fighters) and Muslim Brotherhood, in reality, being cover names for the Egyptian Police, whose stations were nests of subversion.

The terrorists were agents for Nasser's aim of removing the British and French from the Middle East and forming an Arab superstate that could assert itself as the leading power in the region. The Egyptian strongman found the Soviet Union eager to provide support, via not only huge quantities of tanks and modern Mig-15 and Mig-17 fighters, but also an offer of finance to build the Aswan dam. This crucial construction project was to have been funded by the USA, Britain and the World Bank and it would enable Nasser to provide Egyptian industry with cheap hydroelectricity and also lead to the creation of vast areas of fertile farmland in the Lower Nile. However, angry at Egypt's thriving relationship with the USSR, and anxious that the new Soviet arms were being acquired for an attack on Israel, the Americans pulled the plug on financing the dam. This provoked a furious Nasser to accelerate the return of the Suez Canal to Egypt. He needed the revenue that was raised through charging toll fees to enable the Aswan dam project to get underway.

But a treaty signed in 1954 had allowed Britain to retain its controlling interest in the Suez Canal Company until the late 1960s. Pre-positioned military equipment was permitted, together with permission for intervention by Britain, if it considered free passage of shipping was obstructed.

The Americans did not see ownership of the canal as something worth going to war over, particularly as it would inflame opinion in the so-called 'non-aligned' nations. Chief among the 'non-aligned' was India, which was innately hostile towards its former colonial power and not a natural ally of the USA, but, like others in its camp, had useful votes at the United Nations with which the Americans could counter the Soviets and Chinese. Against this, the British and the French, the latter burning to attack Egypt for allegedly sponsoring terrorism in their much-prized colony of Algeria, sought to use Israel as a counter.

Nasser made his move against the British on 26 July 1956, committing an act of revenge and assertion of national pride that was greeted with satisfaction in many parts of the world where similar desires thrived. Britain was not in a fit state to respond, for it had been bankrupted by two world wars. In the late 1940s, its socialist government had been forced to go to the USA to borrow billions of pounds to create a Welfare State at home, while persisting in maintaining colonies around the globe.

Reeling in shock at the audacity of Nasser's move, Britain declared a state of emergency on 2 August. The Conservative government declared it was determined to restore the Suez Canal to British ownership - and recover the nation's pride. But the Americans were not the only ones who thought it not worth the candle. On 14 August 1956 the *Daily Mirror*'s front page headline screamed:

No war over Egypt!

The Labour Party was soon in blatant opposition to a military operation, while the United Nations refused to give its authorization for such a venture. In fact, feeling inside Eden's own government was so strong that two ministers and his personal press secretary resigned in protest. The senior officers of the UK's armed forces were far from happy about doing the Prime Minister's bidding, but still got together with their French counterparts to make appropriate plans. The French had already formulated a strategy for attacking Egypt with the Israelis, who were extremely worried that Britain's withdrawal from the Canal Zone cleared the way for an attack by the Arab world's largest army. Britain agreed that a pre-emptive strike across the Sinai Peninsula would provide the perfect pretext for intervention, allegedly in the name of the international community, to separate the two combatants.

The 6th Fleet was put on full alert on 28 October, as the Americans knew something was going to happen around the end of the month and, sure enough, the Israeli Army was unleashed on 29 October, easily sweeping aside four Egyptian divisions. The British and French duly called on the two sides to preserve the integrity of the canal, a gossamer fig leaf for the real objective, which was, of course, regime change and securing domination over the Canal Zone.

It was hoped, based on unreliable intelligence sources quoting widespread discontent with Nasser's rule, that, once the troops landed, the Egyptians would rise up and depose the colonel. In reality, it would not happen, as hatred of Israel and distrust of France and Britain was stronger than any dislike of Nasser who, meanwhile, refused to agree to a ceasefire.

On 30 October, the two US Navy carriers in the eastern Mediterranean, the USS *Coral Sea* and USS *Randolph*, their accompanying escort vessels and support ships, were ordered to keep a tight watch on the British and French fleets. A mission to evacuate 2,000 American nationals from Egypt and Israel was activated the same day. Meanwhile back in the USA, two carriers, a cruiser and destroyers were put on notice to sail to the Mediterranean. Five US Navy auxiliary transport ships arrived at Alexandria on 31 October where they picked up more than 1,000 of the evacuees, with convoys of trucks and cars bringing more US citizens from

The American carrier USS Randolph, *which led US Navy interference with Anglo-French operations off Suez.* USNHC.

Cairo. US Air Force transports airlifted evacuees from an Israeli airport, while three destroyers steamed into Haifa to complete the operation.

Hostilities between the Egyptians and British began on 31 October, when the cruiser HMS *Newfoundland* was involved in a clash in the Gulf of Suez, at the southern end of the Canal.

> Newfoundland *was on shipping protection patrol when she encountered the frigate. The Egyptian ship failed to answer the cruiser's challenge and refused to stop when ordered to do so.*[3]

The fleeing Egyptian frigate, called the *Domiat*, did, however, fire at the *Newfoundland*, causing some damage. But the British cruiser's 6-inch guns made short work of the *Domiat*, sinking her within six minutes, with the *Newfoundland* plucking sixty-nine survivors from the sea.

A desire to obscure collusion with the Israelis forced the British invasion fleet to wait at Malta before setting sail on the 1,000-mile voyage to the Nile.

The 90,000 sailors, airmen and soldiers involved in Operation Musketeer - half of them British - had trained hard and were confident of success. If the British servicemen were unsettled by the strength of opposition at home, they put it to the backs of their minds and got on with doing their government's bidding. Two thirds of the 500 aircraft involved were British, as were 100 out of 130 naval vessels. There were five Royal Navy carriers: *Theseus* and *Ocean* - carrying Royal Marines and helicopters - together with *Eagle*, *Bulwark* and *Albion* and their embarked strike jets. Landing Ship Tanks (LSTs) and Landing Craft Tanks (LCTs) had been brought out of mothballs on the Clyde and sent to the Mediterranean, to carry part of the seaborne assault force. Two days after the Israelis began their thrust into Sinai, RAF and French Air Force bombers, together with aircraft carriers, which had gone ahead of the main force, began a series of strikes on Egyptian military installations in and around Port Said. On 5 November British and French paratroopers were dropped to seize key objectives, including airfields and port installations. The following day the UK's 3 Commando Brigade spearheaded the assault from the sea, with 40 and 42 Commandos at the tip of the spear. Pressing on fast into Port Said to link up with the Paras, the brigade's floating reserve - 45 Commando, embarked in *Ocean* and *Theseus* - was called in to clear the urban areas behind its sister units and prevent them from being cut off. This heralded a remarkable moment in military history - the first mass helicopter assault from the sea in the face of enemy fire.

> *The first sticks of men were already on the flight-deck at 0400 as the naval gunfire barrage commenced in support of the craft making their final approach to the beach some seven miles away.* [4]

To launch the heli-borne assault, *Ocean* and *Theseus* positioned themselves directly astern of the naval bombardment force. The six Whirlwinds and six Sycamores from the Army/RAF Joint Helicopter Unit (JHU), embarked in *Ocean*, and eight Whirlwinds from 845 Naval Air Squadron, in *Theseus,* were soon packed with marines.

> *The Whirlwinds, without seats or doors, to save weight, and with minimum fuel for such a short flight, could just stagger off the deck with six men each.* [5]

A total of 415 men and twenty-three tons of stores were landed within eighty-three minutes and to do this the helicopters had to make a 100-mile round trip over open sea, each time. Although the enemy was failing to inflict serious losses, 45 Commando was subjected to a devastating strafing run by a Fleet Air Arm Sea Fury fighter that had mistaken the marines for Egyptian soldiers.

Thirty-one British and French servicemen lost their lives during Operation Musketeer, with nine of them Royal Marines, a surprisingly light butcher's bill, but the real fatal blow was to the Anglo-French position in the Middle East. The Suez Crisis '...exposed the myth that Britain and France were still great powers, capable of acting without the support of the United States.'[6] It has also been observed that Nasser's Suez Canal take-over showed the world that '...the former colonial powers no longer had the means or the will to protect their assets and that their great ally, the United States of America, would not support them in a crisis.'[7]

At the United Nations on 2

The British strike carrier Eagle, around the time of Suez. Goodman Collection.

November the USA had secured the passing of a resolution demanding an end to the fighting.

Both the Soviet Union and China were among the sixty-three nations that supported the Americans, while Britain, France and Israel could muster support only from Australia and New Zealand. Beginning to lose its nerve, the British government had announced on 3 November that it would agree to a ceasefire, depending on Israel and Egypt doing the same. The United Nations voted overwhelmingly on 4 November in favour of sending peacekeepers to police the Canal Zone and the next day, even as British paratroopers were jumping out over Port Said, the UK confirmed its agreement to intervention by the UN force. The fact that the Russians - who were at the time brutally suppressing an uprising in Hungary - had suggested to the Americans that a joint US-Soviet intervention force should be put together to stop the fighting had, perhaps, acted like a cold shower for the British government. Fortunately, President Eisenhower immediately ruled out the Russian proposal, but it showed how bad things had become. But, even though the USA was not about to join forces with the Russians, a further twelve US Navy destroyers set sail from the east coast.

Isolated, with oil supplies disrupted due to the fighting around the canal, which had been blocked by the Egyptians sinking half a dozen vessels, so forcing cargo vessels, tankers and passenger liners to take the long route around the Cape, and with gold and currency reserves flooding out of the country due to a collapse in economic confidence, Britain realized that it had no option but to bow to international opinion. France followed suit and a ceasefire came into effect on 7 November.

On the eastern coast of the USA, the carriers *Forrestal* and *Franklin D. Roosevelt* and accompanying task groups sailed from Norfolk, with orders to position themselves close to the Azores and await further orders.

Meanwhile, in HMS *Eagle*, a young pilot who had been shot down while attacking Egyptian tanks, but rescued by one of the carrier's helicopters, had just been given a check-up by a naval surgeon when he was handed his mail. It included a letter from his anti-war sister-in-law. She told him that he should not be fighting 'because the whole campaign was immoral.' [8]

The UK's servicemen shrugged off such comments, consoling themselves with the knowledge that they had achieved their military objectives with surprisingly low casualties during one of the most complex all-arms operations since the Second World War.

The feeling was that MUSKETEER as a whole had been well done, whatever the politicians said. [9]

At the time of Suez, the Gulf was a forgotten zone where clapped-out Royal Navy warships, and their long-suffering crews, maintained patrols that were more akin to the imperial policing roles of the Victorian era.

But Nasser's tactics with regard to the Suez Canal may have been partly inspired by the success of the Iranians, who nationalized the Anglo-Iranian Oil Company in the summer of 1951. Iran at the time was ruled by a fervently anti-British National

Front government, headed by Prime Minister Dr Mohammad Mossadegh, a forerunner of Nasser and Saddam when it came to confronting the West's interference in, and exploitation of, the Middle East and its natural resources. On becoming Prime Minister, Mossadegh had introduced an Oil Nationalization Bill and, because anti-British sentiment was running high in Iran, in late June 1951 the Royal Navy reinforced its presence in the Gulf.

On 1 June 1951 the Reuters news agency reported that the tank landing ship *Messina* was being transferred from the Mediterranean Fleet to the Gulf. This seemed to indicate that British intervention could include an amphibious operation to land troops and evacuate British citizens. The *Messina* was soon at the Iranian oil port of Abadan on the Shatt al Arab. On 20 June 1951, the Iranian government ordered the nationalization of the Anglo-Iranian Oil Company to be taken forward. The next move by the British, in the so-called Abadan Crisis was to send the cruiser *Mauritius* into the northern Gulf, on stand-by to protect British citizens.

> *Morale soared among Britons in the Persian oilfields today as the cruiser* Mauritius *entered the Shatt al Arab River, near Abadan.*[10]

There were reports that the British Army was preparing to send more troops to the Gulf, to show that the UK had the means to intervene forcefully. However, officially, the British were trying to keep things cool. The British Ambassador to Iran, Sir Francis Shepherd, told a Tehran press conference that the presence of the British cruiser in the Shatt al Arab was the 'logical extension of the Persian Government's present intransigent policy'.

The Ambassador refused to say how long *Mauritius* would be there but observed that, although British lives were not seriously under threat, she would continue to keep a watching brief.

Steaming for the northern Gulf to back-up the *Mauritius* was the frigate HMS *Wild Goose*, which had been at Malta when the crisis blew up. On 30 June it was revealed that the cruiser *Euryalus* was preparing to sail from Malta, too.

Sitting inside the metal box that was the *Mauritius*, at the height of the summer when temperatures reached 40 degrees centigrade, was sapping British sailors physically and mentally and on 11 July she was allowed to go upstream to give her crew some shore leave in Basra. The sloop *Flamingo*, which had been at Basra, came down to keep watch off Abadan. The Admiralty had announced that the *Euryalus*, which had been 'specially fitted for tropical waters',[11] would be a permanent relief for the *Mauritius*. On 14 July it emerged that the landing ship *Dieppe* was being sent to Abadan, to relieve the *Messina*, the former said to be carrying landing craft. Meanwhile, in another part of the ongoing gunboat diplomacy orchestrated by Britain, as it continued to argue with the Iranian government about whether or not it would accept the nationalization, four destroyers were moved from the Mediterranean to the Red Sea, from where they would be able to reinforce the Royal Navy presence in the Gulf more swiftly.

Back at Basra, after a couple of days shore leave to enable her sailors to cool off, the *Mauritius* took up station off Abadan, but with the prospect of exercise at sea in the northern Gulf later in July, after the *Euryalus* arrived. One sailor aboard the *Euraylus* later recalled that, during the cruiser's time in the Gulf, regardless of her

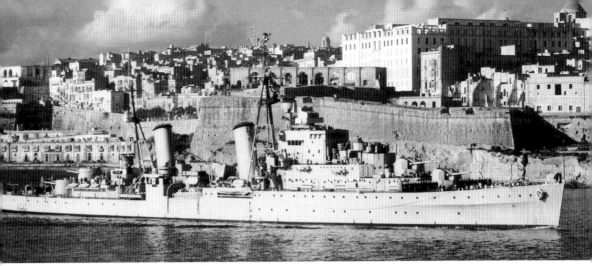

HMS Euryalus *at Malta in the summer of 1951, on her way to reinforce the British naval presence in the Gulf during the Abadan Crisis.* Goodman Collection.

so-called 'tropicalization', her sailors were forced to take sixteen salt tablets a day to maintain their health and that they were afflicted with tropical boils. A programme of regular salt water showers on the upper deck was introduced to combat the boils but, when the cruiser was called on to carry out an evacuation of UK citizens from Abadan, some of the oil mens' wives were embarrassed by the sight of naked sailors taking their cure.[12] But it was not just the sailors that suffered, for it was so hot on the upper deck of the *Euryalus* that:

> Even the ship's cat had to have shoes made to walk on the deck.[13]

In mid-September, the *Mauritius* was sent back to Abadan to cut short the agony of the *Euryalus*'s sailors. The *Mauritius* dropped anchor on the Iraqi side of the Shatt al Arab, only a few hundred yards from the Iranian port, with the destroyer *Armada* just astern of her, to add emphasis to the message that the UK was still ready to intervene, to protect the lives of more than 300 British oil workers still in Iran. The Americans had by then agreed to mediate between the British and the Iranians, with the latter offering compensation of not more than £10 million to the Anglo-Iranian Oil Company, for the loss of its assets.

This did not please the British who continued to keep an expanded naval presence in the northern Gulf. The British companies that had run the Iranian oil fields had shut down production that August, when their employees' residence permits were revoked, and the Abadan Crisis continued into 1952, with Iran forcing UK consulates to close. The Iranians tried also to resume oil production but the flow was inefficient. Mossadegh put up a spirited defence of the oil nationalization at the United Nations and also at the International Court in the Hague, which came to regard it as a legitimate act. But, when Mossadegh moved to take control of the Army, the Shah objected and the Iranian Prime Minister resigned. However, he was reinstated after a popular revolt. Mossadegh finally managed to take control of the Army and continued to cleanse Iran of Western influence, by expelling foreigners. The Americans and British decided it was time to act. The Central Intelligence Agency (CIA) and British intelligence are alleged to have assisted the Shah and anti-government Army units in staging an attempted coup in the spring of 1953. After months of turmoil, in which Mossadegh and his government tenaciously hung on to power, in the August the Army and the Shah finally seized control of Iran.

Mossadegh was imprisoned for three years and then placed under house arrest until his death, from cancer, in 1964. In the wake of Mossadegh being deposed, the Iranians invited foreign companies, including the former Anglo-Iranian Oil Company (now British Petroleum), to run their oil industry, but it was very difficult to raise production back to pre-1951 levels.

Pursuing pirates and slavers was the main business of Royal Navy warships in the Gulf, which was, along its western shores, mainly dominated by sheikhs keen to exploit their oil wealth under the security provided by the White Ensign.

Still maintaining the British presence in the Gulf in 1953 was HMS *Wild Goose*; a Black Swan class sloop launched in October 1942 and designed to hunt German submarines in the Atlantic. As part of the renowned 2nd Escort Group, under Captain 'Johnnie' Walker, her war record had included a part in the sinking of several U-boats.

By the early 1950s, *Wild Goose* was suffering badly from a climate that she was simply not designed to endure. With no air conditioning and cramped accommodation, matters were made worse by rotten food, with sailors fighting over anything that was not too fetid or riven with insects.

The *Wild Goose* was also infested with cockroaches and overrun with rats, which were not shy of invading sailors' hammocks during the night. Naturally, the British matelots' reserves of black humour bolstered them, with a little help from the bottle, as one of the sloop's crew remarked some years later.

The only thing that kept you going was the daily tot of rum [14]

Wild Goose shared her duties with *Wren, Flamingo* and *Modeste*, all of them, like her, Second World War-era Black Swan sloops. Such a presence was not going to deter any major threat to British interests and would always need rapid reinforcement from more powerful units.

In the wake of the Abadan Crisis and Suez, it was inevitable that other countries under the sway of Britain would seek to divest themselves of the last garments of threadbare colonial obligation. On 14 July 1958, the Free Officers' Group, led by Brigadier Abdul Karim Qasim, staged a bloody coup against Iraq's pro-British government, assassinating not only the country's prime minister but also slaughtering its royal family. It appeared that the pan-Arab movement that had seen Egypt and Syria merge into the United Arab Republic would now draw Iraq into its fold. However, the Iraqis were determined to pursue their own path, disliking the influence of the USSR in the other two states. Several unsuccessful attempts by the pro-Syrian, socialist-based Ba'ath Party were made to kill Qasim, including one in October 1959 that involved the twenty-two-year-old Saddam Hussein, who afterwards fled into exile in first Syria then Egypt.

Battling unrest at home, Qasim sought to bond his country by addressing the question of Iraq's disputed claim for a small oil-rich emirate to the south that looked ripe for invasion - Kuwait. The emirate of Kuwait is in fact older than the United States of America, having been established around 1700, when Arab tribes settled on the coast through lack of water in the interior.

Kuwait was soon an important centre of trade, with Britain an aggressive

The Second World War-era frigate HMS Wild Goose *makes a tight turn while on deployment in the Indian Ocean in the late 1940s.* Goodman Collection.

exploiter of commercial possibilities in the region and using the emirate as a staging post for the Persian Gulf-Aleppo Mail Service.

In 1899, the British concluded an agreement with Kuwait to provide its defence as a protectorate of the Empire, for the Kuwaitis feared domination by the Turks and neighbouring Arabs. They also allowed Britain to conduct their foreign affairs. At that time Iraq did not exist other than as a collection of provinces in the Ottoman Empire - Mosul (in the north), Baghdad (centre) and Basra (in the south). However, after the defeat of Turkey in the First World War the map of the Middle East was redrawn, allegedly to give the Arabs their freedom but, in reality, it was a carve up to give the British and French control.

Iraq was created under a British mandate authorized by the League of Nations, but several of Iraq's Arab tribes rose up against British military occupation to fight for their freedom. With fossil fuels an increasingly important factor in the world economy, the British were not about to relinquish their hold on the world's most promising oil-producing region and so they made the pliable Hashemites, who had recently been ejected from Syria, Iraq's royal family.

From 1932, Iraq was supposedly an independent kingdom, but such was British influence that anything contrary to London's wishes was unlikely to stand for long, as the UK ran its defence and foreign policies. However, just as the territorial ambitions of both Germany and Russia over the centuries have stuck to the same course, despite changes in leadership from royal families to dictatorships, so Iraq has hungered to consume Kuwait regardless of who has been in power in Baghdad. And again, as with Germany and Russia, restricted access to the sea has been one of the major driving forces behind those ambitions.

In the post-First World War settlement, Iraq was granted only nineteen miles of coastline - hemmed in by the Persians to the east and Kuwaitis to the west.

In the late 1930s, having reluctantly accepted that its border with Iran should run down the middle of the Shatt al Arab, Iraq sought to lease Kuwaiti territory, so it could create a deep-water port, but Britain was not in favour of this. Frustrated by this, the Iraqis decided to launch a campaign of subversion within Kuwait to overthrow the ruling Sabah family, but this made little headway.

In 1939, Iraq marshalled its military forces in the south of the country around

31

Basra and seemed to be threatening an invasion of Kuwait. However, Britain warned it would intervene forcefully to prevent this and so Iraq's military plans came to nothing. In March 1940, a pro-Nazi, Arab nationalist coup overthrew the royal family and government, but the British invaded Iraq in 1941 and restored both to power despite the best efforts of Hitler's Luftwaffe, which sent squadrons to help the resistance.

The revolutionaries who struck in the summer of 1958 were therefore compelled by the bitter memory of British interference. Furthermore, Qasim hoped to emulate Nasser by destroying British influence, finally 'retrieving' Kuwait, which had become a major oil producer, and so making itself an even more tempting target for an ambitious Iraq.

In mid-June 1961, the Anglo-Kuwaiti treaty of 1899 was replaced with a new agreement that gave Kuwait full independence, but with a provision allowing British military assistance if it was threatened by a neighbour.

Within a week of Kuwait gaining independence, Iraq stated that it would annex it, with Qasim accusing the Kuwaitis of being 'irresponsible people under the sway of imperialism'. [15] On 30 June, the Iraqis ordered two brigades towards the Kuwait border - some 12,000 men against Kuwait's paltry border protection force of around 1,500 soldiers. The same day the Kuwaitis asked Britain for military assistance. This was never in doubt, for not only was Kuwait's oil vital to the UK economy, so were vast sums invested in British banks by the ruling family. At the time, 42 Commando was embarked in a helicopter carrier already East of Suez. HMS *Bulwark* had set off, on what was her first deployment since being converted to the helicopter role, in March 1960 and, as Iraqi troops massed on the Kuwaiti border, she was visiting Pakistan. Steaming into the Gulf, *Bulwark* was off Kuwait by 1 July, with the 600 marines of 42 Commando flown ashore in her embarked helicopters.

The sun was blazing and the temperature reached 120 in the shade as British forces landed [16]

Meanwhile, on 2 July, elements of 45 Commando were flown in from Aden while forces based in Bahrain headed north, including the LST *Striker* carrying Centurion tanks, while the Royal Air Force dispatched Hunter strike jets. The current Gulf patrol ship when the crisis erupted was the frigate HMS *Loch Alvie*, while Loch class sister ships *Loch Ruthven* and *Loch Fyne* were ordered to Kuwaiti waters from the Indian Ocean.

A detachment of Royal Marines from the *Loch Alvie* was put ashore to boost numbers, while a team of forward observers from the ship was sent into the desert in case Naval Gunfire Support (NGS) was required. The aircraft carrier HMS *Victorious* was ordered to head for the Gulf along with the frigate *Lincoln* and destroyer *Cassandra*. Meanwhile, the aircraft carrier *Centaur* and three destroyers - *Saintes*, *Camperdown* and *Finnistere* - together with the frigates *Llandaff* and *Yarmouth*, fleet oiler *Olna* and the LST *Messina* (carrying more Centurion tanks) were told to set course for the trouble zone. The *Centaur* and her escort vessels arrived at Port Said on 5 July to begin a passage through the Suez Canal.

A shipping agent who handles British naval vessels, said officials of the Suez Canal Authority had assured him that all facilities would be made available for a speedy passage. [17]

Because there were fears the Iraqis might resort to mining the northern Gulf, the mine sweepers *Rodington* and *Ashton* were also sent. On 7 July four coastal mine-sweepers - *Walkerton*, *Crofton*, *Burnaston* and *Leverton* - together with a tug were reportedly steaming through the Suez Canal and headed for the northern Gulf. Forty-five British warships were ultimately concentrated in the Gulf region, providing a powerful demonstration of intent that was criticized by Egypt, the Soviet Union and Ceylon. British paratroopers were ordered to Kuwait from their bases in the Mediterranean, but Turkey, banning the RAF from flying over its territory, delayed their arrival. The combined British ground force assembled within a week was only 6,000-strong, but it was more than capable of dealing with Iraq's obsolete Russian-origin armour and poorly commanded troops. The operations centre for the force was the amphibious ship HMS *Meon*, with *Bulwark*'s radar keeping watch for Iraqi air attack.[18]

The decisive battle, if it came, would be for the Mutla Ridge, which dominated the most likely route of advance for Iraqi troops towards Kuwait City and therefore the Royal Marines were dug in along it. The heat was so severe that eggs could be fried '...on the hull of a Centurion tank if ...not already hard boiled in the sun and the troops made instant coffee with water straight from the jerrican.' [19]

Two gallons of liquid were needed per person and the Royal Navy's Whirlwind helicopters provided a lifeline by flying ice and water to the front line troops. [20] *Bulwark*'s role as a floating airbase for those helicopters, particularly in the face of

The commando carrier HMS Bulwark, with Royal Marines embarked, somewhere 'East of Suez' in the 1960s.
Goodman Collection.

a harsh desert climate that swiftly wore out machinery and aircrews, was of course equally important and she was also used as a means of providing the marines with a rest and recreation area.

The climate had begun to take its toll on the marines within a few days of landing, with at least '24 prostrated by heat exhaustion' by 5 July. [21] A dozen of them were flown back to the *Bulwark*'s sick bay for treatment.

While the British troops sweated it out, their government exerted diplomatic pressure on Iraq and the Arab League was persuaded to assemble a deterrent force to replace the UK's by the autumn. It had not been easy as the truculent United Arab Republic had, on 6 July, issued a demand for an immediate withdrawal of British troops from Kuwait.

The British government responded by stating that its chief objective was to guarantee Kuwait's security and whether that was with its own troops or those of the Arab League did not matter. American newspapers were meanwhile sniping from the sidelines, suggesting that British gunboat diplomacy was increasing tension.

> *It may be that what Kassem (sic) has most wanted is to forestall President Nasser of the United Arab Republic from taking control of the tiny kingdom and its incredible oil reserves,* opined the *Washington Post* on 5 July.
>
> *But, with the arrival of British forces, the situation has gone beyond a game of chess and could become a round of Russian roulette.*

Meanwhile, the *Chicago Tribune* suggested that Britain was motivated purely by the need to preserve its oil interests:

> *Kuwait is a vast oil pool, with reserves estimated at twice those of the United States. British interests exploit half of the oil production and 40 per cent of Britain's oil requirements come from the country.*

The *Centaur* and her task group had paused at Malta to await further developments in the crisis and the Ministry of Defence acknowledged that 'excessively trying climactic conditions' were forcing a rotation of vessels, and ground units, in the northern Gulf.

On 14 July the Iraqis stepped up the pressure by staging a display of military might.

> *A huge map that showed Kuwait as part of Iraq faced foreign diplomats in Baghdad today as they watched a two-and-a-half-hour military parade which marked the third anniversary of the revolution that brought Maj.-Gen Kassem (sic) to power.* [22]

In the meantime, in Kuwait, with more Army units arriving, 42 Commando was able to re-embark in *Bulwark* on 21 July while 45 Commando had flown back to Aden on 18 July.

When *Victorious* arrived she became the command centre for all air power including the RAF jets that had been forward deployed to the Gulf. The presence of the carriers off shore, with only a minimal military infrastructure in Kuwait, was vital in sustaining the force that persuaded the Iraqis to back down. However, they had not given up and in October began making menacing noises about annexing Kuwait yet again. Britain responded by reinforcing naval forces in the Gulf and once more the Iraqis backed down.

CHAPTER TWO

PUTTING DOWN THE BURDEN

The creaking old tub HMS *Loch Alvie*, which had started her life in the Second World War with the Royal Canadian Navy, in the dying days of the Battle of the Atlantic, had, by 1962, steamed on way past her sell by date. Handed back to the Royal Navy post-war, the *Loch Alvie* had received a modernization in the 1950s that concentrated on giving her a twin 4-inch gun mounting and half a dozen 40mm anti-aircraft cannons. Despite the fact that *Loch Alvie* was destined to spend her twilight years in the Middle East, she was still not provided with air conditioning that might make her crew's life bearable.

However, by early 1962, the first of a new generation of modern warships - the Type 81, or Tribal class, frigates - was ready, following major work to rectify propulsion problems, to depart Devonport and replace *Loch Alvie* on the Gulf patrol. Serving in HMS *Ashanti*, as she departed the UK for East of Suez, was Sub Lieutenant Christopher Craig, who carried the honour of being the ship's diving officer but had his eye on the sky and a future as a naval aviator. Although he would make his name as an intrepid frigate captain during the Falklands War twenty years later, Chris Craig was to become very familiar with the turbulent waters of the Gulf in the three decades that followed his maiden deployment in *Ashanti*. The Tribals were remarkable for being purpose-built for service East of Suez, at a time when the UK's defence budget was under pressure from cutbacks and the retreat from Empire was about to pick up pace. Most importantly of all, for a ship that would spend a number of years in the Gulf, *Ashanti* had air conditioning and also possessed accommodation for Royal Marines, the latter tasked with carrying out boarding of

The Tribal class frigate HMS Ashanti *spent a good proportion of her career in the Gulf.* Goodman Collection.

F117

suspect shipping. For the main role of the Royal Navy in the Gulf remained hunting for smugglers and other brigands of the seas, although the threat from Iraq meant constant vigilance in waters off Kuwait.

The Tribals were the first frigates designed to embark a helicopter as a full-time part of the ship's capability and the Wasp, which was about to enter service, would be able to project anti-submarine killing power over the horizon, via its homing torpedoes and depth charges, while also conducting surface search missions.

Together with the Country class destroyers built at the same time, the Tribals pioneered the use of highly responsive Combined Steam and Gas propulsion (COSAG), which had never before been used in a major British warship. In conjunction with the steam turbine, the gas turbine could boost *Ashanti*'s top speed to 28 knots, which would prove useful in chasing small boats in the Gulf. The *Ashanti* reached Bahrain on 14 March, going alongside at the British naval base, which had recently been expanded to accommodate additional naval units in case the threat from Iraq arose again. Ten days later, *Ashanti* left in company with *Loch Alvie*, to conduct a week of exercises at sea that included live firing. Having bid farewell to *Loch Alvie*, the *Ashanti* made a flag-flying visit to the Iranian port of Bandar Abbas, which did not impress Sub Lieutenant Craig.

> *It was a dreadful, scrubby little place but we visited Iran as friends and allies, so we tried quite hard to make a good impression, but it was hard work. There were millions of people living in Bandar Abbas, but from seaward it looked like a cemetery and nothing changes that impression when you are ashore.*

Within a few days *Ashanti* was beyond the Gulf, paying a visit to Muscat in Oman, an altogether more pleasant experience for Sub Lieutenant Craig.

> *For a few days I went off and flew maritime patrols with the Sultan of Oman's Air Force, which I found consisted of three piston Provosts and three Beavers, with a pilot team of nine RAF pilots all on assignment from the UK. It was a wonderful job and they loved it. There were about thirty landing strips spread throughout Oman at their disposal and it was real seat of the pants flying. You would drop into a strip, refuel your own aircraft from cans, and hope it took off again etc etc, so it was all great fun. The main objective of the maritime patrols was trying to spot dhows that might be up to no good off the Sultan's shores.*

In the early 1960s, Aden in southern Arabia, from where 45 Commando had flown to defend Kuwait, was still an important British military base, with refuelling facilities for Royal Navy ships. It was, therefore, not uncommon for warships on the Gulf patrol to take a detour down there and when *Ashanti* called in during mid-April she met up with the *Loch Fyne*, which was about to conclude her time on station.

After sticking around for the Queen's Birthday Parade, *Ashanti* departed Aden to resume her patrolling duties.

Such was the imperial routine of warships deployed East of Suez in the early to mid-1960s. *Ashanti* took up more than her fair share of the burden, as did other members of her class, including HMS *Tartar*. When Chris Craig returned to the

Middle East he had completed his training as a helicopter pilot and was flying from the carrier *Eagle*, when she spent some time off Aden, providing support for British troops engaged in a gruelling counter-terrorist campaign. Egypt's Nasser was providing backing for Marxist guerillas, who were determined that, when Britain finally pulled out of Aden, any so-called democratic government that might be left behind would be snuffed out at birth. The days of Queen's Birthday Parades were, by the mid-1960s, long gone and Lieutenant Craig found himself flying essential supplies to the troops in bandit country.

> *Eagle was deployed off the east coast of Africa and off southern Arabia during '64, '65 and '66. While we spent a lot of time off Beira in Mozambique enforcing the blockade that was intended to punish Rhodesia for its Unilateral Declaration of Independence, we also spent a good deal of time up off Aden in support of operations by the Royal Marines in the mountains. The Eagle's helicopters ran provisions and water up to the British positions. We would join the Royals for a drink and a chat before we departed back to Eagle and, in 1965, we also had limited periods of a few days deployed forward, with our Wessex I helicopters, to help them out with some fetching and carrying.*

The UK's major obligation to safe-guarding its remaining dependencies in the Gulf, chiefly the Trucial States of Umm al-Qaiwain, Sharjah, Fujairah, Dubai, Ajman and Abu Dhabi, and its major military base at Bahrain, would require *Ashanti* and other British warships to spend years on deployment in the region. When *Ashanti* returned to Devonport in late September 1965, having departed Plymouth the previous October, her sailors were reunited not only with their wives and sweethearts, but also a grateful British Petroleum executive. The local newspaper explained why:

> *Highlight of the cruise was on March 29 when, as previously reported,* Ashanti *made a five-hour dash to the aid of the BP tanker,* British Queen, *ablaze in the Persian Gulf. On board* Ashanti *in the Sound today, Mr P.A. Medcraft, general manager of BP tankers, presented the ship's company with 'thank you' tokens for their efforts during the fire. It took the form of a £50 cheque for the ship's welfare fund and six silver tankards for the wardroom. Presenting the tokens, Mr Medcraft said: 'It goes without saying that it is a great comfort to us of the Merchant Navy to know your assistance is available in times of emergency.'*[1]

The *Ashanti* was recorded as having spent 150 days at sea, covering 50,000 miles 'patrolling long stretches of desolate coast on the lookout for arms-smugglers and other law-breakers'.[2]

When *Ashanti* returned to Devonport in July 1967, from a Gulf deployment of similar length, she brought back tales that, again, characterized the unsung, but vitally important, work carried out by patrolling warships. During a tour of ports in the Trucial States, the *Ashanti* helped uphold British prestige by acting as home to ten goats, presented to the senior naval officer in the Gulf by the grateful ruler of Abu Dhabi, who was eager to show his appreciation of the security offered by the White Ensign. To have refused the gift would have been a mortal insult to the Sheikh, so *Ashanti*'s otherwise well-scrubbed, and no doubt more fragrant, decks had to tolerate the toilet habits and odours of goats, until the animals could be dropped off in Bahrain.

During the same deployment *Ashanti* spent three months out of the Gulf, on the Beira Patrol, and supporting embattled British troops in Aden. At the western end of the southern Arabian peninsula, the long, drawn out trauma of the withdrawal from Aden, completed at the end of 1967, was the most visible sign of a British government that had decided to abandon all but a minimal presence East of Suez by the 1970s. And it was the Royal Navy that would pay a very heavy price for such a decision.

There have been few more grievous blows inflicted upon the Royal Navy in the past 100 years than the shocking decision to axe its entire fixed-wing carrier force. But to the Labour government of 1964 - 1970, such a dramatic move was an absolute necessity, for Britain was experiencing a drawn-out, economic nervous breakdown. The years of Prime Minister Harold Macmillan's boom had gone bust in spectacular style. It therefore seemed obscene to the new socialist administration that the UK might maintain the remnants of empire at the potential expense of the Welfare State.

The fate of the Royal Navy was, much more than the other two armed forces, tied up with the withdrawal from empire. It had been the White Ensign that had safeguarded the sea-lanes connecting the various colonies. The British fleet reached its peak in 1914, when it was, without doubt, the world's most powerful and, just over thirty years later, having played a major part in achieving victory in two world wars, it finally yielded the crown of sovereign of the seas to the US Navy. This mirrored the place of the two countries in the world - the former supreme imperial power succeeded by the rising military and industrial giant.

Having entered a period of severe decline, which in reality had started during the First World War, Britain seemed, during the second half of the twentieth century, to spurn most cruelly that which it had loved so much - the Royal Navy. The Army was necessary to confront the massed tank formations of the Warsaw Pact in central Europe, while the Royal Air Force was similarly deeply committed to the same crucial theatre. But the Navy seemed to have little function outside policing the safe withdrawal from empire, conveying the other two armed forces back to Europe where they were badly needed. The Royal Navy could, however, prove decisive in the Atlantic, keeping Sea Lines of Communication (SLOC) open in the face of a growing Soviet submarine threat, and the decision in 1962 to invest in Polaris missile-carrying submarines, to provide the UK's independent nuclear deterrent, provided another vital role.

Power projection was not, however, seen as necessary, with the possible exception of needing to insert an amphibious reinforcement force into NATO's Norwegian northern flank. The very commando brigade and naval helicopters that had stormed ashore at Suez in 1956 saved Kuwait from invasion in 1961, and held the line against Marxist insurgents in Aden, would soon be wintering in frozen wastes close to the Russian border. Within such scenarios there was perceived to be no desperate need for big carriers, as air support could be provided by the RAF, flying from a much bigger aircraft carrier - the UK itself - or by the air forces of NATO. Indeed it was the RAF - still smarting from losing the plum role of providing the nuclear deterrent - that had deliberately undermined the case for a new generation of Royal Navy carriers even before the final decision was taken to withdraw from East of Suez.

However, it was still being proposed that a new class of British aircraft carriers should be built, possibly up to five-strong. The Royal Navy had tried, and failed, to win over the air force by explaining that the new carriers would be platforms for aircraft flown by both Royal Navy and RAF aircrews, who would belong to a Joint Services Seaborne Force. Forty years on this has, in fact, become a reality, as the Royal Navy and RAF operate Joint Force Harrier, which is itself a precursor to Joint air groups flying from the two new 50,000 tons carriers that the Royal Navy is planning to bring into service by 2015.

Back in the early 1960s, it was explained that three carriers at least were needed to even guarantee meeting NATO commitments, never mind East of Suez, for one ship could expect to be on deployment, another preparing to take over while the third would be in refit. The new carriers would embark an air wing forty strong: F-4 Phantom fighters and Buccaneer strike jets as well as Airborne Early Warning (AEW) aircraft and Anti-Submarine Warfare (ASW) helicopters. Had they been built, the new carriers would not have been expected to leave service until the early years of the twenty-first century. If such ships had existed, an Argentinian invasion of the Falklands in 1982 might not have been viable. Certainly, re-taking the islands would have been less costly for the Royal Navy, which would have had both the AEW aircraft to detect enemy aircraft further away and the ability, via long-range interceptors armed with radar-homing missiles, to destroy them before they got in range to launch their own weapons. But it was decided that there would be no new ships and the existing aircraft carriers and commando carriers would be run on until the mid-1970s. When this decision was revealed in early 1966, it prompted both the First Sea Lord and Navy Minister to resign.

> ...the trauma throughout the navy was intense. [3]

But the Navy had not helped itself:

> The naval case was weakened by the Naval Staff's refusal to accept less costly ships than the proposed 50,000 ton, fixed-wing carriers. [4]

The RAF had proposed a small carrier should be operated in conjunction with new F-111 long-range bombers, but this had not found favour with the Admiralty, who argued that such a proposal would not provide adequate capability. By the end of 1967, Britain had not only withdrawn from its major base at Aden, it had also disbanded the Mediterranean Fleet and the decision to axe the Royal Navy appointment of Flag Officer Carriers was an ominous sign. And the situation did not improve, for, with a deepening economic crisis plunging Britain further into the red, in early 1968 the Government made more cuts in defence spending and decided surviving commitments East of Suez could not be maintained at all. Both Bahrain and Singapore were to be closed rather than remaining active into the 1970s. The withdrawal from these last outposts East of Suez, with the exception of Hong Kong, would be completed by 1971, and, in the same year, all of the remaining aircraft carriers would be retired from service. The RAF did not escape pain, as it was

The Hermes, *which was destined to be the last of the Royal Navy's big carriers, weathers heavy seas.* Goodman Collection.

decided not to buy the F-111s and most of its overseas bases were closed. NATO commitments were to be almost the full extent of British defence policy. However, under Foreign Office pressure, there was a requirement to continue enforcement of the embargo against Rhodesia and the UK was also committed to the Five Power Defence Agreement in the Far East. The seven carriers that had allowed Britain to exercise global presence with a real power projection capability throughout the 1950s and 1960s, ultimately suffered a long, drawn-out demise. By 1966 *Centaur* had become a depot ship and was sent to the breakers in the early 1970s. *Albion*, which had been converted to a commando carrier in the early 1960s, had gone to the breakers by 1972. The *Bulwark*, which was converted to an ASW ship, survived until the mid-1980s before being sent for scrap. *Hermes* was briefly an ASW carrier before receiving Sea Harrier strike-fighters in the late 1970s and serving as the Royal Navy flagship during the Falklands War. *Eagle* was decommissioned in the early 1970s and had been broken up by the end of the decade. *Victorious* was retired from service and sold for scrap in the summer of 1969. *Ark Royal* was to be the last remaining Conventional Take-off and Landing (CTOL) aircraft carrier in the Royal Navy, but she did not make it into the 1980s, paying off in early 1979 and sent for scrap the following year.

The British retreat from East of Suez left a power vacuum in the Gulf, for the US Navy was in no position to add another major commitment. It was in the vanguard of the Cold War at sea, countering a rapidly growing Soviet naval presence around the globe, but particularly in the Atlantic, Mediterranean and Pacific, and the Americans also had plenty to keep them occupied in south-east Asia.

To make matters worse, in 1968 the Russians began deploying their own

The USS Duxbury Bay, *while deployed to the Gulf in the 1960s, as command ship for the small US Navy presence.* USNHC.

naval forces to the Indian Ocean while the United States was deeply mired in the conflict in Vietnam and could not spare the forces to take over Britain's role as protector of the Gulf. [5]

That does not mean there was no American naval presence in the Gulf, far from it. The Gulf had been important to the USA since the Second World War, not only because of its oil, but also through its key strategic position on the southern flank of the Soviet Union. During the war, the supply route via the Gulf and overland through Iran had been vital in keeping Russia in the fight against the Nazis. In the late 1940s the US Navy established a Middle East Task Force, which aimed mainly to show the flag in Arabian waters and off the coast of east Africa. Between 1949 and the late 1960s a trio of former seaplane tenders served as flagships for the US Navy in the Middle East. The first of these was the USS *Duxbury Bay*, which, in March 1949, spent four weeks as flagship of the US Navy's Commander Persian Gulf, while on her way home from a world cruise.

Over the next seventeen years the *Duxbury Bay* carried out fifteen tours of duty as flagship of Commander, Middle East Force (MIDEASTFOR). She shared the duty with the *Greenwich Bay* and *Valcour*, like them was painted white, to reflect the heat, and received modifications to equip her better for the flagship role. In late August 1951, when the Abadan Crisis was at its peak, the *Greenwich Bay* had cut short a visit to Bombay to head back into the Gulf, so that the commander of American naval forces in the Middle East could keep an eye on the situation. By 1965 the *Valcour* was the sole Middle East flagship, the other two vessels having been retired from service. This entailed *Valcour* being base-ported at Bahrain from the spring of 1966, a precursor of the British withdrawal from the region. Until the end of the 1960s, the MIDEASTFOR was usually composed of the command ship and a couple of frigates or destroyers. Aside from a watching brief over American interests in the region, the US Navy's vessels were also tasked with standing by to provide humanitarian aid and disaster relief anywhere from Ethiopia to the northern Gulf. Service in the US Navy's warships, which generally did not have air conditioning, could be as tough as in the Royal Navy's, although the food was generally better.

41

The tank landing ship USS Barnstable County, heading south through the Suez Canal in the early 1970s, a potent symbol of the fleet that would now guarantee security 'East of Suez'.
Jonathan Eastland/AJAX News & Feature Service.

In the UK, a new Conservative government, elected to power in 1970, was no more likely to reverse the decision to abandon fixed-wing carrier aviation than the previous administration. However, it appreciated that, diminished though the Royal Navy was, it was important to maintain a presence of some sort East of Suez, where there were still interests vital to Britain that needed safeguarding.

In his first major statement, the new Defence Secretary, Lord Carrington, said at the end of October 1970 that five frigates and/or destroyers would stay East of Suez, including one off Hong Kong and one in the Gulf. [6]

The Tribal class frigates flew the flag for Britain in the Gulf into the late 1970s and the occasional presence of a task group in the Indian Ocean would show that the UK still had some regard for its vital interests and obligations East of Suez.

There would, however, be no major military bases in Arabia, but when the British departed from Bahrain and the Trucial States gained their independence in 1971, the Americans immediately moved in.

> When Bahrain became a sovereign state in 1971, the US Navy worked out an agreement to take over piers, radio transmitters, warehouses, and other facilities left vacant by the departing British. [7]

The Royal Navy still proved its utility and, for example, in late January 1971, HMS *Ashanti* assisted a Finnish tanker in distress in the Gulf. The frigate launched her Wasp helicopter, which lowered two members of the engineering department onto the 96,000 tons *Pegny*. The tanker had suffered a catastrophic loss of electric power that prevented her from re-starting her engines and the *Ashanti* went alongside her to put across power cables that enabled the *Pegny* to get her steam turbines up-and-running again.

By January 1972, the amphibious transport ship *La Salle*, which had been converted for service as permanent Middle East flagship, had replaced USS *Valcour*. But even though the US Navy was stepping into the Royal Navy's shoes, it would be a few years before it had cause to send a carrier battle group into the Gulf. It would do so on a forlorn mission to retrieve national pride that ended in disaster and brought the reputation of the USA lower than ever.

CHAPTER THREE

THE PRESSURE COOKER

When, in 1975, the image of an American helicopter lifting off from the roof of the US Embassy in Saigon, with desperate humanity clawing at its skids, was broadcast around the world, it represented the humiliation of a superpower that had, for all its supposed military might and claims of victory on the battlefield, been defeated. Brought so low by communism's shock troops in Vietnam, the demoralized American military found itself presented with a new failure of arms just five years later. A scorched piece of desert was the stage for another powerful drama captured on camera - that of an Iranian cleric inspecting the bones of a US Marine Corps airman who had, just a few hours before, been burned to death, as a mission to rescue Americans held hostage in Tehran ended in disaster. This was the nadir of American power in the Gulf region, which found itself in dread of a revolutionary Islamic republic, for when the Shah fled Iran in early 1979, the USA's so-called 'Twin Pillars' security policy, that had safeguarded Western interests, came crashing down.

In the wake of Britain's withdrawal from the Gulf, the administration of President Richard Nixon, which in the early 1970s was in the process of disentangling the USA from Vietnam, had seen no good reason to get militarily entangled somewhere else.

The 'Twin Pillars' approach was therefore formulated, using proxies to pursue American security interests in the Gulf, more specifically via Iran and Saudi Arabia, the former being the military and economic giant of the region. This enabled permanent US military commitment to be limited to the US Navy's MIDEASTFOR. Despite outbreaks of nationalism in the 1950s, such as the one that led to the nationalization of its oil industry, in the early 1970s Iran appeared to be firmly in the pro-Western camp, with the Shah's secret police keeping a tight grip on dissent. America supplied arms to the Iranians that no other foreign country would be allowed to own, including seventy-seven F-14 air superiority fighters and their formidable Phoenix long-range radar-guided missiles. With his considerable oil wealth, the Shah also bought 188 F-4 Phantom fighters, while from Britain he obtained more than 800 Chieftains to complement his 800 US-built tanks. By the mid-1970s, the Iranian Navy was the most powerful in the region, although that wasn't saying much, as investment in maritime forces at that time in the Gulf was low compared with ground forces.

Iran's modern ships were supplied by Britain, France and the USA and, chief among the Shah's surface combatants, was a quartet of guided-missile frigates built

STRIKE FROM THE SEA

by UK-based Vosper Thornycroft in the late 1960s and commissioned into service between May 1971 and June 1972. But, when the corrupt monarchy was swept away and Iran was declared an Islamic Republic, the very same formidable weaponry was suddenly in the hands of a regime led by Ayatollah Ruhollah Khomeini, who referred to America as 'the Great Satan' and saw the Arabs across the Gulf as corrupt vassals of Western imperialism. The Ayatollah's hostility towards the West was exceeded only by his hatred of the Ba'athist regime in Iraq. Qasim had been deposed in early 1963 in a Ba'ath Party coup, with Saddam Hussein returning from exile shortly after.

The Army seized control of the country back from the Ba'athists, but the latter staged another take-over in 1968 and this time held onto power. Over the next ten years, Saddam rose up through the ranks, gaining a key appointment as head of the party's security organization, which enabled him to remove opponents and consolidate his power still further.

Saddam could see conflict with Iran was coming and he believed that the incumbent President of Iraq, Ahmad Hassan al-Bakr, would not be strong enough for the trials that lay ahead. Saddam made his big move to gain ultimate power in mid-July 1979, seizing the post of chairman of the Revolutionary Command Council and President and General Secretary of the Ba'ath Party. Khomeini had come into contact with Saddam during thirteen years of exile in Iraq, having been forced to flee Iran in the early 1960s for leading opposition to the Shah. In late 1978 Saddam had ordered Khomeini expelled from Iraq during a crackdown on dissent among the Shia Arabs, who made up sixty per cent of the population. This was also done to please the Shah, with whom the Iraqis had found common cause in suppressing the Shias. The most senior positions in the Ba'ath Party, the armed forces and other key elements of the state were awarded to Sunni Arabs, like Saddam, who made only twenty per cent of the population, the rest of Iraq's ethnic mix being composed mainly of Sunni Kurds. But the enmity between the Iraqi dictator and Iran's new ruler was based on more than just differences between strains of Islam - the two men also held violently opposed views on how state and religion should function. Khomeini believed that religion and politics were one, whereas Saddam favoured the secular approach in which the two were separate. The Iraqi dictator would not bow before anyone, not even God.

Having lost its most important pillar of security in the Gulf region, America faced the prospect of either finding a replacement or taking up the burden.

It would be years before Saudi Arabia could build up its armed forces sufficiently and the Gulf States were even more ill-equipped to deal with the Iranian threat. Because of the obvious hostility between Saddam and Khomeini, Iraq might have seemed the logical choice for an American proxy.

However, with Egypt signing the Camp David peace accord with Israel in 1978, Saddam had sought to position himself as a latter-day Nasser who would lead the Arabs to their ultimate goal of destroying the Jewish state. This put Iraq in conflict with the USA, which was Israel's main benefactor.

A reinvigorated US Navy presence in the Gulf was a realistic means of creating a defence against Iran, because it meant a minimal footprint by non-Muslim forces in Arab countries. There was never any question of America failing to live up to its Gulf obligations, because it simply could not abandon the region, for the world economy depended on Arabian oil. In 1978 the Middle East was responsible for supplying: sixty per cent of Europe's oil; seventy-eight per cent of Japan's; twenty-six per cent of North America's; thirty-seven per cent of Australia's and thirty-seven per cent of Latin America's. [1]

Maintaining political stability and the free flow of oil to the global economy have been the overarching objectives of U.S. foreign policy in the Persian Gulf for almost half a century. The U.S. Navy has been one of the primary instruments of that policy, in both peace and war. [2]

The number of destroyers and frigates in MIDEASTFOR was increased and the carrier USS *Constellation* visited the Gulf in 1974. It was a demonstration of the fact that '...the United States, rather than Britain, henceforth would have the responsibility for policing the Gulf.'[3] However, carriers were not permanently deployed in the Gulf itself, but rather in the north Arabian Sea. The operating procedures for carriers at the time required more sea space than the US Navy felt the comparatively narrow and shallow Gulf provided. Additionally, the fact that the Iranian land mass loomed over the entire Gulf meant any warships operating within its confines would have very little time to react to attacks coming from the north-east. The US Navy's carrier force had been worked hard in Vietnam and, in 1976, when former US Navy nuclear submarine engineer officer Jimmy Carter became

The US Marines, and the assault ships that carried them, such as the USS Shreveport, here, would become veterans of service in the Gulf from the 1970s onwards. US Navy/AJAX.

The USS Enterprise *was the world's first nuclear-powered aircraft carrier and is pictured, in the early years of her career.* US Navy.

President, the American fleet expected to receive some form of regeneration. This was not to be, for the Carter administration decided to recoup some of the massive cost of Vietnam, by ordering the cancellation of further ships in the new Nimitz class carrier programme after number three (the *Carl Vinson*). The first two - *Nimitz* and *Dwight D. Eisenhower* - had been laid down between 1968 and 1970, when the Vietnam War was at its height and making great demands on carrier air power. But, now the sheer expense of creating the new carriers and their Carrier Battle Groups (CBGs) naturally made them big targets for cutbacks. Each Nimitz class vessel cost $2.5 billion to build, with a further $17 billion to create and operate the frigates, destroyers, cruisers and supply ships that made up the rest of the CBG.[4]

In another similarity to the situation in the UK of the 1960s, the US Air Force had, for several years, been lobbying behind-the-scenes to prevent the *Nimitz* class programme from draining too much of the overall defence budget.

The US Air Force also came to loathe another US Navy pet project - the Tomahawk Land Attack Missile (TLAM) programme, which aimed to give warships the ability to hit targets deep inland, a job the air force considered its province.

However, political pressure from senators and congressmen, who were worried about the impact on jobs and the future viability of the ship building industry, forced the Carter administration to order a fourth Nimitz (*Theodore Roosevelt*), while the need to preserve a technological edge over the Soviets meant that TLAM would come to fruition.

A major driving force behind cuts in defence spending was Jimmy Carter's belief, that if the USA scaled back its own military budgets, the Soviets would follow suit, so taking the steam out of the Cold War arms race and helping foster world peace. However, the Russians saw such a move as weakness and carried on with their ambitious arms programmes, including a massive investment in an ocean-going fleet that would be able to challenge the US Navy anywhere on the Seven Seas. In a further echo of the British government's mindset of the late 1960s, the Carter administration wanted to concentrate on NATO and discard expeditionary warfare and its expensive assets. However, the US Navy's top brass dug their heels in and pushed on with the five-ship Tarawa class amphibious assault carrier programme, which had started in 1971 and would conclude in 1978. While carriers did make big, fat targets for Soviet weapons, there was no denying that they had, since the Second World War, been the pre-eminent warships, providing deterrence against possible aggression by their mere presence off a hostile coast, as well as unleashing awesome power projection force if needed. In any event, even if hit by missiles, it was reckoned the Nimitz class super-carriers could shrug off all-but-catastrophic damage and keep going. However, there was no escaping the fact that the sheer cost was daunting and there were attempts, even within the US Navy, to pursue smaller, but more numerous, carriers. But there was concern that these vessels would remain attractive targets - and would be more easily destroyed - while lacking powerful air groups to inflict decisive damage on an enemy or defend themselves. New carriers were desperately needed to provide the US Navy with the numbers necessary to maintain a presence around the world. Nuclear-powered ships provided greater endurance than conventionally-powered vessels, so more time on station could be squeezed out of them. The much-reconstructed Second World War-era Midway class carriers - *Midway*, *Franklin D. Roosevelt* and *Coral Sea* - were most in need of replacement, having all been laid down between October 1943 and July 1944 and commissioned between September 1945 and October 1947. By the summer of 1975 the *Midway* was forward-based in Japan, the *Coral Sea* was base-ported in the USA and, like the name ship of the class, due to serve on at least into the 1980s, while the *Franklin D. Roosevelt*, the least capable and least reconstructed of the trio, was by 1977 on her way to the breakers' yard.

Of the other nine non-Nimitz class carriers in commission in 1977, only one was nuclear-powered. The carriers of the Forrestal class - *Forrestal*, *Saratoga*, *Ranger* and *Independence* - and Kitty Hawk class - *Kitty Hawk*, *America*, *Constellation* and *John F. Kennedy* - were constructed during the 1950s and 1960s. The US governments of the day had been alarmed by the potential cost of atomic warships during the construction of the world's first nuclear-powered carrier, the USS *Enterprise*, commissioned into service in late 1961.

In 1977, as a precursor to today's Central Command (CENTCOM), the USA set up an organization in the Gulf region known as the Rapid Deployment Force (RDF). This was no more than a command framework, however, as it had no dedicated ground troops or air forces.

President Carter's use of sea power was cautious, reflecting his liberal outlook - a man of good intentions who did not want the world to think ill of him. In December 1978, with unrest in Iran clearly reaching boiling point, the USS *Constellation* was ordered with her battle group to Arabian waters,

> ...with the avowed intention of manifesting American concern at the chaotic situation in Iran, but move cancelled a few days later after Soviet protests at gunboat diplomacy. Outcome damaging to American prestige.[5]

However, the Carter administration did finally follow through, but in typically hesitant style, with the deployment of the *Constellation* carrier battle group to the Arabian Sea in March 1979. The carrier's presence was supposed to deter the revolutionaries from menacing US citizens in Iran, reassure Saudi Arabia that America was committed to stability in the Gulf and warn the Russians to stay out. But, to avoid further accusations of gunboat diplomacy, it was sent without too much publicity.

With the revolution exploding in Iran, Lieutenant Mike Scherr found his Knox class frigate, the USS *Donald B. Beary*, directed south through the Suez Canal. The American warship was headed into a seething cauldron where civil war in the Yemen also raised tension and the aggressive presence of Soviet naval vessels only made things worse.

The *Constellation*'s CBG was some weeks away from arriving in the region, so Lieutenant Scherr's Surface Action Group (SAG) was the nearest available US Navy reinforcement.

> One night on the Mid Watch from 00.00-04.00, our ship, together with the destroyer USS Davis *and frigate USS* Richard L. Page, *was approaching Sicily when we received a Flash message that contained only one line: Proceed east at best speed. We turned around, brought the second boiler on line, and headed east down the centre of the Med.*
>
> *In the morning we received another Flash message indicating that we could expect ninety days sustained independent operations. We still had no idea as to what we were doing or where we were going. The next day we were given a point for under-way replenishment and soon we spotted a fleet tanker with the Romeo flag at the dip (indicating she was ready to bring us alongside). We still did not know what was up and where we were to get ammo, food, parts etc. We had no clue how everything we needed got to that ship, in a day-and-a-half. We were finally told to continue down the axis of the Med and turn right at the Suez Canal, only we did not have permission to enter Egypt. We did not have charts for the Canal, Red Sea, the Indian Ocean or the Gulf. We did, however, have our Canal Certificate. The State Department and the personal intervention of President Anwar al-Sadat brokered our entry into the Canal. When we arrived in Egyptian waters a US Navy Captain met the ships and delivered the charts - he was assigned to the Pentagon, flew out to Egypt to deliver the charts, and flew directly back to Washington. We entered Port Said and moored for the night. We waited for the formation of the next day's convoy for passage through the Canal. The bottom of Port Said was a junk heap and we ended up with a fouled anchor so this delayed our underway time. I was sent to the foc'sle to see to the problem and we finally got the anchor off the bottom. We proceeded down the canal and since the US was really not welcome - this was less than six years after the 1973 Arab-Israeli War - the trip was very tense. The Egyptians had many pieces of armor and defense installations along the west side of the canal and had bulldozed the abandoned Israeli positions on the east. The tracking of our ship's bridge by an Egyptian gun at a range of 50-100 yards was very uncomfortable. We then got held up in the Great Bitter Lake for twenty-four hours, as a civilian tanker had run aground in the lower part of the canal. We still felt very uneasy; not having maneuverability, with many guns pointed in our direction*

and impounded ships rusting at anchor in the lake since the war. We finally got out of the canal and headed down the Red Sea, still not knowing our mission or destination. We were sent to the only friendly port around, the French naval base in Djibouti, for fuel and instructions. It turned out our little Squadron was to double the US presence in the Indian Ocean Theater. The other US forces - the Mideast Force flagship and two destroyers - were in the Gulf, evacuating US and Western European civilians from Iran, so they were fully occupied. However, there was a little war between North and South Yemen, with the communist South beating the North and threatening to close the Bab al Mandab strait, so impeding the free passage of shipping. Our job therefore, was to patrol the Bab al Mandab along with another US Navy frigate. But, then we were called to Bahrain where they needed the services of our helicopter for long-range reconnaissance. Normally single screw frigates did not steam 3,000 miles alone, but off we went. Because of the situation we were at a condition III steaming watch (wartime manning of systems and weapons) and had ammunition loaded in the ammo handling system of the 5-inch gun mount. On our transit across the south coast of the Arabian Peninsula we were counting tankers and other shipping. About the 10 March our helicopter's radar warning receiver was lit up by a Soviet gun's Fire Control Radar. The pilot closed us as fast as possible and put the hangar between himself and the radar and then slid over at deck level and landed (not a normal procedure). Our Captain decided to close with the Russian and find out what was going on. As we closed, I suggested going to General Quarters, but the Captain did not want to provoke the Soviets, being so far from any support. I then asked permission to man the 5-inch mount. This was denied, but we were allowed to stand-by. My sailors had somehow heard what was going on and manned up themselves. I asked about the mount and was told the hydraulics were lit off and warmed up. When I looked down from the bridge to the foc'sle I saw, in the blazing heat, my Gunners' mates were leaning on the life lines, which is not normally allowed, with long sleeves rolled down, shirts buttoned at the neck and trousers tucked into boots, in short in battle dress, smiling up at me. They had flak jackets, helmets laid out in the mount, and all was ready for whatever was over the horizon. As we came upon the Soviet destroyer, which was an old Kotlin class, the ship was at swim call and getting her crew out of the water. We had caught them with their pants down, but they were apparently at GQ with all guns - four 5-inch and four quad 45mm anti-aircraft mounts - pointed in our direction. We closed to 2,000 yards to see what he was doing. The guns tracked us. As we turned away, our skipper signaled the Soviet by flashing light: "I wish you a pleasant voyage". We went onto Bahrain, changed a Variable-Depth Sonar Transducer, picked up supplies and headed back to Djibouti. We joined up with the Constellation and her escorts. They had been on the way home to San Diego at the end of a 6-month Western Pacific deployment. Shortly we were detached from the CBG to go look for the Soviet Foxtrot submarine that was out there. It was an easy ASW operation; the Foxtrot was in port *near Somalia. We closed the anchorage, but could not go inside the twelve-mile limit. We were to keep the sub under visual observation, which is hard to do from twelve miles. So, with good navigation we got as close as possible, and, with large gunfire spotting binoculars, we went up to the Radar platform, about 105ft up, to watch the sub for a week. With the Connie CBG in the Indian Ocean, our squadron was sent back to the Med and passed through the canal without incident.*

The storming of the US Embassy in Tehran on 4 November 1979, by hundreds of 'students' who had been whipped into a frenzy by Ayatollah Khomeini's fiery rhetoric against the 'Great Satan', would lead to a nuclear-powered carrier being drawn into the confines of the Gulf itself. Sixty-six embassy workers and US diplomats were taken hostage, along with three other American citizens at the Iranian Foreign Ministry. The deployment of another carrier battle group to the Indian Ocean coincided with the release of thirteen of the hostages between 18 and 20 November, but the situation appeared to reach deadlock thereafter, the Iranians not easily cowed by the brandishing of the 'big stick'.

The Soviet invasion of Afghanistan over Christmas 1979, to save a communist regime from fervently Islamic Afghan tribesmen, deepened American anxiety and an Indian Ocean battle group was deployed regularly from that point on - to the so-called Camel Station - within striking distance of both Iran and Afghanistan. The battle group was built around either a Pacific-based carrier, from the 7th Fleet, or one drawn from the 6th Fleet and the requirement for this deployment rather shattered the idea of concentrating on NATO commitments.

By late April 1980 nearly thirty US Navy warships were in the Arabian Sea, preparing to launch a daring mission to rescue the Tehran hostages. Operation Eagle Claw would come from two directions: US Air Force transport aircraft flying Special Forces troops into Iran from Egypt and Oman, while eight helicopters were launched from the USS *Nimitz*.

The US Marine Corps-operated RH-53D Sea Stallions were minesweeping aircraft and would, therefore, arouse less curiosity than the troop-carrying variant of the same helicopter, if parked out in the open on the carrier flight-deck. To meet the *Nimitz* the helicopters were transported to Diego Garcia, a tiny British island in the vastness of the Indian Ocean that was also home to a massive American military base. Once the helicopters were aboard, the *Nimitz* headed for the Gulf and, by the evening of 24 April, was fifty miles off the Iranian coast, launching her part of Eagle Claw at 7.30 pm.

The RH-53s were to fly to a landing strip, called Desert One, some 260 miles south of the Iranian capital, where they would meet with one MC-130 troop carrier and three EC-130E tanker aircraft, together with 120 soldiers from Delta Force and the Rangers. The helicopters would then take the assault force to Tehran. After they had been prised from the hands of their captors, the hostages would be flown by the RH-53s to a captured airfield where giant C-141 Starlifter jets would be waiting to take them to freedom. Any attempts by Iranian jets to intercept them were to be neutralized by F-14s from the *Nimitz*. Eagle Claw was a complex plan and it began to go wrong from the beginning. Special Forces troops, keeping watch over a road near to the Desert One airstrip, first of all had to stop a bus and detain its forty-five passengers and then, when a petrol tanker and a car came along, were forced to open fire. The petrol tanker exploded but the car got away, making it inevitable that the alarm would be raised. Meanwhile, two hours and forty minutes after taking off from the *Nimitz*, one of the RH-53s suffered severe rotor problems and had to be landed and abandoned, its crew being picked up by one of the other helicopters. Then, after the RH-53s encountered sandstorms, another suffered several failures in key systems and had to fly back to the *Nimitz*. But the worst happened after the helicopters reached Desert One. Because of the incident with the vehicles on the road, and the fact that another RH-53 had become non-operational on arrival, there were now not enough helicopters to safely carry on with the mission, and so the decision was taken to abort Eagle Claw. The C-130s would fly back to Oman with the Special Forces troops while the helicopters would return to the *Nimitz* after re-fuelling. To enable them all to top up with fuel from one of the EC-130s, the helicopters had to change positions, but, due to its weight and thin air at high altitude, one of the Sea Stallions was unable to sustain its hover and crashed onto the tanker aircraft. Both burst into flames, with the five aircrew in the C-130 and three US Marines in the RH-53 killed. In a state of shock, the mission commanders ordered the surviving helicopters to be abandoned at Desert One along with jeeps and other equipment. The rescue force and helicopter aircrews then flew back to Oman aboard the three remaining C-130s. With the dawn came the Iranians and the gleeful cleric who picked through the smouldering wreckage and held up the bones of dead US servicemen for the world to see how humbled, and incompetent, the 'Great Satan' was. Certainly Jimmy Carter's presidency received a blow that was a major factor in the Democrats losing office in the presidential elections of the same year.

> *The last shreds of Jimmy Carter's credibility were also consumed by the flames.* [6]

The remaining Tehran hostages would be released from captivity on 20 January 1981; the day Ronald Reagan began his presidency. It was a move designed to encourage the USA to provide spares for the Iranian armed forces' US-origin weapons systems, as Iran was at war with Iraq.

A month after the failed hostage rescue there was an attempted coup by pro-Shah military officers and in the July another was launched but like the first, it failed. The Iranian opposition collapsed when the Shah died that summer, leading Saddam to conclude that it was now highly unlikely that an American-backed group could solve the Iranian problem. He believed that, as time went on, Khomeini's grip would tighten and that the likelihood of Iran fomenting a Shia rebellion inside Iraq, as a precursor to invasion, would grow. So, on 22 September 1980, Iraqi forces had invaded Iran and, despite their sluggishness, managed to capture the port of Khorramshahr.

But Saddam was not, of course, acting purely out of fear, for the traditional Iraqi desire to gain broader access to the sea was also a factor and seizing control of both sides of the Shatt al Arab Waterway was, therefore, a primary objective. The capture of Iran's oil-rich province of Khuzistan was another Iraqi aim, in what became known as the Iran-Iraq War.

It so happened that when war broke out in the northern Gulf, the Royal Navy and the US Navy were scheduled to conduct an exercise in the Indian Ocean that was to draw in a total of 25 naval vessels, 170 aircraft and 18,000 men. It was a rare excursion for a British task group beyond the NATO area. The task group flagship was the County class destroyer HMS *Antrim*, accompanied by the Leander class frigate *Galatea* and Type 21 frigate *Alacrity*, which, plus RFA vessels, carried on, as scheduled, to the Far East. Due to the increased tension in the Middle East, two other members of the task group, the destroyer *Coventry* and frigate *Naiad*, were retained in the area of the Gulf and Arabian Sea.

There was no aircraft carrier available for leading such a deployment, as, at the time, the sole remaining ship of the type in commission, *Hermes*, was busy preparing to take on her new role as a jump jet carrier. The first of a new class of three carriers, *Invincible*, had been commissioned in July 1980 but was still being worked up to full operational pitch.

Meanwhile in the Far East, the *Alacrity* received orders to patrol the waters of Hormuz. Her eager young Commanding Officer was none other than Commander Chris Craig.

> *I had taken over in Hong Kong and everything was going swimmingly in my first week in charge when, on 14 October, at 23.00, I received a signal onboard* Alacrity *to sail with all despatch for the Gulf.* Alacrity *conducted a very fast transit across the Indian Ocean, exercising Action Stations, carrying out high seas firings, sorting out war organization and generally galvanizing the ship for a very uncertain future. We experienced a lot of difficulty over fuel. I had signalled my fuel state on departure, but there was a bit of a problem in working out how I was going to get more before I ran out, just short of the American supply ships up in the Gulf and the northern Arabian Sea. In the end, on 17 October, I fuelled from the Australian ship HMAS* Supply *in company with the frigate HMAS* Derwent. *We were on the fringe of a tropical cyclone, which made the process quite entertaining. Eventually, after a lot of disconnects and a fair bit of drama we ended up getting our fuel. A day-and-a-half later we were approaching Hormuz. The* Midway *and* Eisenhower *were the two US carriers on station and they had their operating areas in the northern Arabian Sea. We transited past them and, after doing a little bit of shadowing and teasing of a Russian Krivak Class frigate that was, in turn, shadowing the* Eisenhower, *we met up with the resident USN tanker, which was the* Hassayampa. *We carried out a re-fuelling with her on the 22 October and the next day rendezvoused with the Type 42 destroyer HMS* Coventry *and the RFA* Olwen, *which had been the resident Gulf ships, along with the frigate HMS* Naiad, *which was also in the area. On 26 October we ended up playing cat-and-mouse with a Russian vessel that was snooping around off Muscat. Five days later we carried out replenishment from the RFA* Stromness, *and on 3 November,* Coventry *departed and* Alacrity *became the senior ship of British forces in the Gulf. On 5 November* Alacrity *did a*

replenishment from Blue Rover *and I flew into Seeb in Oman to attend some meetings. We did a lot more patrolling and then, finally,* Antrim *came up from the south-east and, on 12 November, we handed over to her. The next day we started home, but, on 15 November, we conducted a night encounter exercise with the French Navy off Djibouti and then passed back through the Suez Canal, headed across the Mediterranean and back up to the UK. Obviously, for a starry-eyed first frigate command it was quite an exciting beginning.*

The *Alacrity* had played her part in the opening cycle of the Armilla Patrol, as the Royal Navy's now constant commitment to the Gulf was to be known. Thereafter, the deploying ships would come direct from the UK, with the next vessels assigned being the Type 42 destroyer *Birmingham* and Type 21 frigate *Avenger*, leaving in the October and arriving back home in March 1981.

As the war between Iran and Iraq raged on, the Americans increased force levels in the Arabian Sea and the Gulf to almost forty warships. The USS *Dwight D. Eisenhower* returned to the USA in late December 1980, having completed a deployment that had lasted for 251 days, 152 of them a single stretch at sea without a break. Her escorts were the cruisers *Carolina* and *Virginia*, all three warships proving conclusively the stamina of nuclear propulsion.

During the next eight years the US Navy would maintain at least one CBG in the northern Arabian Sea. Within the Gulf itself it deployed a reinforced presence of cruisers, destroyers and frigates under the banner Joint Task Force Middle East.

In October 1981 the British County class destroyer HMS *Glamorgan* left Portsmouth as flagship of Flag Officer, First Flotilla, Rear Admiral Sandy Woodward, bound for the Middle East. Joining *Glamorgan* were three frigates and a trio of RFAs. The British were headed for a rendezvous in the Arabian Sea with an American CBG led by the USS *Coral Sea*. During an exercise the Royal Navy played the part of an attacking 'enemy' force.

The frigates were all anti-submarine ships and not capable of doing serious harm to an aircraft carrier, short of ramming it. Only Glamorgan, *with her four Exocets and effective range of twenty miles, could inflict real damage on the* Coral Sea. [7]

Just a few months later Rear Admiral Woodward would be facing Argentinian Exocets that claimed the destroyer *Sheffield*. She had only just completed a tour of duty on Armilla when Argentina invaded the Falklands in April 1982 and was immediately ordered to the South Atlantic. The Type 21 frigate *Active*, which had been in the Gulf with *Sheffield*, returned to the UK first, before going south. The new Type 22 frigate *Broadsword*, frigate *Yarmouth* and tanker *Plumleaf* were on their way to the Gulf and had already reached the Mediterranean, but they too were soon on their way to the Falklands. The destroyer *Cardiff*, which was on stand-down from the Gulf in Mombasa, also received orders to sail south. With so many Royal Navy warships and auxiliaries diverted to the Falklands, New Zealand offered to help out in the Gulf. Consequently, between June and August 1982, the frigate HMNZS *Canterbury* was on the Armilla Patrol alongside two different Leanders, HMS *Ajax* and HMS *Aurora*, supported by the RFA *Gold Rover*. New Zealand also

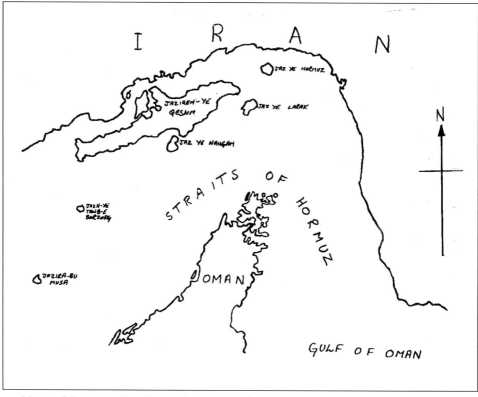

Most of the world's oil supply passed through the Strait of Hormuz, where Iran frequently provoked a response from the US Navy. This map was drawn by a sailor in the British frigate London, *for the ship's newspaper.*
Crowter/D. Littlejohns Collection.

sent the frigate *Waikato*, which relieved *Canterbury* in August 1982 and patrolled alongside *Aurora* and then *Alacrity*, the latter having seen distinguished war service in the South Atlantic under Commander Chris Craig.

In August 1982, the Iraqis declared most of the northern Gulf an exclusion zone, including Iran's vital Kharg Island oil terminal and any ships seen in the vicinity were warned they would be attacked by aircraft armed with Exocet anti-shipping missiles. That September, enraged by the support being given to the Iraqis by the Gulf states, and angered by France supplying Super Etendard strike jets that could extend the Exocet threat, Ayatollah Khomeini made a thinly veiled threat to cut off the oil trade with the West by closing the Strait of Hormuz.

This was not an idle boast, for the Iranians had anti-shipping missile batteries, but the scale of interference depended on whether or not the benefits of doing such a thing would outweigh the problems it would cause.

Dominance over the Strait of Hormuz is split between Oman and Iran and, after Britain withdrew from East of Suez, the Iranians seized some strategically placed islands on the Gulf side of the Strait that gave them even greater influence. One hundred tankers a day passed through Hormuz, so there were plenty of targets for the Iranians to attack, except the Iraqis did not rely entirely on exporting their oil by sea and closing the Strait outright would most likely provoke a very strong response from the West.

A campaign of harassment by Iranian naval vessels and Revolutionary Guard fast boats was mounted, with the aim of punishing those supporting Iraq with war loans, such as the Gulf states, or supplying them with weapons or other support, such as the USA and European countries.

While fewer than fifty merchant ships were attacked in the Gulf between 1980 and 1983, nearly eighty would fall victim in 1984. The main Iranian naval bases were at Bandar Abbas in the south, in a good position to dominate Hormuz, and at Bushahr, Kharg Island and Khorramshahr, well placed to cause trouble in the northern Gulf.

Although Iran was ostensibly denied spares, technical support, and munitions from the West, in fact covert shipments of weapons and spare parts from the USA and other Western nations, together with supplies from China, Vietnam and Israel, were vital to keeping the Iranian war machine running.

The Iranians' US-built F-4 Phantoms were operational, along with their Maverick missiles and their helicopters were also soon on the prowl against Arab tankers and other merchant ships. However, the effectiveness of strikes was limited, as the vessels were huge and, therefore, not easy to sink or even to slow down.

The Iraqis, on the other hand, had only naval bases at Umm Qasr and Basra, but they did have a good supply of Exocets for their Super Etendards.

In March 1984 a Greek tanker was hit with an Iraqi Exocet and in the April a Panamanian-registered tanker off Kharg fell victim to a similar strike.

The Iranians attacked an oil tanker flying the Kuwaiti flag in mid-May and then another merchant ship, this time belonging to Saudi Arabia, when the latter was inside Saudi territorial waters. In early June, the Iraqis managed to sink a Turkish-registered tanker in the northern Gulf but an Iranian Phantom seeking to attack shipping was shot down close to the Saudi coast.

In 1986 the Iranians captured the al-Faw and started to launch anti-shipping missiles across the water, in an attempt to hit ships at anchor off Kuwait's main oil terminal. By the beginning of 1987 the Iranians had made seventy attacks on shipping in the Gulf while the Iraqis had notched up 132. [8]

Commander 'Sharkey' Ward was a Sea Harrier pilot during the Falklands War of 1982, downing three Argentinian aircraft in air combat but, by the late 1980s, he had left the Royal Navy and was running a small security company called Defence Analysts Limited (DAL). The conflict in the Gulf between Iran and Iraq seemed to demand DAL's attention, especially as its highly relevant freelance skills could be used to counter those of the hired hands piloting Iraqi strike jets. 'We realized that oil tankers suffering air attack on the Kharg Island 'shuttle' might well be saved from total destruction through the 'hands on appliance' of various safety measures,' explained Commander Ward some years later.

This shuttle was the main Iranian oil export route between Kharg Island in the North and the Strait of Hormuz in the South. Exocet-armed Iraqi fighter jets piloted by highly paid ex-patriate pilots represented the threat. For

55

each tanker hit a pilot would receive a bonus; and a new Mercedes would be waiting on the tarmac when he returned from his mission. But, it was difficult to convince the oil shipping magnates that our services could be beneficial in financial terms. We overcame this by talking with the insurers Lloyd's of London, explaining the possible benefits of our services. As a result, one of the underwriters agreed to discount the war insurance rates for Gulf oil tankers protected by DAL and by the amount of cash that we were to charge for our services. And so Project Xenephon was launched, with an ex-Special Forces operator and various physical safety measures installed onboard each tanker, operating in what had become dubbed 'Exocet Alley'. A retired Special Boat Squadron officer provided these operators to us.

The safety measures instituted aboard the tankers included: Advice to the Master on precise routing; damage control training for ships' crews (something else that tapped into the Royal Navy's excellent training and practice); reducing secondary injuries from blast by covering all bridge windows with a special plastic film; sandbagging various key points on deck; providing armoured protection for key personnel on the bridge; applying First Aid to casualties following an attack; towing a radar reflector decoy astern of the ship. A key lesson that the ex-Royal Navy Sea Harrier pilot's organization conveyed to the tanker Masters and crews was that sticking with the hit vessel was better than abandoning her. However, the desire to flee was understandable. 'An Exocet coming inboard in an oil tanker is a horrifying experience,' acknowledged Commander Ward.

The catastrophic rupture of a main oil cargo tank is inevitably followed by a raging inferno that cannot be contained by onboard fire-fighting resources. In the immediate aftermath of impact, the first reaction of the crew is to abandon ship - usually ably led by the Master! Our operators' most important duties were to dissuade the Master and crew from immediately manning the lifeboats; to assess the damage; to treat casualties; to call for assistance and to contain the fire. In all, DAL operators were involved in twelve missile/air attacks that resulted in generally serious damage to the ship. Without DAL onboard control and assistance, most of these tankers would have been lost to fire; instead of which, they were saved and personal injury was kept to a minimum. But it was no easy ride. Our only operator casualty was an ex-SBS specialist. When his ship was moored and embarking oil at Kharg Island, the Iraqis launched a strafing attack, which caused minimal damage to the vessel's hull but peppered the bridge with high velocity cannon rounds. Our man was badly injured, having had no time to take cover behind the armour plating. He had shards of glass in his chest and abdomen and other injuries including a severed Achilles tendon. Iranian medics rushed onboard and whisked him ashore - where they knelt on him to keep him still while removing the main shards of glass from his wounds. Apart from his health, our main worry now was recovering our chap from the clutches of the Iranian military, who had always viewed our operators with overt suspicion. Luckily, the shipping concern that we were working for used their considerable influence with the Iranian authorities to recover the ex-SBS man, within the space of about twelve hours.

On the night of 17 May 1987, an American warship fell victim to two Exocets. The pilot who launched the missiles, from one of Iraq's newly acquired Mirage F-1 fighters, later claimed that he mistook the Perry class frigate USS *Stark* for an Iranian tanker. The *Stark* was eighty miles to the north-east of Bahrain when she was hit and her Rules of Engagement (ROE) instructed her that she was to exert a neutral presence. She therefore had no clearance to fire before a potential aggressor did. A US Air Force Airborne Warning and Control (AWAC) aircraft flying from Saudi Arabia had advised the Stark the Iraqis had F-1s on the prowl and shortly after 9.00pm the frigate picked up one with her own radar. Despite this, *Stark* did not raise her readiness levels.

> *...the ship's super-rapid blooming offboard Chaff (SRBOC) launchers are not armed, her phalanx anti-missile Gatling gun is turned off, and her .50-caliber machine guns are unloaded.* [9]

The F-1 launched its first missile little more than twenty miles from the *Stark* and, as the Exocet sped towards its target, the US warship asked the pilot of the strike jet to identify himself. Sixty seconds before the first missile hit the warship on her port side, *Stark* finally armed her chaff launchers and readied her weapons systems. The second missile hit within seconds of the first and incredibly, although both missiles were spotted by lookouts, neither the ship's radar nor the Electronic Support Measures (ESM) detected them. [10]

Thirty-seven American sailors were killed, for one of the missiles detonated next to a mess deck. Part of the first missile carved a path of destruction eighty feet through the ship and then punched out the starboard side. In fact, only one of the warheads actually blew up, but fuel from both missiles ignited, causing serious fires that melted sections of the warship's aluminium superstructure. Burning propellant from the first missile shot into accommodation areas and also ruptured the primary water main for firefighting equipment. The second Exocet struck just eight feet away from the first missile's impact point, detonating between three feet and five feet within the hull, creating a large blast zone. [11]

Because of inefficient drainage, water used to fight the fires collected inside the ship and almost caused her to capsize. Additional pumps were flown out to the *Stark* by a US Navy helicopter based in Bahrain, which also flew injured sailors ashore for treatment.

> *Damage control is magnificent. Although fires reach a temperature of 1,800 degrees F, melting parts of the aluminium superstructure, and the weight of water sprayed into the conflagration causes the vessel to list 26 degrees to port, the* Stark's *men save their ship.* [12]

The American warships *Waddell* and *Conyngham*, both destroyers, moved in to lend assistance, while the British frigates *Broadsword* and *Active* happened to be nearby as well and offered help. With daybreak the two Royal Navy warships moved closer to the stricken *Stark*, providing cover against any further attacks.

At the same time as the American frigate was hit, a Norwegian tanker was set ablaze during an attack by Iranian boats off Saudi Arabia while a Russian vessel was

The stricken frigate USS Stark, still smoking and listing to port, the morning after being hit by two Iraqi Exocet missiles. US Navy.

damaged by a mine strike off Kuwait.

Despite the damage, the *Stark* was able to return to the USA under her own steam, where she was repaired, at a cost in excess of $100 million, and returned to service.

With the air threat so high, the Royal Navy had begun to deploy its more modern air-warfare ships to the Gulf whenever possible. Experience in the Falklands War had shown the combination of the Sea Dart long-range SAM system, carried by the Type 42 destroyers, combined with the shorter range Sea Wolf SAM, carried by Type 22 frigates and some Leanders, was effective.

In the immediate aftermath of the *Stark* attack, the air defences of British frigates on patrol in the Gulf were boosted with the provision of shoulder-launched SAMs to teams of embarked Royal Marines. The *Broadsword* and *Active* were also given new rules of engagement:

> *Captains of both ships have been given orders to shoot first and ask questions afterwards if they feel any unknown aircraft is likely to put their ships at risk.*[13]

The *Active*, with her antiquated Sea Cat SAM system, was the most vulnerable of the two British frigates and therefore appreciated the boost to air defences provided by the Royal Marines. Meanwhile, Iraqi government spokesman Tariq Aziz told a press conference that, as there had been no attempt to interrogate the F-1 pilot by radio, he had assumed the warship in his path was Iranian.

A subsequent inquiry found that human error was to blame and the ship's Commanding Officer and her Tactical Action Officer were both given letters of reprimand and resigned their commissions. [14]

At the inquiry questions were raised about the readiness of the *Stark*, her design, and the rules of engagement issued to her captain.

> *Following the attacks, these rules were changed to permit U.S. warships to fire on nearby aircraft that were acting 'suspiciously'.* [15]

In practical terms, measures were taken to enable American warships in the Gulf to handle the dreadful aftermath of missile strikes better, including extra breathing apparatus for damage control teams and smoke penetration (thermal imaging) cameras, to provide more efficient location of casualties. The thermal imaging cameras were obtained from the UK, having proved their usefulness during the Falklands War, in which several Royal Navy warships were sunk or badly damaged. The ships' Close-in Weapon System (CIWS) and automated weapon systems were also refined.

After three years of enduring attacks on its tankers, Kuwait, which was still bank rolling the Iraqi war effort and therefore had every reason to expect an escalation in the Iranian assault on its trade, was ready to consider radical measures to gain protection. The Soviets, who were supplying vast quantities of arms to Saddam, and were keen to establish a naval presence in the Gulf, had previously indicated that they would look favourably on the idea of providing protection for Kuwaiti tankers, re-flagged as Russian vessels. Extremely alarmed by this prospect, America immediately offered to provide escorts for Kuwaiti vessels that had been re-flagged as US ships.

So, American warships began close escort of merchant vessels in July 1987, but in the UK some politicians cautioned against Britain joining the USA, for fear of getting sucked into the fighting. The MP for *Active* and *Broadsword*'s home base of Devonport, and former Labour Foreign Secretary and Navy Minister, Dr David Owen, was reported as saying that he feared UK warships could be attacked if British protection was provided to re-flagged merchant ships.

> *Nobody doubts that the Americans could sail through the Gulf with their Reaganite guns blazing. The danger for us is that unlike the Americans our ships don't have any air cover and are therefore much more vulnerable.* [16]

On 21 July, Dr Owen had suggested that a multi-national flotilla should be established, involving both the Russians and the Chinese, to provide escort for merchant ships. British Prime Minister Margaret Thatcher was, however, persuaded that re-flagged merchant vessels should soon be offered the protection of British warships. The UK Defence Secretary, George Younger, revealed that he had given Royal Navy warships authority to defend themselves or any British merchant ships under attack. The Type 42 air-defence destroyer *Cardiff* had by this time reinforced the Armilla frigates and all three Royal Navy warships were supported by the RFA tanker *Orangeleaf*, herself vulnerable to Iranian or Iraqi attack. The Defence Secretary stressed that, despite robust ROE, the British warships were neutral in the conflict. The minister said:

> *We have found through all this war - and we have been there longer than anyone else - on all the occasions that our naval ships have been accompanying any British ships they have not been attacked. We are entirely non-provocative...we are not aiming to attack anybody at all...I believe that will be respected...*

However, Mr Younger cautioned that, if British vessels were attacked, 'they would have to defend themselves.' [17]

On 22 July, four Iranian F-4s made a threatening run towards Kuwaiti re-flagged tankers under escort from American warships as they passed through the Strait of Hormuz. The strike jets turned away after being warned off via radio by the escort force flagship, the guided-missile cruiser USS *Fox*. The cruiser's CO, Captain William Mathis, explained that the F-4s took off from a military airbase near Bandar Abbas but 'stayed inside their territorial limits as they came down towards us.' The risks were not restricted to the air though, with the *Fox* forced to take evasive action to avoid a small Iranian fishing boat that would not move out of her way.

The US Navy's escort task was dubbed Operation Earnest Will, and it was while she was being protected by three US Navy warships, and underway from the UAE to Kuwait, that the 400,000 tons re-flagged tanker *Bridgeton* hit a mine, which turned out to be a First World War-era Russian design, but she did not sink.

> *The explosion was clearly audible as a loud* boom *aboard the destroyer* USS Kidd, *which was one mile to the left and about half a mile to the rear of the* Bridgeton. [18]

The *Kidd* was one of four guided-missile destroyers built for the Shah of Iran in the late 1970s, but acquired by the US Navy after the revolution of 1979. Now she was command ship of the escort force and received a plaintive radio message from the *Bridgeton*:

> *We've been hit! We've been hit!* [19]

The *Kidd's* CO, Commander Daniel Murphy, ordered the escort ships to slow down and extra lookouts were immediately posted on the American warships' upper decks to spot any other mines floating in the vicinity. Aboard the *Kidd* that meant:

> *At least nine sailors were on the bow, some armed with M-14 rifles to fire at any suspicious objects in the water.* [20]

It was the first of many such incidents and, with the US Navy being weak in the area of modern Mine Counter-Measure Vessels (MCMVs), in early August a request was passed from the Pentagon to the UK Ministry of Defence, asking for the deployment of sophisticated Royal Navy MCMVs to the Gulf. However, the US request met with a 'no' from Margaret Thatcher. A similar request submitted to Germany was also greeted with a negative. While Britain had agreed to provide warship escorts for British-flagged merchant vessels through the Strait of Hormuz and as far as Bahrain, it was felt that the presence of MCMVs would only increase tension. In the meantime, Iran declared a 'day of hatred' for the USA and promised attacks on US-escorted convoys. The commander of US Navy forces in the Gulf, Rear Admiral Harold Bernsen, was in no doubt that Iran's fiery rhetoric would result in attacks:

> *I have every reason to expect that they are going to do something.* [21]

That turned out to be a series of naval exercises, involving thousands of volunteer fighters, belonging to the Islamic Revolutionary Guard Corps under the ominous codename 'Martyrdom'. Tehran warned British and American warships to stay clear of its coastal waters or it would 'severely confront them'. [22]

Meanwhile, America staged its own show of strength by launching a mock invasion of Somalia, in cooperation with that country's armed forces. The Pentagon made no secret of the fact that it was sending ashore thousands of US Marines from an amphibious warfare task group, to test how swiftly it could insert a similar force into the Gulf to secure oilfields in Saudi Arabia or Kuwait. The detection of what might be shore-based Iranian Anti-Shipping Missile (ASM) battteries, using their radars to try and acquire targets in the Strait of Hormuz, further increased the tension. As US Navy Electronic Warfare (EW) aircraft from a carrier in the Gulf of Oman tried to jam the Iranian radar, warning of an imminent attack was flashed to all American warships in the region. It was soon determined that the radar in question belonged not to a Silkworm ASM battery but to a ground station making a general sweep of the Strait. However, the Americans were so jumpy that even the chairman of the US Joint Chiefs of Staff, Admiral William Crowe, was called to his office in the Pentagon, in the early hours, during the emergency. On 6 August the USA repeated its appeal for British and German MCMVs.

> *The Americans, bruised by the first rebuff, claim Britain has a duty to help the U.S. maintain its role in policing the Gulf and protecting oil tankers. But that has not altered Mrs Thatcher's insistence that Britain keep a low profile.*[23]

The UK was worried, along with other European nations, that contributing additional warships to ensure the safe passage of the pro-Iraqi Kuwaiti tankers might provoke Iran into more aggressive action against merchant ships, not less. However, by 11 August, following the appearance of more mines in the Gulf, the UK had changed its mind about the MCMVs, as George Younger revealed.

> *News of further mining in the Gulf area over the last 48 hours shows that a new situation has arisen...The Government has therefore decided to equip the Armilla Patrol with a minesweeping capability to enable it to continue to carry out its task effectively.*[24]

The decision had followed a crisis meeting at 10 Downing Street, chaired by Mrs Thatcher. Four highly effective Hunt class MCMVs - *Bicester, Hurworth, Brecon* and *Brockelsby* - plus the *Abdiel*, as tasking ship, were on their way, along with the frigates *Andromeda* and *Brazen* and the destroyer *Edinburgh*. The forward repair ship RFA *Diligence* was also sent, from the Falklands, to stand-by to repair warships damaged by mines or missiles and provide general engineering support. The *Abdiel*

A British Hunt class mine-hunter rafted up next to HMS Herald *in the Gulf.* ACME Photographic.

would be replaced the following year by the survey ship HMS *Herald* while MCMVs from Holland and Belgium were also soon operating alongside the Royal Navy's.

The Labour opposition greeted the Tory government's change of heart over the mine-hunter force with warnings about escalating the conflict, with Shadow Foreign Secretary Gerald Kaufman calling the move 'a very serious reversal'.[25] By November, the US Navy had managed to send eight RH-53s aboard the assault carrier USS *Guadalcanal*, which had been committed to the MCMV role, together with half-a-dozen 1950s vintage small coastal minesweepers.

In March 1988, the British government revealed that ten mines had been found and destroyed by Royal Navy mine-hunters in the Gulf and that, between July and December 1987, an impressive 405 merchant ships had been escorted through Hormuz.

The increased level of US Navy participation - with many more ships being sent into an intense threat environment which they had no experience of - worried Tanker War veterans like Sharkey Ward. Through its work aboard tankers running the Exocet gauntlet, the former Royal Navy jet fighter pilot's DAL organization had gained some very valuable intelligence concerning operations in the war zone, particularly with regard to activities within the Iranian twelve-mile limit.

> It was very apparent that the USN warship commanders had not had adequate briefing about the Gulf airspace. To most of them, anything that moved in the air was a threat, whether it happened to be flying within recognized civil aviation airways or not. On one occasion, a US warship stationed itself close to Dubai, anchoring under the main approach to the international airport. Action stations were called whenever an airliner made its approach and one could hear the ship calling on the international emergency frequency: 'Unknown aircraft, you are approaching a US Navy warship. Turn away or we may be forced to open fire!' Incidents such as this triggered me to write to the White House, advising the President that unless the US Navy became better briefed on Gulf airspace and operations, there was likely to be a regrettable incident, i.e. an American warship was likely to engage and shoot down a civil airliner or perhaps a sheik's private jet. The White House acknowledged my letter but took no action.

To avoid giving the impression that they were becoming directly embroiled in local conflicts, British warships merely 'accompanied' a merchant vessel. Aboard the frigate HMS *Andromeda*, a Sea Wolf Leander, twenty-two year-old Acting Able Seaman Gary Davies came eyeball to eyeball with the Iranians as they threatened UK-flagged ships.

> At the time, the Iranians were being particularly aggressive. Our job was simply to escort British-flagged vessels so that any aggressor would think twice about getting involved. In all we made forty-eight transits, accompanying more than 5.6 million tonnes of shipping, although unofficially it was much more, as vessels from other flags would take advantage of our presence and attach themselves to our mini-convoy for the extra security it provided.
>
> I remember most of them being Japanese. The trade was obviously

The British tanker Isomeria *under escort from HMS* Andromeda, *at the height of the Tanker War. Note the lifeboats made ready for boarding by the tanker's anxious crew.* Gary Davies.

lucrative despite the high risks, with about eight ships a week being attacked. We heard rumours that some Ship Masters were being offered $10,000 per round trip. The most memorable incident from our numerous transits was a close encounter with an Iranian frigate. The date was 8 September 1987 and we were taking the Shell tanker Isomeria *out of the Gulf when the Iranian warship appeared out of the haze. Just seven months earlier the same frigate had fired five Sea Killer anti-shipping missiles at the same, then unprotected, tanker, but all had missed. I couldn't help wondering what kind of fireball there would be if a tanker went up in flames just half a mile away from us! The frigate was identified as the* Sahand *and it all got a bit interesting when she closed to within a mile of us and challenged the* Isomeria *to identify herself. At the time I was acting as a lookout and my job was to report what I could see down to the Operations Room. I had a direct comms link to the Chief Gunner who was getting quite excited at the other end as the 'bandit' moved in! I had to provide a running commentary of what I could see. It all came to a head when I witnessed the smaller 35mm gun on the stern of the Iranian warship being slowly, but surely, trained in our direction. As the situation developed we upped speed and closed the gap to our charge. Everyone kept their cool. It became apparent that the Iranians were doing a bit of maintenance but there was obviously some brinkmanship involved - there's a time and a place for everything, including gun maintenance, and this wasn't it. Having stayed with us for a few hours, the Iranian ship suddenly veered away to interrogate a Japanese tanker going the other way.*

On 22 September 1987 an Iranian landing craft called the *Iran Ajr* was intercepted north-east of Bahrain and captured by US forces. Because the US Navy lacked the right kind of helicopters for armed interdiction of surface vessels, US Army MH-6 helicopter gunships were embarked in American warships and it was one of these aircraft, from the frigate USS *Jarrett*, that found the *Iran Ajr* laying mines. Her progress was halted by rockets from the MH-6.

The frigate USS Samuel B. Roberts, *which struck a mine in the Gulf.*
M. Welsford.

The boarding parties, who found that the mines were of the same type that damaged the *Bridgeton*, wasted no time in sinking the *Iran Ajr* and, stung by this, Iranian Revolutionary Guard armed speed boats attacked RH-53s making aerial sweeps.

Just a few hours prior to the *Iran Ajr* interception, the British-flagged tanker *Gentle Breeze* had been attacked to the south of Kuwait, by a gunboat that fired more than a dozen small calibre shells into her.

And the missile menace had not gone away. In October 1987, an Iranian Silkworm missile, launched by a land-based battery in the al-Faw hit the Kuwaiti-owned, re-flagged Tanker *Sea Isle City*. This provoked an American assault on 19 October, against two oil platforms suspected of being used by the Iranians to coordinate attacks or to launch them. The resident Iranian troops were given time to leave before the destroyers *Hoel, Kidd, Leftwich* and *John Young* poured more than 1,000 shells into the platforms.

In the meantime, the Iraqis had been attacking shipping and Iranian oil terminals further and further south, close to the United Arab Emirates and Hormuz. Indeed official United Nations' figures recorded that both sides in the Gulf had attacked 167 ships during 1987.

Therefore, the threats now stretched from the bottom of the Gulf to the top and nowhere was a rear area, where relaxed routines could be followed, as the Perry class frigate USS *Samuel B. Roberts* discovered on 14 April 1988, while involved in tanker escort duties. Keen-eyed sailors aboard the frigate had spotted at least three tethered mines floating close to the surface nearby, but, as she carefully withdrew stern first from what was clearly a minefield, she struck a mine containing 250lbs of explosives and suffered catastrophic damage. The gash ripped in her side was

64

twenty-two feet long while her keel suffered a nine feet tear. The crew battled severe flooding, while vain attempts were made to restore her propulsion, but somehow, over the next seven hours, the warship's sailors managed to keep her afloat.

Intense fires were aggravated by the use of aluminium in construction...[26]

Yet, despite the damage, not one of the *Roberts'* sailors had been killed. After preliminary repairs at Dubai, the frigate went back to the USA on the back of a Dutch heavy-lift ship and was repaired at a cost of around $38 million. An examination of the danger area the *Samuel B. Roberts* had strayed into revealed mines of Iranian origin and this provoked an operation that turned into the biggest surface action involving the US Navy since the Second World War.

Operation Praying Mantis was launched on 18 April and, over a period of forty-eight hours, Joint Task Force Middle East attacked a pair of oil platforms - the Sassan and Sirri, just off the UAE , both of which were suspected of being Iranian bases. The Americans also went in search of one of the British-built Iranian frigates, the *Sabalan*, that had been carrying out attacks on shipping.

Three Surface Action Groups (SAGs) were put together to tackle each of the targets: Bravo, composed of the destroyers *Lynde McCormick* and *Merrill* and reinforced by the assault ship *Trenton*, took on the Sassan; Charlie, composed of the cruiser *Wainwright* and two frigates, *Simpson* and *Bagley* attacked the Sirri; Delta, composed of the destroyers *Joseph Strauss* and *O' Brien* and the frigate *Jack Williams*, hunted the *Sabalan*.[27]

As with the October 1987 attack on platforms, the Iranians were given time to evacuate the Sassan, but some chose to stay and fired on the ships of SAG Bravo with a 35mm anti-aircraft gun. A well-aimed 5-inch shell from the *Merrill* silenced the Iranian gun.[28] US Navy explosive experts placed charges on the rig to destroy it and these, together with rockets from US Marine Corps Cobra gunships dismantled it. However, during this assault one of the Cobras was either shot down or suffered a catastrophic mechanical failure, with its two crew killed. SAG Charlie similarly destroyed the Sirri platform. The Iranians hit back by sending their navy out to fight. One of their fast attack craft, the *Joshan*, made a sortie towards SAG Charlie, firing a Harpoon anti-shipping missile, which the Americans distracted with countermeasures. The *Joshan* was herself destroyed via the unusual application of SM-1 anti-air missiles, which had been adapted for the surface-to-surface role, and fired by both the *Wainwright* and the *Simpson*. The *Wainwright's* 5-inch gun and *Simpson's* 76mm finished the job, with the *Joshan* suffering fifteen of her sailors killed and twenty-nine wounded.

When a pair of Iranian Phantoms, carrying Mavericks, tried to intervene, the *Wainwright* loosed off some SM-2 anti-air missiles that winged one of them and persuaded both to turn away.

Some Revolutionary Guard speed boats made a lunge towards the American warships, but were attacked themselves by US Navy strike jets from the carrier USS *Enterprise*, and, with one of the craft destroyed, the rest retreated from the scene. While the *Sabalan* was sheltering in Bandar Abbas, the Iranians did order the *Sahand* to go out and do battle. Despite being warned to back off, she launched a missile, which failed to hit anything. In return Harpoon missiles from the *Simpson* wrecked

Sahand, which was bombed by Intruders, the latter being forced to evade SAMs fired by the Iranian frigate. Gunfire from the American warships finished her off. Now the *Sabalan* also entered the fray, firing missiles, but she too came off badly, hit by a bomb and left dead in the water. The *Sabalan* could easily have been sunk, but the White House, which was monitoring the incident on a minute-by-minute basis, instructed the commanders on the spot not to do so.

Despite this crushing defeat at the hands of the Americans, the Iranians continued to harass Western naval vessels and merchant ships. The first such attack came within hours of the US Navy assault on the rigs.

> *A British tanker and a US-operated oil rig were shelled by an Iranian warship today in a tit-for-tat attack in the Gulf.* [29]

The tanker was the 112,744 tons *York Marine* and the oil rig belonged to Sharjah, both attacked by the Iranians less than three hours after the conclusion of Praying Mantis.

With the situation remaining tense, Sharkey Ward feared that soon there might be a tragedy in which many innocent civilians would die.

> *One year later, almost to the day that I wrote to the White House, an A300 Airbus en-route from Iran to Dubai was shot down.*

On 3 July, Iranian fast boats attacked the Ticonderoga class cruiser USS *Vincennes*. Equipped with the powerful AEGIS combat system, she was receiving a comprehensive picture of the entire Gulf, which, to her command team, appeared to show she was the target of a coordinated revenge mission. Embroiled in running battles with the Iranian boats, during which both of the *Vincennes'* 5-inch guns engaged targets, her radar seemed to indicate an incoming air attack from an Iranian strike jet. But the two Standard SM-2 anti-air missiles the *Vincennes* fired did not bring down an F-4 or F-14, but the Iranian airliner, carrying 290 people, all of whom died. The American warship had requested that the radar contact identify itself a number of times, with no response. Radar operators in the Combat Information Center mistook a climb away from the *Vincennes* for a dive towards her and, on receiving that information, the CO had believed he had no choice but to shoot the mystery aircraft down. [30]

The Iranians were understandably furious and made very strong representations to the American government, which offered to pay compensation to the families of those killed. An inquiry blamed the tragedy on sailors in the *Vincennes* failing to interpret the information provided by their equipment properly, but there was a suggestion that an identification signal from an Iranian military aircraft on an airfield across the water may have contributed to the fatal confusion. [31]

A lull of ten days in the Gulf was broken when the Iranians attacked a Japanese-owned tanker sailing by Farsi Island. The Panamanian-registered *Universal Monarch* suffered a severe fire in her engine room that her crew struggled to contain. The frigate USS *Nicholas* picked up the tanker's distress calls and immediately launched her MH-6 helicopters to ensure the Iranians could not attack the tanker again. As they approached, the American helicopters were fired upon by a couple of Iranian fast boats. Giving chase, the MH-6s fired rockets, damaging one of the Iranian vessels.

The British frigate HMS London *escorts a tanker through the Strait of Hormuz.* D. Littlejohns Collection.

This was the tense situation that the British Type 22 frigate HMS *London* sailed into just a few weeks later. The *London* had been called out to the Gulf in a hurry when one of the British warships already on station - HMS *Charybdis* - suffered fuel contamination. After exercises with an American CBG, led by the USS *Forrestal*, in the Arabian Sea, the *London* began escorting tankers in and out of the Strait of Hormuz. *London*'s Commanding Officer was Captain Doug Littlejohns, who had come to the frigate from commanding a nuclear-powered attack submarine. He had always imagined he would be stalking merchant ships from beneath the waves rather than protecting them against the threat of missile attack.

There were congregation points - one outside for tankers going in and another inside the Gulf for ships needing an escort to come out through the Strait of Hormuz. There was tremendous liaison between the MoD and the owners of the tankers. When you arrived at a congregation point you made contact with the tankers and then tried to get them in line, the ship going up and down like some sort of sheep dog. The Iranians would sometimes send their warships out to sail up and down parallel to the convoy. I remember one of their British-built frigates actually trained his guns on us. I didn't take too kindly to that and I got on the radio and said to him: 'I would really prefer you don't do that!' He turned his guns away. London *also made a few air contacts on her radar and we had to watch out for mines. Then we had an incident where we had a report of some Iranian missile boats leaving an island base. I had my Lynxes in the air, armed with Sea Skua anti-shipping missiles, just in case, and an Airborne Early Warning Sea King from the RFA that was with us had them on radar. We saw this lot coming at us, but they then turned around and went back in to wherever they had come from. There was an American warship at anchor at Dubai and he had the Iranians on his screen as well. There was a lot of iron-mongery in the Gulf and it could pose its own hazards sometimes, you know, the sheer number of warships in there. In the Gulf the* London *was permitted a higher level of threat than normal - my Principal Warfare Officer had permission to fire if I was not available to give the nod. There wasn't a submarine threat at that time but there was obviously an air threat and it was proven and of course there were the mines.*

In the meantime, the US Navy seemed keen to learn from its mistakes and, in the wake of the *Vincennes* incident, Commander Ward and other executives of DAL were invited to the State Department and the Pentagon to discuss the possibility of providing onboard training and intelligence advice to US warships in the Gulf. 'We addressed Chief of Naval Operations and his senior Admirals as well as a combined audience of all US Intelligence Agencies,' recalled Commander Ward.

They, quite rightly, were keen to find out how good our knowledge of the Gulf actually was. We answered many questions before what was presented as 'the crippler'. A Lieutenant Commander declared that his Admiral and his associated staff had been puzzling over a detailed satellite photo of Gulf waters for the previous nine months. In the photo, there was a dhow with what appeared to be parallel rails stretching out over the water. Was this a mine-laying dhow? By chance, the CNO in his briefing to us had mentioned that the American fleet had lost interest in mine warfare more than ten years previously - and now the US Navy was feeling very vulnerable. As soon as one of our guys looked at the photograph, he gave the answer to what had mystified the US Navy for some time: 'Gentlemen, this is a picture of a dhow that is fishing for shrimp! The parallel rails are simply the bamboo poles that suspend the shrimp net in the water!' Having satisfied the US Intelligence Services' curiosity, we were informed by the Pentagon that a contract for our services onboard all US warships in the Gulf would be forthcoming. Sadly, a twelve per cent defence budget cut was announced before the contract was signed and it went down the chute.

Simultaneously, the Iran-Iraq war was in its final weeks. Iran had suffered hundreds of thousands of soldiers killed, with thousands of civilian casualties during Iraqi air raids and missile attacks on cities, including Tehran. In April 1988 the Iraqis had regained the al-Faw and all other territory lost since the beginning of the war. However, even though it appeared to be gaining the upper hand, Iraq had achieved none of its original war aims and, like Iran, had suffered hundreds of thousands of dead. In fact 375,000 Iraqis were killed or wounded while the Iranians suffered over a million casualties. [32]

In mid-July 1988 the Iranians agreed to a UN brokered ceasefire and a month later the fighting really did stop, even though some expected it would be used as a cover by the Iraqis to launch an offensive.

It was due to take effect at midnight and everyone was very jumpy. Intelligence sources had told us that the Iraqis were going to make a sneak attack. [33]

Even after the ceasefire it was still felt necessary to escort merchant ships and it was while she was engaged in just such a duty that HMS *Southampton* was in collision with a British-flagged container vessel in the Gulf of Oman on 4 September 1988. The Type 42 destroyer suffered a nine feet gash along her waterline between the Sea Dart SAM launcher and the bridge. Heavily down by the bows, somehow her damage control teams managed to keep her afloat while the *London* sailed to her assistance. The *Southampton*'s bridge was also damaged, with much of her radar and communications equipment put out of action. The *Southampton* would

The RFA Diligence *comes to the rescue, as the destroyer HMS* Southampton *strives to stay afloat.* D. Littlejohns Collection.

eventually be transported back to the UK on the back of a heavy-lift vessel and, after extensive repairs, was returned to service in 1991.

By late September 1988 the US Navy had scaled back the intensity of its operations, and ceased providing close escorts for merchant ships, but it still kept its guard up, by offering 'zone defence'. In the December, Earnest Will was declared to be at an end, the US Navy having protected 270 merchant ships in 136 convoys, with only one - the *Bridgeton* - damaged while under escort. [34]

The American sailors who said farewell to the war zone took with them not only memories of running the gauntlet of missiles and mines, but also a climate that had an intensity like no other they had experienced. One US Navy Gulf veteran later recalled:

> *It could still be quite hot during the build-up to the high summer. I always felt fortunate I did not smoke, as those who did had to go outside whenever the interior Smoking Lamp was out. The deck railings would get so hot during the worst summer months that you could not touch them without getting a low-degree burn. When the smoking lamp was out, our guys were generally forced to go to the fantail, where the smoking lamp was usually always open, but they got blasted with hot winds from the environment and, if underway at respectable speed, hit with hot air from the gas turbines venting out the stacks. Radar was another interesting issue during certain months. These sirocco winds would come either out of Iran or the Kuwaiti-Saudi desert border areas. To a ship's radar operator sitting at his console, it could look like his screen was being eaten up by some strange amoeba, as the sirocco would consume the radar console screen inch-by-inch, as the advancing winds and sand storm got closer and closer blinding everybody. Never saw that in the Eastern Mediterranean and certainly nowhere in the Pacific.*

In January 1989 the UK MOD decided that, after the return of the three Hunt class MCMVs then on deployment (*Berkley, Cottesmore* and *Chiddingfold*), the British mine countermeasures force would be withdrawn from the Gulf along with the *Herald*.

69

And, with the end of the Iran-Iraq War, one of the three British frigates and destroyers deployed was put on a longer leash, in the Arabian Sea and the Indian Ocean area. By the late 1980s, for the Royal Navy the Gulf commitment had come to represent a quarter of its sea time, with between six and nine warships committed to the deployment, either on patrol, working up to go or, in maintenance after a spell on Armilla.[35] It had demonstrated that Britain was prepared to defend her interests in the Gulf region even if she no longer had fixed-wing carriers to deploy. For the initially hesitant UK the escorting of merchant ships during the Tanker War had been a resounding success.

Not a single merchant ship 'accompanied' by British warships was ever attacked, never mind damaged. [36]

For the USA, the resolve of its navy during the war had demonstrated to the Gulf region that it could be relied upon to stay the course, showing determination despite the loss of lives and damage to warships. The US Navy had helped to '...dissipate the memory of Washington's lack of resolve during the Tehran hostage crisis...' [37].

Above all the US Navy, in conjunction with the Royal Navy and warships from other Western fleets, had kept the oil flowing to the world economy. However, in containing the alleged Iranian threat, the leading Western powers and the Gulf states had provided a great deal of assistance to a brutal dictator who would in time pose an even greater danger to world security.

CHAPTER FOUR

ARABIAN BLITZKRIEG

The name Saddam can be literally translated into English as 'he who confronts' and its spirit defined the dictator of Iraq from his earliest years. Allegedly born in the summer of 1939, Saddam Hussein never knew his father, who was either murdered or absconded shortly after the future tyrant was born into poverty in a village outside the town of Tikrit, to the north-west of Baghdad. Tikrit is reputedly the birthplace of the legendary Saladin, who vanquished Christian crusaders and rolled back their occupation of Palestine in the twelfth century. Saddam always regarded the fact that he was brought into the world close by Saladin's birthplace, as deeply significant.

Tikrit was also home to Saddam's uncle, Khairallah Tulfah, a fanatical Arab nationalist and neo-Nazi army officer who supported the abortive attempt to break free from British influence in 1941. Jailed for his part in the revolt, Saddam's uncle cultivated a hatred of the British and the Jews, passing on those views, and his virulently nationalistic beliefs, to his nephew. As a boy, the troublesome Saddam swiftly learned to enjoy brutality, terrorizing his classmates at school, threatening to kill teachers who displeased him and disembowelling cats for fun.

Having gained a basic education, Saddam tried, and failed, to become an army officer, but soon found the opportunities for mayhem offered by extreme politics to his liking. Both uncle and nephew saw the newly formed Ba'ath Party as the answer to Iraq's needs and Saddam's main talent was as a street enforcer, beating up, and in some cases murdering, opponents of the Ba'athists. This was Saddam's university of life, equipping him with the ferocious animal instinct and flair for violence he would need to claw his way up through the Ba'ath Party and gain control of Iraq.

But, having been little travelled, aside from his exile in Syria and Egypt following the failed assassination attempt on Qasim in late 1959, and a trip to France to see the type of nuclear reactor Iraq would one day use to drive its nuclear arms programme, Saddam would always find it difficult to understand the psychology of foreigners. He proved equally ignorant of military affairs, with many of the worst defeats in the Iran-Iraq War due to Saddam's incompetence, although anyone who tried to tell him to stay out of matters of strategy did not live long.

And so, in the summer of 1990, Saddam thought he could use brute force to get his way in a dispute with Kuwait, while believing that neither the USA nor anybody else would do anything about it. Anyone within the regime who thought he should choose caution was too scared to say so.

On 2 August, Saddam's elite Republican Guard swept across the border and into

Kuwait City, meeting little significant opposition.

The build-up of Iraqi troops close to the border with Kuwait had been no secret, but the most American and British intelligence experts expected, was a temporary incursion into the oilfields. The international community simply did not believe that a nation that had just endured one of the longest and most bloody wars of the twentieth century would, two years after its conclusion, start another conflict.

A US Navy carrier and her CBG, hovering offshore in the Gulf, might have given Saddam pause for thought. However, while the American fleet had occasionally sent its big carriers into the Gulf, its senior officers remained concerned that there was not the room for manoeuvre and the Iranian threat, so amply demonstrated in the 1980s, was simply too serious. Despite a major CENTCOM planning exercise held during July 1990, in which it was demonstrated that Saudi Arabia could not be defended properly by carrier air power if the ships stayed outside the Gulf, the US Navy had not been prepared to change its mind.

The decision by Britain in 1961, to deploy carriers into the Gulf when trouble looked likely had prevented an Iraqi invasion of Kuwait. However, General Qasim was not quite the gambler that Saddam was and the Iraqi Army of 1990 was the fourth largest in the world, even bigger than the USA's.

Saddam had ordered the invasion because he was burning with a sense of injustice. Having acted as a bulwark against radical Islam spreading to the oil-rich Gulf sheikhdoms, and also a proxy for the West, Iraq was being rewarded for its suffering with demands by both Kuwait and Saudi Arabia for the repayment of billions of dollars of war loans. The Kuwaitis were accused by Iraq of slant drilling, from their side of the border, into Iraq's portion of the Rumaila oilfield. Saddam demanded that not only should the war loans be written off but that Iraq be allowed to drill for oil on the Kuwaiti side of the Rumaila. The Iraqi dictator also suggested that the Gulf states should provide him with more 'loans' to help restore his country's economy. A decrease in oil production was also demanded, to enable a rise in the price per barrel, which would be another means of boosting Iraqi revenues.

Saddam suggested that, at the very least, Kuwait should hand over the islands of Bubiyan and Warbah, finally broadening Iraq's access to the sea. If the Iraqi Army occupied significant parts of Saudi Arabia as well as Kuwait, then Saddam would control nearly half the world's known oil reserves and he would be able to hold the international community to ransom, with the power to destroy the global economy by disrupting the smooth flow of oil.

Underlying this dispute between brother Arabs was Saddam's desire to fulfill what he believed was his manifest destiny, as the leading warlord of the Middle East. He would have the ability to avenge himself on the West, for all the ills it had allegedly visited upon the Arab world over the years, and also give him the power he needed to destroy Israel and liberate Palestine.

Reclaiming the whole of Kuwait as the 'lost province' of Iraq, unjustly ripped away by the British, was the seemingly easy, first step. Such a pretext for invasion was, as far as Saddam was concerned, the perfect justification for war, as it was all the fault of the West for robbing Iraq of Kuwait in the first place.

In February 1990, at a meeting of Arab leaders in Jordan, Saddam not only hinted that he might use force to obtain the billions he needed to prop up Iraq's economy, but suggested US Navy ships should remove themselves from the Gulf permanently. The Iraqi dictator also declared that it was useless for the Gulf states to look for protection from America. It would not have the staying power in any crisis, if it meant bodybags on the same scale as the Beirut bombing that forced the USA to leave the Lebanon.

While such statements could be dismissed as posturing by a strongman, to improve his credibility on the Arab Street, disturbing evidence of Saddam's weapons of mass destruction (WMD) ambitions had also been coming to light.

British customs officials had seized component parts for a supergun that could fire shells hundreds of miles. Then, not only in the UK but also in the USA and other countries, customs officials seized triggers and various other key components for nuclear weapons, all destined for Iraq. Saddam boasted on television that he already had much of the material needed to create the bomb. Fortunately, an Israeli air strike on the French-built Osirac nuclear reactor, near Baghdad, in June 1981, had destroyed a key enabler in Iraq's nuclear weapons programme.

On 25 July 1990 the American ambassador to Iraq had indicated to Saddam that the USA was little interested in intervening in the dispute between Kuwait and Baghdad. It did not help that the Kuwaitis and Saudis were one minute defiant and the next ready to do secret deals and offer Saddam drilling rights and more 'loans'.

On 30 July it was obvious to the military and intelligence communities of both the USA and Britain that Iraq was about to invade Kuwait. However, during the build-up of Iraqi forces on their borders, the Kuwaitis had not asked for military assistance, nor had the Saudis, for fear of provoking Saddam. The Saudi ruling family was particularly worried about outraging Islamic fundamentalists who could be expected to object strongly to the presence of non-Muslim troops on the holy soil of Arabia.

The presence of warships in international waters did not present the same problem, but none of the Royal Navy's Gulf deployment units had received an indication that a new threat to the stability of the Middle East was on the verge of exploding. At Mombasa, Lieutenant Commander Jeremy Stocker was about to take a week's leave when he was called back to his ship, the frigate HMS *Jupiter*.

News of the invasion was met with some astonishment. As far as the Armilla ships were concerned there had been no prior indication that such an

The Leander class frigate HMS Jupiter **leaves Portsmouth in May 1990, bound for the Gulf.** M. Welsford.

F60

event was imminent, or my ship would never have left the Gulf to start a tour of East Africa. For a few days we remained at Mombasa while the British government and the MOD decided how to react. Then the message came through for Jupiter *to head back to the Gulf to join up with* York *and* Battleaxe, *and the supply ship* RFA Orangeleaf, *the other ships of Armilla Patrol Group 'Whiskey'.*

There was no way the 40,000-strong Saudi military and the remnants of the Kuwaiti Army, which had fled across the border, could resist 250,000 Iraqi troops now massing in Kuwait, and so it was plain that military intervention by the USA, and possibly other Western nations, would be needed.

In the meantime, both British Prime Minister Margaret Thatcher and US President George H. Bush, who held talks in Colorado shortly after Saddam's troops invaded, agreed that trade sanctions should be implemented immediately.

On 3 August the United Nations Security Council unanimously passed Resolution 660, which demanded a complete Iraqi withdrawal from Kuwait. Three days later it passed Resolution 661, imposing sanctions and a trade embargo on Iraq. This prohibited the import and export of all goods except medical and humanitarian supplies and would need to be implemented by a sizeable naval force.

The USS *Independence* battle group, which also included two cruisers, at least one destroyer and two frigates, had been in the Indian Ocean for a number of weeks and was now close to the Gulf. Within four weeks nearly 40,000 US troops would be in Saudi Arabia, to hopefully draw a line in the sand that Saddam dared not cross. However, at least a quarter of a million US troops would be needed to push the Iraqis out of Kuwait and no offensive military action would be possible until the turn of the year.

Meanwhile US Navy warships belonging to Joint Task Force Middle East were already in the northern Gulf, along with the command ship USS *La Salle*, the *York* and *Orangeleaf*. They were the first line of defence at sea when Operation Desert Shield was initiated on 7 August, the umbrella under which a US-led military

A dolphin precedes the RFA Orangeleaf in the Gulf. McCaig Collection.

coalition, which included European and Arab nations standing shoulder-to-shoulder, aimed to prevent the Iraqi Army from moving any further south. The challenge ahead was considerable. On 8 August, President George H. Bush made a live television broadcast to the world, in which he stated:

> This is not an American problem, a European or a Middle East problem. It is a world problem.

Comparing the situation confronting the international community in August 1990 with that which faced the world in the late 1930s, when Hitler was allowed to annex territory without armed intervention by the leading powers, President Bush stated:

> If history teaches us anything it is that we must resist aggression or it will destroy all our freedoms.

As he ordered troops to the Saudi desert and additional warships to leave for the Middle East, President Bush cautioned:

> It may take us time and some considerable effort... [1]

In the UK, Devonport MP David Owen warned against comparisons with the 1930s. 'It is a unique situation,' he told a local newspaper.

> Let's not make too many comparisons with Hitler during the 1930s...We face a proven dictator... a man who has used gas. The world has to face this challenge. [2]

However, Seth Carus, an expert at the US Naval War College Foundation provided a more cutting analysis:

> If I had to put money down, I would say the odds greatly favour a direct military confrontation between the United States and Iraq, possibly on a large scale. [3]

In Dr Owen's home city of Plymouth, Royal Navy spokesmen were officially denying that ships were being prepared to reinforce the Royal Navy presence in the Gulf, but reliable defence sources suggested that the frigates HMS *London* and HMS *Brazen* would soon sail for the Middle East. In fact, prior to the crisis, the Royal Navy's deployment cycle had already designated that *Brazen* should depart for the Gulf in the September, along with *London* and the destroyer *Liverpool*. The deployment would take place earlier than scheduled, but with *Cardiff* in place of *Liverpool*. The Portsmouth-based *Cardiff* had only just returned to the UK from a Gulf patrol and was therefore the ideal ship to deploy, as she was fully worked up and retained the necessary modifications for the high threat level in-theatre. These included additional communications equipment and counter-measures, such as infrared decoy rockets.[4] Also at Portsmouth, the destroyer HMS *Gloucester* was preparing to go. The Hampshire naval city was furthermore gripped with rumours that a carrier, either *Invincible* or *Ark Royal*, would be sent to the Gulf, carrying Sea Harrier fighters to provide protection for the Armilla Patrol ships.

Meanwhile, across the Atlantic, on 7 August the *Saratoga* CBG had departed Mayport, Florida. The *Saratoga* was accompanied by the AEGIS-equipped cruiser *Philippine Sea*, the guided-missile destroyers *Spruance* and *Sampson* and the frigate *Elmer Montgomery*.

The battleship *Wisconsin*, based at Norfolk, Virginia, sailed the same day, her

One of many Desert Shield patches worn by the men and women of the Coalition forces. Ray Bean/STILL MOTIONS Collection.

battle group including the guided-missile cruiser *Biddle*, frigate *Thomas C. Hart* and destroyer-tender *Yellowstone*. On 8 August a US Navy spokesman confirmed that a total of fifteen ships had left various American naval bases in the previous forty-eight hours. As in the UK, spokesmen claimed it was all part of the usual pattern of scheduled deployments, but an undeclared Amphibious Ready Group, centred on the *Inchon*, met up with the *Wisconsin* and her escorts.

At the same time, the *Dwight D. Eisenhower* and her battle group passed through the Suez Canal. The Mighty Ike's CBG included the cruiser *Ticonderoga*, destroyers *Scott* and *John Rodgers*, and frigate *John L. Hall*. Also with the *Eisenhower* were the nuclear-powered attack submarines *Spadefish* and *Oklahoma City*, both armed with TLAMS, which had yet to be fired in anger but would soon make their debut.

The prospect of many thousands of infidels in Saudi Arabia was something that filled one young man with horror and hatred. Recently returned from fighting the Soviets in Afghanistan, Osama bin Laden, son of a mega-rich construction magnate with close ties to the Saudi royal family, suggested that he could provide thousands of Muslim fighters, including those of his Al-Qaeda organization, to kick the Iraqis out of Kuwait. [5] The Saudi government gave bin Laden's offer some thought, as they were as keen as he was to keep Westerners off their soil but, it was clear that lightly-armed mujahadeen were not going to be able to do much against the tanks, heavy artillery and non-conventional weapons of the world's fourth largest army. Only a superpower like the USA could help the Saudis remove the Iraqis from their front doorstep. Bin Laden who believed his fighters would have been invincible because of their Faith stayed in Saudi Arabia and fumed. He had formed a hatred of the West, and the USA in particular, over the previous decade in which he, like many thousands of young Muslims, had become radicalized by the struggle against the Russians in Afghanistan. A devoutly religious man, bin Laden and his fanatical confederates would not rest until all current, or former, Muslim lands, from Spain to Indonesia, had been cleansed of what they saw as Western corruption. The entry of thousands of Western troops into Saudi Arabia, in 1990, was the match that lit the blue touch paper that would detonate a series of atrocities against the USA and its allies in the late 1990s, and culminate in the 2001 attacks on New York and Washington.

But that was a completely unforseen threat for an America keen to wind down its expensive military-industrial complex after winning the Cold War. The day Saddam's troops invaded Kuwait, President Bush had proposed a twenty-five per cent cut in the US armed forces by 1995. But the American military, being a resolutely can-do organization, with the world's most powerful economy behind it, never did anything by halves, even with huge defence cuts looming. The taps were turned full on and whatever was needed to do the job in Kuwait would be provided.

But the British, equally keen to reap the post-Cold War 'Peace Dividend', were typically determined to get away with going to war on a shoestring if at all possible. Logic dictated that, if a sizeable task group was to be assembled in the Gulf, then a carrier would be needed as flagship, but the UK government decided to delay a decision as long as possible, until it was clear which way the situation was going to develop.

The *Ark* had returned to Portsmouth on 4 July, for a major assisted maintenance period and to give her crew their summer leave. Aside from receiving major alterations to her living spaces, to accommodate women sailors - being sent to sea in British warships for the first time in 1990 - work on the *Ark* included an important update to the ship's Action Data Automation Weapon System (ADAWS) software.

With deployment of a carrier ruled out in the short term, another Gulf flagship had to be found and the Type 22 (Batch 2) frigate *London* was selected for the job. She already had powerful surveillance and command systems, but was now equipped with additional, high-powered communications kit, to enable her to carry out her new role.

An awful lot of naval hardware was converging on the Gulf region, or being prepared for deployment, and it was all, obviously, far more than needed for 'normal operations' as the spokesmen were claiming. Within a week of the invasion even the Russians, who would not be part of the coalition, had two warships heading for the region and the French, who would be semi-detached players, had sent a frigate into the Gulf within a few days of the crisis blowing up.

A total of eighteen nations ultimately made up the Allied naval armada, including Australia, Canada, France, Italy and the Netherlands. Even Kuwait managed to contribute two, missile-armed attack craft that had escaped from the Iraqis. Eight Kuwaiti missile boats, armed with Exocets, had been captured, but it was doubtful their missiles systems were working.

The imposition of sanctions - and the use of naval forces to enforce a trade embargo on Iraq - was meant to show Saddam that the international community meant business, the only problem being that the Iraqi dictator understood the psychology of democracy about as well as the West understood his twisted megalomania.

While the embargo was a useful means of building the coalition, very few senior people in the US government believed that sanctions alone would achieve the objective of ejecting Iraqi troops from Kuwait. For a start, the embargo was certainly not President Bush's long-term plan, despite some in his own administration and a few of his allies saying that it should be the full extent of pressure to get Saddam out of Kuwait.

'The embargo will inevitably leak; and the hostility of average Arabs towards us will likely grow,' said President Bush. 'The long haul may squeeze Saddam, but it is not exactly favourable to us.' [6]

That was not the position in many European capitals.

It is clear that the EC regards the Security Council resolutions as the indispensable determinant of action. Any step the US took beyond the resolutions would lose European support. [7]

With Jordan refusing to join the coalition and Iran remaining strongly anti-US, there were clearly potential gaps in the embargo. In Jordan there was popular support for Saddam and it also stood to lose a great deal of trade with Iraq via its port of Aqaba on the Red Sea. Iraq's oil pipeline through Turkey and Saudi Arabia was cut off, but the Baghdad to Aqaba road provided a route for supplies. While Jordan prevaricated over an embargo, President Bush warned King Hussein the US Navy would close Aqaba - Iraq's so-called 'overland port'. Another American fear was that an Iraqi ship might be scuttled in the Suez Canal.

But regardless of the embargo, for some countries trade had to continue with Iraq, as their national economies depended on it - for example, Sri Lanka exported thousands of kilogrammes of tea to Iraq, while others exported rice. But it was felt that, as one hole leads to another, the embargo had to be solid to stand any chance of working at all. That meant absolutely nothing could get through. Iraq faced severe difficulties as it imported most of its necessary basic foods. Ironically it got a substantial amount of them from the USA, including wheat, corn, rice, soybean meal and eggs. [8]

It might seem obvious that the whole point of having the Gulf clogged up with warships was to employ them in actually enforcing the embargo. However, there was a major divergence of opinion on this matter, between the US and UK on one hand and other European nations and Canada on the other. According to the news magazine *Newsweek*, other nations were not 100 per cent happy about the USA being in charge of the embargo and wanted to wait for evidence of sanctions-busting by the Iraqis. The French and the Russians in particular bridled at the way things were developing.

Some said that ships bound for Iraq were being deterred and turned around anyway without the embargo needing to be actively enforced.

Events, however, settled the issue. President Bush ordered CENTCOM to begin enforcement of the embargo on 16 August and, as soon as it saw the opportunity to display serious intent, the US Navy seized it.

> ...*the US and Britain thought the existing resolutions entitled them to use force to stop the Iraqi ships. France, Canada and other EC states thought not.*[9]

The clearly empty Iraqi tankers sailed on regardless of the shots from the frigates USS *Reid* and USS *Robert G. Bradley*, so the US Navy shadowed them and prepared, to send boarding parties across the following morning. Another Iraqi tanker, this time fully laden with oil, also stormed past American warships and was fired at, without stopping. The warships kept contact with the vessel and awaited orders to disable the tanker with gunfire and effect a boarding. However, this was not authorized, as Washington felt that it might cause the coalition to fracture, or even provoke Iraq into launching an attack. A Chinese merchant ship had, however, been inspected on 18 August by a team from the cruiser USS *England*, while, in the Red Sea, off Aqaba, the destroyer USS *Scott* diverted a Cypriot ship away from the port after the captain admitted he was carrying cargo bound for Iraq.

However, a pause in interceptions was ordered while the USA held discussions with its allies to reach an agreement on how to apply the embargo. The Western

European Union (WEU) gave its blessing to the use of force, if necessary, and on 25 August, the UN issued permission too. The enforcement began officially, with the international community's blessing, on 31 August, when an American warship intercepted an Iraqi tanker. By then the three British warships were settling down to a routine. Lieutenant Commander Stocker in *Jupiter* spent the majority of his time at sea monitoring shipping in the lower Gulf:

> *...a six - seven day patrol would be followed by a forty-eight hour stand-off in one of the ports in the southern Gulf - Dubai, Abu Dhabi and Bahrain being the most visited. The enormous port of Jebel Ali, a few miles down the coast from Dubai, became, in-effect, a forward operating base where ships conducted routine maintenance. 'Runs ashore', that is shore leave, are not a usual feature of naval operations in a potential war zone, but ships in port were regarded as important signals of reassurance to the Gulf states, who all felt threatened by further aggression. In September the world's media announced that, for the first time, a British warship, that is* Jupiter, *had intercepted and interrogated a merchant ship inside the Gulf. While we were pleased to hit the headlines in such a positive way, in fact this was simply the first occasion where the media had been aware of it. Such actions had been underway on a daily basis for weeks. Once a ship had been positively identified, it could be checked against the patterns of merchant ship traffic we were expecting. In cases of doubt, a small boarding party would be sent across to verify the ship's identity, cargo and destination.*

And so the Gulf slipped into its phoney war period in which, especially for the crews of the warships, it was hard to believe that danger existed over the horizon or that war might break out at any moment. However, as Operations Officer and a watchkeeping Principal Warfare Officer of the *Jupiter*, Lieutenant Commander Stocker only needed to recall previous casualties at sea to keep sharp.

> *Few serious attempts were made by Iraq to break the blockade and an air of some unreality had fallen in the Coalition warships. The serious purpose of our activities was evident and so was the potential threat from the Iraqi Air Force. The fate of the USS* Stark, *at the hands of an Iraqi Mirage, was uppermost in my mind. Even periodic sorties by similar aircraft - from a friendly Gulf state - caused some consternation when their radar emissions were detected. On the other hand, the actual daily routine of six hour defence watches, training evolutions and a port visit every ten days, felt more like a peacetime exercise.*

But, there had been speculation that Saddam might strike back at the warships enforcing the embargo. Rumours circulated in the USA and UK that at least one biological agent was being produced by Iraq, possibly botulism, cholera or anthrax to be used in aerosol form, so that, if a warship was holed by an Iraqi weapon, an aircraft could then spray the ship.

> *If Saddam could spread BW as a fine aerosol cloud, even an aircraft carrier would be vulnerable.* [10]

The major US Navy striking forces in place were the USS *Independence* CBG in the Gulf of Oman and the USS *Dwight D. Eisenhower* CBG in the Red Sea, while there

The USS Independence *at sea in the early 1990s.* USNHC.

Once she was through the Suez Canal, the Eisenhower's F-18s drew a line in the sky that Saddam dared not cross.

Iain Ballantyne.

were eight MEF ships in the Gulf itself. Among the aviators of the *Independence*, confidence was high, with the Commander of the carrier's air wing, Captain Jay Yakeley, observing that when the shooting started there could be no doubt of Saddam's fate.

> *In a day he would be decimated. It would be over in a day.* [11]

More than 37,000 US Marines were deployed in the Gulf and there was speculation that a massive air and amphibious assault might be launched on Kuwait City, to release the 2,500 US citizens, 4,000 British, and more than 1,000 from other countries being held hostage by Iraqi troops.

However, it would be a severe gamble without the overwhelming force that was not yet in place. The invasion of Panama in December 1989 was a good example of just such a raid, but against more powerful and numerous Iraqi forces it would not be so easy to pull off. It never happened and the hostages were taken to Iraq to act as 'Human Shields', protecting military installations with their presence on site.

The 'human shields' were ultimately released, as a vain ploy by Saddam to gain influence with the West.

As autumn drew on, it was clear that, while many countries were contributing ships, few of them, with the exception of the USA and Britain, would do anything if it came to war. Germany deployed five minesweepers, but to the eastern Mediterranean, which at least freed up similar US ships for service in the Gulf. Canada had agreed to send three naval vessels, while Japan wanted to send minesweepers but its constitution might prevent the ships from entering the Gulf during hostilities. Against popular opinion - but with all political parties at least united behind the government - the Australians deployed three naval vessels to the Gulf towards the end of August: the frigates HMAS *Adelaide* and HMAS *Darwin* and supply ship HMAS *Success*.

Britain's task group was growing by the day, with ships that had earlier been prepared for 'routine deployment' in the Gulf arriving, along with vessels from even further away than the UK.

Possibly the ugliest ship in the British fleet, the RFA *Diligence*, was one of the most crucial coalition vessels and was usually based in the Falklands. Although crewed by Royal Fleet Auxiliary sailors, and commanded by an RFA officer, she was also home to 120 Royal Navy marine engineers. They ran the workshops that

Aboard a British warship, a Royal Navy boarding party rehearses rapid-roping down from a hovering helicopter. Toby Elliott Collection.

made the vessel a floating maintenance facility, an especially vital function in an area like the Gulf, where there was no permanent forward operating base for British naval vessels. In addition to being able to carry out basic maintenance and supply electricity and other 'domestic' services while a ship was berthed alongside her, the

Diligence, in time of conflict, could provide temporary battle damage repairs. Like the Americans, the British relied on the sea to convey their ground forces to the Gulf, with the Falklands War veteran Landing Ship Logistic, RFA *Sir Tristram*, being the first vessel to leave the UK, carrying armoured vehicles belonging to the 7 Armoured Brigade, the so-called Desert Rats, on 28 September. The decision to prepare for the ground assault option had obviously been taken, despite daunting Pentagon estimates of the human cost in any war, which put US casualties alone at 20,000, including 4,000 dead. [12]

On 8 October, in the Gulf of Oman, two coalition interception groups detected Iraqi merchant ships that might be trying to flaunt the embargo. The Basra-registered *Tadmur* was intercepted by HMS *Brazen*, the American destroyer *Goldsborough* and the Australian frigate *Darwin*. As he was first on the scene, *Brazen*'s CO, Commander James Rapp, was given command of the interception and boarding.

> *I was not, in fact, the most senior officer, as the American warship had a senior four-ring Captain and a one star Commodore was embarked in the Australian, but that was the way the system worked. I suppose it was designed to show the embargo enforcement force was not solely a US-led entity. The* Tadmur *boarding, and subsequent investigation of her cargo, was a lengthy affair, lasting about six days. We made contact with what could be a suspect ship one night and boarded her the next day, somewhere off the coast of Oman.'*

The *Brazen*'s Royal Marines took the lead in the boarding, rapid-roping down from the ship's hovering Lynx helicopter. A Squirrel helicopter from the *Darwin* rode shotgun, ready to provide covering fire. A US Coast Guard team, with the necessary specialist search skills, was also soon aboard the Iraqi merchant ship, to carry out a search, and, as *Brazen*'s CO later recalled, they found something interesting:

> *The six tons of rice we found onboard the* Tadmur *was obviously more than the ship's crew needed. Rice was contraband as far as the UN was concerned. So, we then had to find a friendly port where a more thorough investigation could be carried out. Oman was the obvious place and, luckily, the UK Armed Forces Minister was visiting the sultanate at the time and managed to secure agreement for the ship to go into an Omani port. So, we went to anchor, with the* Tadmur *positioned on the* Brazen *and with the American warship nearby. The Australian warship had detached herself by this time. The* Tadmur *had a Coalition boarding party aboard throughout this period and my First Lieutenant was in charge of her. However, when the Iraqi vessel went alongside, and after she was off-loaded, the boarding party was withdrawn along with my First Lieutenant. The* Tadmur *was promptly re-loaded with her cargo of rice and sailed. We therefore had to reboard her, bring the* Tadmur *back into port and off-load her.*

Meanwhile, HMS *Battleaxe* had been the lead ship for her own interception, as she was the first to catch up with the *Al Wasitti*. Not far behind the British Type 22 frigate were the Australian destroyer *Adelaide* and US Navy destroyer *Reasoner*. The new British Gulf task group flagship, *London*, was also nearby having only just arrived. The Iraqi-registered ship was asked to stop and allow a search, but refused, forcing the CO of *Battleaxe*, Captain Andrew Gordon Lennox, to order one of his 20mm cannons to put a warning shot across the vessel's bows.

> *We fired warning shots because the ship did not appear to want to answer us or take part in the inspection...* [13]

Taking the decision to open fire did not just begin and end with the CO of *Battleaxe*. He later explained that he had used satellite communications to consult the task group commander, who in turn discussed the situation with the commander of British forces in the Gulf who, finally, gave the green light after talking it over with senior officers and politicians back in the UK. Two, six-strong Royal Marines' boarding teams then rapid-roped down onto the deck of the ship. The British troops 'compelled the captain to bring the vessel to a stop'.[14] Keeping everyone sharp during boardings, was the thought that Saddam might have ordered suicide squads to secrete themselves in merchant ships, ready to blow them apart once Allied troops were aboard, but the UK marines met no resistance and a team of US Coast Guard inspectors was put aboard the *Al Wasitti*. On finding empty cargo holds they permitted her to go on her way. Despite the situation in the Gulf remaining unresolved, the *Battleaxe*, *Jupiter* and *York* headed home as scheduled. In *Jupiter*, Lieutenant Commander Stocker was not alone in having mixed feelings.

> *There were enough ships in the Gulf, from an increasing number of nations, to handle the tasks. We were back in the UK by mid-November, disappointed to have been pulled back from a live crisis zone, yet also happy to be home. For the forces building up against Saddam back out in the Middle East, it was by no means certain that hostilities would ensue. A lot of people thought a diplomatic deal would be brokered.*

The CO of *Battleaxe*, who had experienced the full horror of war when a previous ship he was serving in, HMS *Ardent*, was sunk during the Falklands conflict, reflected at the time that he hoped '...the situation does not escalate and that the UN embargo is sufficient to persuade Saddam Hussein to withdraw.' [15]

American carriers continued to stay out of the Gulf, although the *Independence* carved out a short stay of four days in early October. The logic for remaining in the northern Arabian Sea was that it would reduce the dangers posed by mines and suicide boats, and also minimize the potential Iranian threat.

As the diplomatic process wore on, the sailors, airmen and ground troops did their best to keep sharp, but it wasn't easy in the morale-sapping heat. To boost morale, senior officers did the rounds of troops in the desert and sailors aboard their various ships. The objective was to assure the servicemen that their job was worthwhile and that the crisis would soon be resolved one way or the other. There were doubts not only about it being worth assembling such a large coalition, if the war option was not to be a serious proposition, but also over whether or not it could be efficiently knitted together.

The Commandant of the US Marine Corps, General Alfred Gray, had visited marines in the Gulf and told them he didn't want to hear anything about bad morale.

> *I don't want to hear any more questions about how long you are gonna be here. We're gonna be here until we get done what has to be done, right?*

An F-14 Tomcat about to launch from the USS Saratoga, *October 1990, keeping the pressure on Saddam.* Ray Bean/STILL MOTIONS Collection.

There'll be no morale problems...because I say there'll be morale. [16]

They gave him a rousing reception for his no-nonsense approach. A fortnight later British forces commander-in-chief, Lieutenant General Sir Peter de la Billière, visited naval vessels at Dubai, including the RFA *Diligence*. The General dismissed talk of sagging morale and was optimistic about the coalition working smoothly.

> *Getting to know my own forces on the land, sea and in the air will help me to co-ordinate Britain's efforts with other allied commanders. I think we will be able to work well together, despite coming from many different nations. My initial impression today is that morale is absolutely fantastic among our forces and we are fortunate they are such a high standard.* [17]

The General's visit coincided with the arrival of the RFA *Sir Tristram* and other ships carrying the British Army heavy equipment and armoured vehicles.

At this time there was controversy over the lack of a unified command structure for the multi-national naval forces. Vice Admiral Henry H. Mauz, who was CO of the US 7th Fleet, as well as commander of US naval forces in the Gulf, said there was no need for such a structure, as he was confident they would all work together without it.

There were sixty-eight ships in the combined force and, by 17 October, they had conducted 2,463 intercepts and 253 boardings, most of them in the Red Sea against traffic going in and out of Aqaba.

By mid-October the US Navy presence alone in the Middle East was fifty-three warships - fifteen in the Gulf, thirty in the northern Arabian Sea and eight in the Red Sea.

Vice Admiral Mauz told a reporter from the local *Gulf News*:

> *I think the word has gotten around quickly that it is impossible to penetrate the embargo. The ships we search are quite co-operative. In fact, the master of the ship usually facilitates the search.*

Ships carrying contraband cargo were diverted to ports where they were scheduled to be held for the duration of the crisis. Minesweepers had just arrived and were deployed just in case, although no mines had been reported so far. Vice Admiral

Mauz, like the UK's General de la Billière maintained that morale was high.

I've visited several of our ships and morale is not a problem. They don't want to spend the rest of their lives here, but they are prepared to wait until our mission is complete. [18]

In mid-November Saddam Hussein told a television interviewer that he was 'prepared to enter into deep dialogue as to the requirements for security in our region'. The Iraqi dictator added: 'We are confident that these parties will reach serious and deep solutions to all the issues, in the forefront of which will be the Palestinian issue.'

However, Saddam avoided giving any meaningful reaction to the United Nations' demand that he pull his troops out of Kuwait. In response, and to emphasize the coalition's determination, the US Navy began deploying the extra muscle it would need to prosecute a war, including the battleship USS *Missouri*, which departed Long Beach on 13 November. By December 1990 it was estimated that the Iraqi military had enough stockpiles to last at least a year and it was clear that, even if Iraq's civilian population started to hurt from the embargo, it would not bother Saddam one bit.

In the first week of December, the USA won a resolution from the UN authorizing the use of force to evict Iraqi troops from Kuwait and the deadline set for Iraq to stage an unconditional withdrawal was 15 January.

But the USA was willing to meet with the Iraqis for last minute peace talks. Alternatives to war included containment - Saddam could withdraw but an embargo on military equipment would be maintained. But to contain him would need troops permanently stationed in Arabia, which was not welcome from an Islamic point of

With the battleship Wisconsin already in the Gulf, her sister ship, the USS Missouri, left Long Beach in mid-November. The 'Mighty Mo' is pictured here in Australian waters in the late 1980s.

Jonathan Eastland/AJAX News & Feature Service.

view. A nightmare scenario envisaged Saddam withdrawing from all but the Rumaila, something likely to destroy coalition unity, as no one would go to war to eject him from an oilfield alone. Saddam would regard himself as being victorious and aggression would have been seen to pay. It would be an unwise precedent to set and would likely bring dreadful disorder to the so-called New World Order.

By now the Royal Navy's Armilla Patrol was part of a larger operation, codenamed Granby, with a joint operational HQ established alongside the Americans in the Saudi capital of Riyadh. On the last day of 1990, HMS *London* joined forces with an American warship and the Australian frigate *Sydney* to intercept the 36,000 tonnes Iraqi oil tanker *Ain Zalah*. While *Sydney*, which had just arrived in theatre, took the role of co-ordinator, *London* and the American warship moved in close, with helicopters from all three warships dropping boarding teams onto the tanker. They met no opposition and a search failed to reveal contraband, so the *Ain Zalah* was allowed to go on her way to Iraq. By the end of the year, the Multinational Interception Force (MIF) had boarded 1,000 ships out of some 7,000 vessels challenged. Between five and ten ships had been boarded each day.[19] Ninety-three per cent of boardings were in the Red Sea [20]. But now the focus was shifting, from embargo enforcement to preparing for combat.

> *...the war that may begin in about six weeks would involve so many weapons never before fired in anger, and so many strategic and tactical doctrines never yet pushed to the ultimate test, that it would be unlike any ever fought before.* [21]

In Portsmouth, the Type 42 air-defence destroyer HMS *Manchester* was preparing to leave on deployment with the *Ark Royal* task group in the New Year, probably for the front line up-threat in the Gulf. The destroyer's Signals Communications Officer, Lieutenant Richard Thomas, experienced a hectic period prior to an emotional Christmas and New Year holiday.

> *At the unit level, though the Captain might have been privy to his part in the campaign plan, we did not have exposure to the overall timeline. We did, however, have a clear directive to prepare the ship and our people as best we could for conflict. This was a huge logistical challenge, what with extra stores and last minute 'bolt-on' extra pieces of equipment. From late November we were at a shortened notice to sail for the Middle East.*

> *This was a particularly hard time for the Ship's Company, as each weekend was possibly your last at home before sailing into the unknown. It was a Sunday in early January when we were contacted at home - my wife and I were staying with her parents - to say the ship would sail for GRANBY this coming week. Lots of tears and a spoiled Sunday roast, but also relief that the uncertainty and waiting were over - we were off.*

CHAPTER FIVE

MOVING IN HARM'S WAY

I n early January 1991, with little more than a week to go before the United Nations deadline for Iraqi troops to leave Kuwait ran out, the RAF base at Brize Norton in rural Oxfordshire was a hive of activity. Every night half a dozen flights took off for the Middle East, no matter how bad the weather. While the majority of people living in the communities that dotted the surrounding landscape worried about the possibility of snow inconveniencing their trip to work in the morning, inside the fence of the military base, airmen, soldiers and sailors were wondering what fate might await them in the deserts of the Gulf.

Chief Petty Officer Mark Baker boarded an RAF VC10 transport jet, destined for the RFA *Diligence* and, during the long flight to the Middle East, reflected on what he had left behind and what he might face.

> *Leaving home was the worst part. My wife tried to put on a brave face but she was terribly upset. I was in the Falklands War and experienced some grim moments. It won't stop me doing my job, but you can't help thinking back to the last time and wishing you weren't going into another war.*[1]

Just a few days after CPO Baker joined his ship at Dubai, further north, off Qatar, the Royal Navy's task group held its final combined training exercise before war. Exercise Deep Heat was held between 6 and 8 January, and included 'rescuing' a crippled vessel under air attack. This required some dramatic manoeuvres from participating warships and mock strafing runs by RAF Jaguar strike jets, which, for some British sailors, brought back memories of 'bomb alley' in San Carlos water during the Falklands War. One of them was the Royal Navy task group Commanding Officer, Commodore Chris Craig, who, during a brief visit to the destroyer HMS *Gloucester*, reflected on the past and what might lie over the horizon:

> *We have got to consider the worst case...That could mean conflict with the nation of Iraq.*[2]

The British naval commander went on to say that he hoped the collective experience of his ships' commanders, many of them blooded in the Falklands, would stand the ships under his command in good stead. Deep Heat culminated in a firepower demonstration off Qatar. It was witnessed by British Prime Minister John Major, who was aboard HMS *London*, as part of a visit to British forces in the Gulf.

> *The destroyers* Gloucester *and* Cardiff *were shrouded in smoke...as they tested their big 4.5-inch guns during the live firing.* London *and* Brazen *also*

The destroyer HMS Cardiff *alongside the RFA* Diligence *at Jebel Ali in the UAE.* McCaig Collection.

took part in the deafening display. While their machine guns riddled targets with tracer bullet holes, the ships' rapid-fire 20mm and 40mm anti-aircraft guns blew them to pieces with cannon shells. The RFAs also joined the deadly cordite chorus, spitting out fire and smoke from their anti-aircraft guns. Then the 'fly boys' of the Royal Air Force gave the radar and missile operators aboard the ships a run for their money. Inter-Services rivalry obliged the fighter-bomber pilots to swoop dangerously low over the Task Group, weaving between the ships just a few feet off the surface of the water. As one pink-painted Jaguar distracted eyes high above the horizon, another zoomed in low, giving the ships no warning, as it dropped brightly burning magnesium flares in place of bombs. For all the exuberant flying, the Navy boys reckoned they had the measure of the fliers, who, they claim, would have been knocked down by missiles before they got anywhere near the Task Group. [3]

The *Gloucester* had already experienced her own real-life adrenalin-pumping call to Action Stations, when it appeared the Iraqi Air Force was about to mount a pre-

An RAF Jaguar strike jet swoops low past one of the British task group's Type 42 destroyers during Exercise Deep Heat. McCaig Collection

emptive strike on the coalition naval forces. As Deep Heat ended, one of the 'Fighting G's' officers, Lieutenant Chris Hodkinson, relived the moment he thought war was about to break out:

I was off duty and lying in my cabin bunk, which is below the bridge. Suddenly I heard the whoosh of chaff rockets going off. Then I heard the operations officer talking urgently with the captain. By then I was wide awake, thinking 'God, this is it!.' [4]

As the chaff from the rockets surrounded *Gloucester* with strips of metal that would, hopefully, make the incoming missile miss its intended target, the warship's alarm klaxons blared. Throwing his anti-flash clothing and flak jacket on, Lieutenant Hodkinson sprinted for his action station.

I went into auto... my mind running through a series of check-lists of things that I had to do to play my part...I couldn't afford for a second to contemplate the possibility of the ship being hit and me being killed. [5]

In *Gloucester's* Ops Room the radar operators watched calmly, as one of the contacts on their screens appeared to be starting an attack run. Another blob, indicating a launched missile, would mean that the moment of truth was only seconds away. Would the Sea Dart missiles and Phalanx Close-in Weapon System (CIWS) be able to destroy the missile and the attack aircraft before the destroyer was crippled or sunk? But the Iraqi aircraft did not launch any missiles and instead reversed direction and flew home, much to everyone's relief, including Lieutenant Hodkinson.

The Iraqi was just giving us a fright, testing us. Whatever was in his mind, he bottled out and turned around. [6]

During another night 'up-threat', *Gloucester's* radar screens showed a whole swarm of Iraqi aircraft heading south towards coalition naval vessels. The US Navy's carrier-based fighter jets were ordered to intercept the Iraqi formation while fingers hovered above firing buttons in Royal Navy and US Navy picket ships. But, once again, the Iraqis were playing chicken and turned around.

As January move into its second week, the massive coalition armada began to flex its muscles, all part of tightening the screws on the Iraqis. The Americans made no secret of the fact that eight amphibious assault ships carrying around 10,000 US Marines and sailors had sailed through the Strait of Hormuz.

The official line was that they were on 'routine operations', but no one believed that for a moment, least of all the local *Gulf News* newspaper. Its 11 January edition noted:

...the aircraft carrier USS Midway *and her battle group will sail into the Gulf for 'routine training' within the next few days.*

The movements of warships thousands of miles away did not escape notice either and the *Gulf News* reported that *Ark Royal* had departed Portsmouth on 10 January headed for exercises in the Mediterranean,

...amid speculation that it might eventually be destined for the Gulf.

The *Ark's* presence in the eastern Mediterranean would, according to *Gulf News*, allow the *John F. Kennedy* to move into the Red Sea.

On 11 January, HMS *Gloucester* once again went to Air Raid Warning Red status when eight Iraqi jets appeared to be heading straight for her. In HMS *London*, monitoring the situation as it evolved, the British task group commander contemplated the layers of defence *Gloucester* had to rely on before suffering a hit:

The destroyer USS Sampson, one of Saratoga's escorts, steams hard in the Gulf. Ray Bean/STILL MOTIONS Collection.

> *If she failed to engage the contacts at extreme range with her Sea Dart missile, they would have the chance to unleash Exocets against any of the picket ships. Thereafter, her remaining defence was the limited 4.5-inch gun and finally the Phalanx...*[7]

Commodore Craig immediately contacted General de la Billière at his HQ in Saudi Arabia, informing his boss that he needed permission to fire. This was granted, but the aircraft turned around and scuttled back to Iraq. There was consternation in Whitehall that a British warship might have started the war early. However, experience in the Falklands War and consideration of the *Stark* incident had made it clear to Commodore Craig that, he who hesitated in modern naval warfare, died.

> *The challenges faced by Royal Navy warships in the Falklands conflict, where we lost the* Sheffield *to Exocet, and the* Stark *in the Gulf five years later, had provided a number of direct lessons. In high-tension operations the demands are many but the primary ones are constant vigilance, no complacency and no soft assumptions about friendly or neutral tracks...the latter do not exist in a high-tension environment. Clear command delegations are necessary within the ship to allow Ops Rooms' crews to act dynamically and aggressively within very firm guidelines, well drilled and well practised wherever and whenever possible. A realistic set of criteria for defining hostile intent is needed, so the Rules of Engagement have got to be sufficiently robust, but obviously judicious, depending upon the international situation at the time. And there is, as ever, quite a lot of benefit from declaring, promulgating and enforcing exclusion zones to safeguard the survivability of warships.*

By 14 January, Commodore Craig could finally provide his warships with the good news that ROE had been modified in light of the incident three days earlier. The UK's ROE were brought into line with the US Navy's and British warships were allowed to fire in self-defence without hesitation if a similar threat emerged. But the danger didn't just come from the air. In early January a Cypriot tanker had struck a mine in the Gulf of Oman, which was obviously hundreds of miles from Kuwait and therefore caused great alarm, with the coalition suspecting it could be one of a number sown by a vessel belonging to Iraq. Another theory was that rough weather had set adrift mines laid during the Iran-Iraq War and they had been carried through the Strait of Hormuz. However, the mine threat was prevalent in the northern Gulf too, as the pilot of *Gloucester*'s Lynx helicopter, Lieutenant Commander David Livingstone, later related:

> ...so the Lynx was carrying out regular mine searches, each time clearing an area...ten miles square. Looking for those mines was annoyingly tedious... [8]

With last-ditch peace talks between US Secretary of State James Baker and Iraqi Foreign Minister Tariq Aziz in Geneva breaking down, tension was at an all-time high and the crews of the British and American warships furthest north were living on the edge. It was clear that the only way home would be to fight and win and certainly, as Lieutenant Hodkinson acknowledged, it was time to get on with the job.

> There is some feeling on the ship that, having been out here so long, we would like to take part in any action to throw Saddam out of Kuwait. [9]

The CO of one British warship was concerned that the sharp edge the Royal Navy task group had honed during Deep Heat would soon wear off.

> The waiting has been an incredible strain on us. We have trained and trained for war but you must never overdo it or you become stale. [10]

After Deep Heat, the *Brazen* had headed south to a port in the UAE where she could carry out final preparations for war, before leaving to take up a position in the southern Gulf as guard ship for the RFAs and mine warfare vessels.

> Last night the supply ship RFA Fort Grange re-supplied the Brazen and survey ship Herald, while proceeding south down the Gulf from the exercise area. The Fort Grange's Sea King helicopters buzzed back and forth with heavy payloads swinging beneath them in nets. Loads were also transferred from Fort Grange to Brazen using pulleys and lines slung between the two vessels...Brazen is now being stripped of non-essential peacetime fittings, such as paintings presented by UK organizations associated with the ship. Curtains and decorative lights in the officers' wardroom will come down and the few wooden ladders still connecting parts of the ship are to be replaced by more fire resistant steel ones. Brazen's crew is tired after five days at sea rehearsing for conflict...They will now enjoy some shore time, as a brief respite from an increasingly tense schedule. [11]

The frigate's sailors were perfectly well aware that the Iraqis had proved their lethal intent in the past, as *Brazen*'s CO, Commander James Rapp, acknowledged.

> There was great uncertainty of course about the exact nature, and level, of threat the Coalition naval forces would face during hostilities. There were the mines and of course Saddam's air force with its Exocet-capable aircraft, which had in recent times been used to attack both merchant shipping and Western warships. Then there was the chemical and biological threat, something else that was a proven danger, as the Iraqis had not hesitated to use such weapons against the Iranians. But, we had a job to do, and so we

As the Gulf teeters on the brink of war, the frigate HMS Brazen takes on supplies from the RFA Fort Grange. Iain Ballantyne.

pushed the understandable anxieties about what the future may hold to the backs of our minds.

Aboard the task group flagship, HMS *London*, as she took up her designated position off Qatar, Commodore Craig contemplated how the COs of his most exposed warships might be feeling as they moved further north.

As I watched Cardiff *move forward on radar, I felt for her commanding officer, Adrian Nance. He had been on board* Sheffield *when she had been destroyed by Exocet in the Falklands. Eight years later, I had him, his memories and his ship utterly exposed in the front line of missile defence - once more against Exocet. I wonder what nightly memories he lived with? They never showed.* [12]

In fact the spectre of the *Sheffield*'s fate in the Falklands War hung over the entire task group. On 4 May 1982, the Type 42 destroyer was hit by an Exocet missile, which struck the warship amidships on the starboard side, just above the waterline and, although the warhead didn't explode, its fuel did, killing several sailors.

Her principal water main had been cut so there was not enough available for effective firefighting, and fires soon gripped the *Sheffield*, sending choking, poisonous fumes from burning electric cables, throughout the ship. Nine years later *Brazen*'s Chief Petty Officer Danny Keay, who headed the frigate's centre section damage control team, was grateful that the lessons of *Sheffield*'s demise had been learned.

> *We now have improved fire-fighting gear and better protective clothing. There are special curtains around the ship's internal doors, which will stop smoke from spreading if we are hit. Every member of a British warship's crew now has a breathing device that looks like a plastic bag with an oxygen bottle attached to it. We did not have these in the Falklands and I'm sure many lives were lost as a result. After putting the bag over your head there is enough oxygen for you to get out of the interior of the ship to the upper deck. It's quite funny really, because as a kid your mum tells you not to put plastic bags on your head, but the Navy tells you to do it because it will save your life.* [13]

The *Brazen*'s water pipe system was also fitted with cut-off taps and entry valves that made sure one hit could not deprive the damage control teams of the means to douse fires. However, the protective clothing the fire-fighting teams had to wear made it almost impossible to tackle fires without rapid heat exhaustion, as Petty Officer George Harding explained:

> *It's crippling. We have to wear four layers of clothing and this makes it almost impossible to fight a fire. In addition to their underclothes, the lads*

have to wear their ordinary overalls, with a chemical warfare suit on top of that and, lastly, a 100 per cent lambs wool fire suit. [14]

This fire suit was designed to scorch, but not burst into flames. However, under the various layers of clothing, and wearing a breathing mask and a hard hat, the sailors needed more than two pints of water an hour to replace lost fluids. During some damage control drills the heat became so intense for some sailors that they collapsed and had to be put on insulin drips to recover. How the damage control teams might fare during the heat of battle did not bear thinking about.

As the sands of time ran out, estimates of casualties that could be expected ranged from 9,000, during a short war, to more than 300,000, including 60,000 dead if it dragged on for months. Both the US Navy and the Royal Navy had established field hospitals in the Saudi desert, but there were also naval doctors and nurses at sea. The Americans had sent two massive hospital ships - the *Comfort* and the *Mercy* - which were converted merchant ships. Together they provided 1,000 beds and twelve

With the minutes to war ticking away, a damage control team on the Gloucester *is put through its* paces. Iain Ballantyne.

operating theatres. Lieutenant Donna Hoffmeier explained *Mercy*'s primary role was to '...rehabilitate patients with lesser injuries so they can return to their units. The secondary mission is to stabilize more seriously ill or injured patients for transporting back to the United States...' [15]

While the two American ships were painted white with huge red crosses, the UK's RFA *Argus*, which was usually an aviation training vessel, had been modified to accommodate a two-floor air conditioned hospital before leaving Britain, and had retained her warship grey paint scheme. Technically this meant she was a legitimate target for the Iraqis because she was not a hospital ship. Termed a 'Primary Casualty Reception Ship', the *Argus* carried a medical team of ten surgeons, forty-one nurses and also forty Royal Marine bandsmen acting as orderlies. She would be expected to stand close to the Kuwait coast, with her large flight-deck ready to receive casualties straight from the battlefield. After initial treatment they would be transferred to a field hospital ashore, or, if they died, retained aboard the *Argus* in one of the ship's mortuaries. Meanwhile in the amphibious assault ships of the US Navy, the Leathernecks of the US Marines were setting their faces for war and, having enjoyed some shore leave after entering the Gulf, were getting back aboard ship to sail for an undisclosed location where they would have one more rehearsal for D-Day against the shores of Kuwait. Their ships - among them *Tarawa* and *Iwo*

Jima - carried the names of Second World War amphibious assaults drenched in blood, where their forefathers had waded ashore under heavy fire. Aboard the assault ship USS *Shreveport*, as she prepared to sail for the final exercise, battalion commander, Colonel T.A. Hobbs was brimming with fight:

> *I am sure my boys, under cover of attack helicopters from the* Shreveport, *can take back the beaches of Kuwait in minutes.*

One of the *Shreveport*'s helicopter gunship pilots was similarly bullish:

> *We are ready to obey the President's orders to kick Saddam out of Kuwait.*[16]

In another echo of the Pacific War, where the US Navy suffered the loss of 10,000 sailors lives in ships supporting marines fighting for the Japanese home islands, the spectre of kamikaze attacks by Iraqi aircraft, or small boats, pushed itself to the fore. The *Shreveport*'s Lieutenant Craig Anthony admitted:

> 'It's a little unsettling. But we are confident that kamikaze attacks would not get through. But even if they did, the Shreveport is a big ship and can soak up a deal of punishment.*

But Lieutenant Anthony hoped that war could still be avoided:

> *I know it doesn't look good at the moment, but I retain some hope that Saddam will pull out and avoid a war that would destroy his country.* [17]

At Bahrain, the battleship *Wisconsin* slid out of harbour on 13 January, her 57, 350 tons bulk low in the water, carrying a full war load of 16-inch shells and Tomahawk cruise missiles. Nearly forty-six years earlier the *Wisconsin*'s big guns had helped bring the Second World War to a close. Soon her guns would roar again, hopefully helping to drive Iraqi occupiers out of Kuwait. The deadline for Iraq to withdraw from the emirate, or face military action, was set for 12.00 am on 16 January and shortly before the deadline Commodore Craig sent a signal from HMS *London* to the task group ships. He hoped that his words would inspire and steel them for what lay ahead:

> *We are about to engage in the greatest endeavour of our lives, on behalf of most of the nations on earth. After weeks of preparation you are entirely ready - with a spirit and resolution that are remarkable. Over the days ahead, total concentration and sustained application will ensure an emphatic victory. May God go with you as you move in harm's way; my best wishes will be with you throughout. Without further orders, all Commanding Officers of Royal Navy ships are, on the outbreak of hostilities, to hoist battle ensigns.*[18]

Aboard the *Wisconsin*, as the hours to the deadline dissolved, the battleship's Roman Catholic chaplain absolved the crew of their sins and then returned to his office for a box of rosaries and a flask of oil to use in anointing the dying. [19]

The USS Wisconsin moves north after slipping out of Bahrain. McCaig Collection.

CHAPTER SIX

APOCALYPSE THEN

As the deadline for his army to leave Kuwait passed, the world expected the Sword of Damocles suspended above the head of Saddam Hussein to descend with terrible swiftness.

The United Nations had authorized 'all necessary means' to effect the departure of the Iraqi occupiers from Kuwait. Certainly the coalition had every kind of 'means' at its disposal, with 700,000 troops, seven US Navy striking groups - five centred on aircraft carriers and two on battleships - 3,400 tanks and close to 1,000 strike jets. The US Navy's carriers and US Marine Corps aviation alone provided 600 combat aircraft.

Against this the Iraqis were able to field, according to Pentagon intelligence reports, 545,000 troops in Kuwait and southern Iraq, 2,000 tanks, hundreds of combat aircraft and at least fifty combat vessels. But, the Allies did not let loose their dogs of war immediately for fear of being seen as too eager. However, as America's Chairman of the Joint Chiefs of Staff, General Colin Powell later explained, they didn't want to wait longer than was necessary.

...for fear of losing credibility and having fresh political obstacles...About two days, I argued, seemed a reasonable compromise. [1]

When it opened in the early hours of 17 January, Operation Desert Storm fired 700 combat aircraft like an arrow at the heart of Saddam's regime, with attacks on key command and control centres in Baghdad itself. Other prime targets during the opening night of attacks included nuclear and chemical weapons research and production plants, for it was no secret that Iraq had developed chemical warheads for its Scud B, Al-Hussein and Al-Abbas missiles. The Iraqis also possessed prodigious numbers of artillery shells containing chemical materials. In the first twenty-four hours of Desert Storm, the Allies flew 1,000 bombing sorties and unleashed 151 cruise missiles, beginning the process of destroying Iraqi combat units in Kuwait and subjecting Iraq's infrastructure to a process of dismemberment.

The most precise weapon in the coalition armoury - the revolutionary TLAM of the US Navy, introduced into service in 1986 - was also one of the least trusted among the Army generals running the coalition war. Colin Powell allegedly told the officer in charge of deciding how to destroy Iraqi targets:

I don't give a damn if you shoot every TLAM the Navy's got, they're still not worth a shit. Any target you intend to destroy with TLAM, put a fighter on it to make sure the target's destroyed. [2]

Neither Powell nor General Schwarzkopf were to make much of this issue in their post-war autobiographies, but the tactical cruise missile was, after all, an untested weapon that promised much, and it was only natural there should be doubts about its ability to deliver. At 2.30 a.m., Baghdad time, as US Army Apache helicopters were destroying Iraqi radar stations to open a gate for the strike jets, the US Navy was launching its untried weapon from warships in the Gulf and the Red Sea. The *San Jacinto* was the first from the Red Sea, the cruiser's superstructure bathed in the glow of the rocket motor's flame and obscured by smoke, as the first ever TLAM to be fired in anger leapt out of its Vertical Launch Silo (VLS). Meanwhile, the destroyer *Paul F. Foster* led the way in the Gulf, although that honour should have gone to the vessel in charge of co-ordinating the cruise missile strikes, the battleship *Wisconsin*. Instead the battleship's Combat Information Center (CIC) team heard the *Foster* proudly declare on the radio net, as her first missile took flight: 'Happy trails!' On the destroyer's upper deck a sailor exclaimed:

There it goes...we just started a war! [3]

In the *Wisconsin* sailors were hard at work, their fingers flying over computer keyboards, as they re-programmed their ship's cruise missiles for unexpected targets. Originally the intention had been to also use warships in the eastern Mediterranean, but Syria and Turkey, the former contributing ground troops to the coalition and the latter a NATO ally, had not given permission for the TLAMs to fly over their territory. The relevant targets had been re-allocated and so *Wisconsin*'s sailors therefore, had to type in pages of revised information. But, around 40 minutes later than the designated firing time, the job was finally finished and the battleship could play her part.

Her Commanding Officer, Captain David Bill, told his crew over the PA to 'stand-by' before counting down 'five-four-three-two-one' to the launch of the first of eight TLAMs the battleship would fire that night. After a heart-stopping delay of a few seconds, it burst from a metal box launcher on the upper deck. [4]

Ironically, because the USA did not need to worry about offending a nation already deeply hostile towards the coalition, the missiles launched from the Gulf flew over Iran. So, as one-by-one TLAMs leapt into the air, trailing a great plume of smoke, their rocket motors falling away and with jet propulsion kicking in as small wings sprang from each missile's body, they headed north-east over mountainous terrain. The problem with plotting a course for TLAMs over the featureless desert that dominated southern Iraq was that, not only was the airspace thick with Allied air traffic, but the missile's guidance system would have no distinguishing features to navigate by. Once a Tomahawk crossed the coast a computer guidance system kicked in, comparing radar readings with a 'map' in the missile's computer brain, a guidance system called Terrain Contour Matching (TERCOM). As it got closer to a target, the missile used a video camera to track its route, by comparing what it saw to the 'map'.

The world would soon know if TLAM was a wonder weapon or a dud. Upon its accuracy and destructive power lay the reputation of the US Navy, which had invested so much in money and time in the weapon.

The men and women who pressed the buttons that sent TLAMs on their way were still imbued with the warrior spirit, rather than being technocrats. Among them was one young man whose ancestors had wielded a different kind of Tomahawk in a more primitive form of warfare - Wesley Old Coyote, one of sixty-four men and women from the Crow Indian tribe serving in the US armed forces in the Gulf. In the *Wisconsin*, Captain Bill was aware that under the martial mask that required his 1,500 officers and men to cheer the missiles on their way, many would be concerned about causing the deaths of innocent people. Giving a speech over the PA that reminded his sailors of the price in human lives that would undoubtedly be paid, the battleship's CO said:

...there's some solace in that the Tomahawk missiles we just fired have gone against military targets. [5]

Two hours after Desert Storm started, President Bush made a live television broadcast to the world from the Oval Office of the White House, in which he said:

We have no argument with the people of Iraq; indeed, for the innocents caught in this conflict I pray for their safety. Our goal is not the conquest of Iraq; it is the liberation of Kuwait. [6]

As the strike jets swarmed north above southern Iraq and the cruise missiles winged over Iran, in the British task group flagship, HMS *London*, Commodore Craig watched a radar screen spellbound by the unfolding spectacle.

I am watching the greatest single-wave assault of destructive power since the Second World War. A mass of aircraft inch their way implacably across the display towards the top left-hand corner - Kuwait and Iraq. Cruise-missile tracks mesh with carrier-launched and shore-based bombers. In sophistication and scale, it is simply unprecedented. [7]

The news that the coalition air offensive had started was relayed to Gary Hurr, a journalist embarked in HMS *Brazen,* only after the bombs and missiles had struck their targets.

I was woken to be told: 'The Americans have launched three attack waves.' Within an hour the 250-strong crew of the Type 22 frigate had been summoned to action stations in case of Iraqi reprisals. [8]

Commander Rapp spoke to *Brazen's* sailors over the ship's PA system, crisply providing them with all the motivation they needed.

Come to action stations fully rigged as if it was an attack on us.

By that Commander Rapp meant that everyone should have their gas masks and NBC suits to hand, together with anti-flash gear. The *Brazen's* job was to protect the vital supply ships *Fort Grange, Orangeleaf* and *Sir Bedivere* from potential Iraqi air attack, so she needed to be sharp. Further north, the *London* continued to monitor the developing air war, her Operations Room staff tensed for any Iraqi response. The American Commander-in-Chief of the multi-national naval task force had asked the British commander to put his Type 42 destroyers, HMS *Cardiff* and HMS *Gloucester*, near the coast of Iran. Commodore Craig had been immediately worried about a repeat of the loss in that earlier conflict of the destroyer HMS *Coventry.* Close in to the Falkland Islands, she had found herself helpless against Argentinian air attack, because background clutter from landward neutralized her air defence

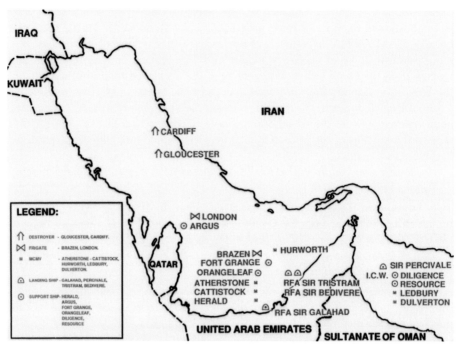

The disposition of British naval units in the Gulf, on the eve of war, in a chart drawn up for the UK naval task group commander. C. Craig Collection.

radar. In the Gulf, Iraqi jets deciding to attack from the direction of Iran would be able to use the background clutter of the coast to obscure themselves, possibly preventing the Type 42s' Sea Darts from getting a good lock-on and coalition warships would not be able to fire while enemy planes were still in Iranian airspace.

It was one of many issues concerning the Commodore, whose staff worked in far from ideal conditions. For example, with no purpose-built flagship facilities, the *London*'s sonar suite - the Sound Room - had been converted into the Commodore's situation room. The opening of hostilities kept the *London*'s sonar staff busy anyway, for they had been seconded to Commodore Craig's staff, in order to run his situation boards and help process signals. Chief Petty Officer Yorkie Cunningham and Petty Officer Bob Burton led the two watches of *London*'s sonar ratings who now worked for the Commodore. Chief Petty Officer Cunningham was on watch with his team when Desert Storm was unleashed:

> *That first night was amazing. The Ops Room displays had hundreds of contacts, so many in fact that they ran out of track numbers. Through in the situation room our job basically consisted of collating information. Every warship and every merchant ship in the operational area had to be kept track of - there were 130 warships alone. We also had to sift the Commodore's signals - he could get 800 in a day and we had to prioritise them.*

Worries about TLAM's effectiveness proved unfounded, with the US Navy claiming that eighty-five per cent of the missiles launched in the first wave hit their targets,

An EA-6B Prowler electronic warfare aircraft returns to the Saratoga *having successfully covered a strike mission.* Ray Bean/STILL MOTIONS Collection.

including the Defence Ministry and the Baghdad Telecommunications Centre. Workers at the General Dynamics plant in the naval city of San Diego, where the missiles were made, cheered when told that US Navy ships had fired the weapons successfully in the opening salvoes of Desert Storm.[9] But the arms factory employees sobered up when they saw the reality of war on their TV screens and realized that many of their neighbours in San Diego, serving aboard warships in the Gulf, were potentially at risk from retaliation.

The first American casualty in the war was US Navy F-18 pilot Lieutenant Commander Michael Speicher, from the *Saratoga* whose aircraft 'vanished in a bright burst' [10] at 4.00 a.m. on 17 January. Action reports suggested that his aircraft had either been shot down by a pursuing Iraqi Mig-25 or collided with the enemy aircraft.

The air defence system the coalition air forces were tasked with penetrating was sophisticated and multi-layered, consisting of many hundreds of AA guns and SAM launchers, all tied together by a formidable French-made command and control system. Over the first forty-eight hours of Desert Storm the plan was to destroy it and neutralize the Iraqi Air Force. Once that was accomplished Saddam's military could be torn apart with impunity, the troops in Kuwait and southern Iraq cut off from their regime commanders in Baghdad and pounded to pieces. To take part in the air war, the US Navy had the *Midway* and the *Ranger* in the Gulf itself while retaining the *Saratoga, John F. Kennedy* and *America* in the Red Sea. A sixth carrier, the *Theodore Roosevelt*, was steaming hard for the war zone but would not arrive in theatre until 22 January.

On the first night of the air war, *John F. Kennedy*'s planes, and those of *Saratoga*, hit targets near Baghdad and airbases in western Iraq, while the USS *America*'s aircraft provided fleet defence over the Red Sea and Saudi Arabia. Aircraft from the *Ranger* and *Midway* attacked targets in southern Iraq, including the port of Basra and Umm Qasr Naval Base. The carriers were in many cases closer to the targets than the airfields of land-based aircraft. Against the 2,000 sorties flown by the coalition in the first twenty-four hours, the disorganized and incompetent Iraqi Air

US Navy F-18 Hornets, such as this one being prepared for launch aboard the Saratoga, were heavily involved in the first night of strikes.
Ray Bean/STILL MOTIONS Collection.

Force could only put up two dozen aircraft, with nearly half of them shot down. On that first night the US Navy scored its only air-to-air victories of the war, when a pair of Hornets from the *Saratoga*, on a bombing run, broke it off for forty seconds to shoot down two Mig-21s, using a combination of heat-seeking Sidewinder and radar-homing Sparrow missiles. True cool-headed professionals, the American pilots resumed their strike mission and successfully bombed an Iraqi airfield.

The US Navy pilots who plunged into the maelstrom on the first night returned to their carriers awestruck by the lethal light show that had greeted them. Commander John Leenhouts, the Executive Officer of an A7-E Crusader squadron flying from the *John F. Kennedy* remarked:

> It looked like the fireworks display at Disney World multiplied by a hundred. [11]

Hornet pilot Lieutenant Tyler Kearly described his first mission as:

> Three and a half hours of boredom and ten minutes of stark terror. [12]

Day two of Desert Storm saw the beginning of an aerial mining campaign in the northern Gulf, the first of its kind by American carrier planes since the Vietnam War.

The USS America, which launched her initial air strikes from the Red Sea, but later moved to the Gulf. Ray Bean/STILL MOTIONS Collection.

A quartet of Intruders, covered by fourteen other planes from the *Ranger*, dropped mines in the mouth of the az-Zubayr River, with the aim of closing the naval facilities at Basra, az-Zubayr and Umm Qasr, so that Iraqi craft could not come out in the northern Gulf. The Iraqis shot down one of the Intruders, with its two-man crew killed. No similar missions were mounted after that and the few mines laid did not prevent the Iraqis from coming out.

However, on the plus side, one senior US Navy commander regarded the swift destruction of the Iraqi air defence system, command infrastructure, and the cutting of communications between Baghdad and Kuwait, as the decisive phase. 'The war was won in the first forty-eight hours,' remarked Rear Admiral George Gee.

Working in the confines of a Type 22 in a major military operation was far from ideal, but in true British style Commodore Craig made do.

> The London *was emphatically cramped as a flagship - often my flag staff officers out-numbered the ship's staff. We ended up with twenty-six ships in the task group at the height of the war and eighteen helicopters to boot. It wasn't easy exercising effective Flag Command of such a large task group from a Type 22, but we improvised. There is no doubt, with hindsight, if one had known we would be involved in such a major conflict that the MOD would have been looking straight away at deploying a two star admiral with his command staff in a carrier. In reality though, the situation was not so clear-cut and perhaps the people in the UK didn't realise it would end up as a full shooting war. What I thought was brave of the MoD and Fleet HQ at Northwood was to persevere with the staff and command structure already in place, to stick with the people who had a handle on the situation. To have effected a command shift in mid-conflict would have been more destructive...out-weighing the benefits of the carrier being sent. A new task group commander would have found re-establishing good links with the Americans very difficult to manage when the missiles were flying.*

Behind the scenes, the decision not to send *Ark Royal* to the Gulf caused great anguish in the Royal Navy. But it could not be helped, as the Government was not prepared to spend the extra money needed to make her suitable for such an intense area of operations. In addition to this reluctance by the Treasury, when it came to funding the modifications to the ship herself, there were also claims that the UK government wasn't prepared to pay for extra engines the Sea Harriers would have needed to operate in the demanding desert environment. Additionally, with memories of the Falklands being so fresh, there was considerable anxiety about operating a carrier in the Gulf itself. Not only was there Saddam's seemingly formidable air force and its many Exocet missiles, there was the considerable Silkworm anti-shipping missile threat and mines were, like the Exocet, already a proven hazard. With the exception of the USS *Independence*'s brief foray the previous autumn, not even the vastly more capable US Navy had, prior to hostilities breaking out in January, dared to deploy a carrier into the Gulf for more than a short period.

As reported by the newspapers in Arabia, *Ark Royal* had departed Portsmouth a week before the air offensive started, with the Type 22 frigate *Sheffield* as close escort and supported by the RFAs *Regent* and *Olmeda*. The *Ark* carried eight Sea Harrier fighters from 801 Naval Air Squadron and eight Sea Kings in anti-submarine, radar picket and transportation roles. A further two Sea Kings were embarked in the *Olmeda*. The main submarine threat was thought to be posed by pro-Saddam Libya, which had been helping the Iraqi dictator break the trade embargo. The Type 42 destroyers *Manchester* and *Exeter* reinforced the task group on 13 January and a few days later the commanding officer of what was known as Task Group 323.2, Rear Admiral John Brigstocke, himself a former captain of *Ark Royal*, embarked in the carrier.

> *On 17 January as Desert Shield became Desert Storm and the Gulf War began in earnest, ARK ROYAL went to defence watches and the SHARs were armed each with four AIM-9L Sidewinder missiles and put on alert. Given the unpredictability of Libya's ruler and the uncertainty of his support for Saddam Hussein, flying was curtailed on the 18th as the Task Group sailed by Libya.* [13]

Having deliberately avoided provoking Colonel Gaddafi to repeat his defiance of the mid-1980s, the *Ark Royal* headed for Cyprus, where the UK still maintained two military bases that were heavily involved in supporting the coalition campaign. On 22 January, as the *Ark* task group reached Cypriot waters, the argument on the exact nature of her role had continued to rage back in the UK. The US Navy had turned up the heat by requesting the British carrier should come at least into the Red Sea, where she could lead the continuing embargo operation that sealed off Aqaba. This would release US Navy warships for combat operations against Iraq. However, despite these entreaties, 'there seemed to be opposition in London to *ARK* playing a more forward role.'

> *...it was not to be...Admiral Brigstocke and his group took up the important but rather frustrating role of surveillance of the vital Mediterranean sea lines of communication upon which the coalition forces in the Gulf depended.* [14]

The British warships were joined by the USS *Virginia*, USS *Philippine Sea*, both cruisers, the nuclear-powered attack submarine USS *Pittsburgh* and the destroyer USS *Spruance*, all of them with TLAM and destined to fire at Iraqi targets after Turkey had given consent. With Scud missiles falling on Israel, the Iraqi threat was far from unrealistic, and a complete UK surveillance picture was meshed with that of the US Navy, the *Ark* working closely with the 6th Fleet flagship *Belknap*. In the absence of air cover from an American carrier in the eastern Mediterranean, the Sea Harriers were probably the most effective Combat Air Patrol available, just in case the Iraqi Air Force or the Libyans found their courage, with two Sea Harriers in the air over the eastern Mediterranean during daylight and at least one at night.

The main function of the coalition fleet in the Gulf was to deny Iraqi forces the use of the sea, and to threaten the occupiers in Kuwait on their seaward flank.

The enemy fleet would be prevented from making attacks or re-supplying their ground troops in Kuwait; the US-UK naval units up-threat in the northern Gulf would be able to conduct bombardment missions against Iraqi positions and they could also launch an amphibious assault.

The Royal Navy could be expected to use its plastic-hulled Hunt class Mine Counter-Measure Vessels close in-shore to clear mines both for the amphibious assault and battleship bombardments. The US Navy had very few vessels capable of this very demanding role and none as advanced as the Hunts. Aggressive search-and-destroy patrols by British Lynx helicopters armed with Sea Skua ASMs - another capability the US Navy did not then possess - could also be decisive in eliminating the Iraqi Navy. The vessels of the RFA were responsible for supplying coalition warships with everything from toilet rolls to ammunition and would be the only vessels of that kind to risk the dangerous waters of the northern Gulf. Another support vessel taking her share of risk was the MCMV command and support ship HMS *Herald* - a white-painted survey ship - with her peace-time crew of 119 increased by forty, which made her every bit as cramped as the *London*. Looking after the health of everyone onboard, and in the MCMVs, was Surgeon Lieutenant Annalisa Judd, assisted by Leading Medical Assistant Kev Shore. LMA Shore later recalled:

> Not only did we have the mine warfare people embarked, we also had five lads from 16th Air Defence Regiment Royal Artillery with their shoulder-launched SAMs to give us some sort of chance if we came under air attack. Of course, a major worry was the potential NBC threat and not long after the war started, we got down to vaccinating people for all sorts of nasties, from anthrax to the plague.

The campaign to eliminate the Iraqi Navy had started on 18 January, with aircraft from the *Ranger* and *Midway* claiming three Iraqi vessels to the east of Bubiyan Island. To rescue downed pilots and search for further enemy units, the Americans prepared a joint force with the Kuwaitis under the US Navy's Commander Dennis G. Morral: the Perry class frigate *Nicholas* and the Kuwaiti patrol craft *al-Sanbouk* and *Istiqlal*.[15] In addition to Navy SEALS, the *Nicholas* embarked a US Coast Guard board and search team, two US Navy Seahawk helicopters and a pair of OH-58D Kiowa Warrior helicopters from the US Army, armed with rockets and guns. The Kiowas also had equipment that could detect radar emissions. Many of the US Army personnel were veterans of similar embarkations during the recent Tanker War. To await calls to rescue downed aviators, the task group was sent right up into the oil platforms of the ad-Dorra field off Kuwait. As there was a very real danger from Silkworm missiles, fast attack boats and strike planes, Commander Morral hoped the surrounding oil platforms would confuse Iraqi search radar. The force moved up on the night of 17 January, with the Kiowas and a Seahawk out in front. The helicopters picked up radar operating from oil platforms, which could only mean enemy troops using them as observation posts to report incoming coalition air strikes to their headquarters in Kuwait or Iraq. Further proof was provided when the *Istiqlal* was fired on as she approached one of the platforms. Withdrawing on 18 January the force went in to deal with the threat, the *Nicholas* sending up a Seahawk and the British contributing a Lynx from *Cardiff* to carry out a supplementary reconnaissance mission. The attack was launched on the evening of 18 January -

coming in low over the sea the Army helicopters fired Hellfire rockets at two platforms, while the *Nicholas* and *Istiqlal* bombarded others with their guns and missiles. Cut to pieces in their ramshackle shelters on the oil platforms, the enemy troops were overwhelmed by the sheer violence of the attack, with five Iraqis killed. At day break on 19 January, it became clear that Iraqis were still holding out on one of the oil platforms, so the frigate and a Kuwaiti boat moved in, but a few warning shots prompted a surrender.

A distinct failure in the coalition containment of Saddam Hussein prior to Desert Storm was not preventing his naval forces from laying mines. In order not to provoke a renewal of hostilities before the coalition was ready, the Allied navies had kept out of the northern Gulf and this gave the Iraqis the opportunity to plant mines 'in a two-belt, 150-mile arc stretching from Bubiyan Island to the Saudi border...'[16]

The minefields contained contact mines, tethered to the bottom, and other so-called 'influence' mines, such as the Italian-origin Manta that was detonated by ships' prop noise and magnetic signature. However, the majority of the mines were contact mines, many of them of a pre-First World War design, but containing around 300lbs of explosives and plenty powerful enough to sink any of the warships in the Gulf. Some of the influence mines were programmed to remain dormant while mine-hunters passed over them and then explode under warships following on. The Iraqi minelayers had been observed at their work and higher command had been warned but no action was taken until, with the beginning of Desert Storm, orders were given for the capture of an Iraqi vessel, in order to obtain charts and other documents that would, hopefully, provide details of the mine threat. In the early hours of 24 January, a Russian-origin Yevgenya class minelayer was spotted alongside a jetty at Qaruh Island, off the coast of Kuwait.

Intruder bombers from the *Theodore Roosevelt* disabled her a few hours later, after she had put to sea, and an American task group, composed of the frigates *Curts* and *Nicholas* and the destroyer *Leftwich*, was sent in to make the capture. With her own Seahawk preceding her, the *Curts* led the way and Iraqi mines were soon spotted nearby, one of them, lying in the frigate's path, was destroyed by machine gun fire from the helicopter. When the Seahawk found the minelayer, it was receiving assistance from another Iraqi vessel lying alongside it. This patrol craft panicked and, breaking away, managed to hit a mine and sink. With US Army helicopters from *Curts* providing cover, the Seahawk moved in over the minelayer and spotted the crew trying to destroy documents and equipment. The helicopter peppered the minelayer with machine-gun bullets, persuading the Iraqi sailors to abandon ship. Twenty-two were rescued and a boarding party put aboard the crippled vessel by *Curts* recovered the remaining documents. The vessel was then sunk by the American frigate's 76mm gun. Having been fired on from Qaruh, the Kiowas attacked Iraqi positions there and a SEAL unit, composed of teams embarked in the three US warships, went ashore and took the surrender of a fifty-three-strong garrison. At just after 5.00 p.m. a SEAL officer pulled up both the Kuwaiti and US flags on Qaruh. For the Kuwaitis this was a joyous moment, for while Qaruh was normally home to a bird sanctuary and had no permanent human population, it was the first piece of their national soil to be liberated.

With his exposed destroyers moved to a better position in the northern Gulf, Commodore Craig's new worry had been that the Iraqis would try and use the cover of Allied aircraft returning from raids on Baghdad to mask an attack. This had duly happened on 24 January but, luckily, an American airborne early-warning aircraft detected the four enemy aircraft very early in their attack run. Next, the US Navy Ticonderoga class missile cruiser *Bunker Hill*, together with HMS *London* and the Type 42s, picked them up on search radars.   But, just as the two British destroyers were about to push the fire button on their Sea Darts, and *London*'s Sea Wolf missile launchers were training towards the danger area, American and Saudi fighters shot down the Iraqi jets. At the height of the action, Commodore Craig had found himself smiling at the cool efficiency with which the Iraqi aircraft had been dealt with. The comprehensive layered defence, that had been so absent in the Falklands nine years earlier, impressed him.

> *The Iraqis sent two Exocet-carrying Mirage F-1s at low-level that were working with Mig-23s as a higher-level distraction. American aircraft took out the high level threat while the Saudis dealt with the F-1s. It was very neatly done. There were so many layers of defence... If the Iraqi aircraft directly threatening us had got through the Saudi F-15s, then the US Navy's F-14s would have been their next hurdle. Only then would we have been expected to deal with them. Everybody was on Actions Stations, all missiles ready. I didn't really feel anxious about it.*

The news magazine *TIME International* painted a dramatic picture of the interception:

> *Four Saudi jet fighters were flying patrol near the Kuwaiti frontier last week when their radios crackled an alert. Peeling off, they intercepted a pair of Iraqi fighters heading towards gulf waters where British warships were operating. Captain Ayedh al-Shamrani swerved his U.S.-built F-15 behind the Mirage F-1s and shot both out of the sky. Returning to base in Dhahran, the Saudi pilot received a hero's welcome. Said the modest Shamrani: 'It was my day.'* [17]

If the fate of *Sheffield* in the Falklands haunted the Royal Navy, it was only natural that the *Stark* and *Vincennes* incidents hovered over the US Navy, which did not want to fall victim to the same errors again. Some senior officers believed, however, that losses due to surface-skimming missiles were almost inevitable. Rear Admiral Daniel March, one of the US Navy's senior front line commanders in the Gulf, later expanded on this by saying:

> *...there was significant potential for them to get through with a couple of assets, suicidal or whatever, with some Exocets...I think we would have taken some losses.* [18]

The F-1s of the 24 January lunge had done well, as by the time they were shot down they were within Exocet range of a variety of British and American warships, including HMS *Cardiff*, HMS *Gloucester*, USS *Mobile Bay*, USS *Bunker Hill* and USS *Worden*, which were close to the Iranian coast. The route the F-1s chose along

The Gloucester *was well up threat, with her Lynx helicopter, here seen parked on her flight deck shortly before hostilities, destroying a number of Iraqi vessels.* Iain Ballantyne.

the Saudi coast was, unknown to them, where the battlespace picture compiled by the Allied air forces met that created by the navies and, because they didn't quite knit, there was a slight lack of clarity.

However, some later analysis of the 24 January incident has suggested that the Iraqi Mirages were not even carrying Exocets, and were instead more interested in bombing oil installations or water desalination plants in Saudi Arabia.

Whatever their intention, the failure of the mission made a great impression on Saddam Hussein. On 25 January, the Soviet Interfax news agency reported that a number of Iraqi Air Force generals had been executed. On 26 January, the Iraqis began to fly their aircraft to Iran, creating fears in the coalition that the latter might allow a mass attack from its air space. Those that fled included more of the deadly Mirage F-1s, some of which were shot down while making their escape bid. Were the Iraqis about to try and use the radar shadow of Iran to make their big foray? Such a mass attack had been in the back of everyone's mind since the start of Desert Storm, from senior officers down to senior ratings such as Yorkie Cunningham in

A sailor aboard the British destroyer Gloucester *keeps a sharp eye out for possible air attack.* Iain Ballantyne.

HMS *London*:

> On 17 January after the balloon went up you thought 'well this is it'.... the Iraqi Air Force is going to come straight over the horizon.

If an Iraqi plane did get through, the battle-hardened Royal Navy put its faith in each warship deploying her own individual layered defence. One of *Brazen's* officers, Sub Lieutenant Paul Appelquist, had explained during Exercise Deep Heat that the frigate would rely on 'seduction, distraction and confusion'.

> The *Brazen can fire off chaff rockets, scattering strips of metal foil that seduce any incoming radar-homing missile away from the ship. If that fails we can distract and confuse radar missiles via other measures. Our Lynx helicopter can also play a part by taking off and flying some distance away and dropping chaff. And if that fails we resort to destruction. We are absolutely confident about Sea Wolf. The system fires two missiles in each salvo, with the first taking out the enemy aircraft or missile. The second destroys any wreckage to make sure it doesn't come on and cause harm.* [19]

The next piece of Kuwaiti territory to be liberated fleetingly was Maradim Island on which it was suspected the Iraqis were operating more observation posts. In the early hours of 29 January the US Navy task group assigned to the task - the assault carrier *Okinawa*, cruiser *Mobile Bay*, destroyer *Caron*, the *Curts* and *Leftwich* - was ready to attack. Sea Stallion and Sea Knight helicopters on the *Okinawa* embarked Kuwaiti and American marines and, after some reconnaissance from attack helicopters, which saw no obvious sign of life, they conducted an aerial assault. The coalition marines discovered arms and radar equipment and documents, which again yielded more useful intelligence, but there were no enemy soldiers. When nearly twenty Iraqi naval vessels were sighted heading south at high speed, the landing force was withdrawn. The same day Iraqi forces had seized the Saudi border town of Khafji, their only serious offensive ground action against the coalition, and, as the US forces withdrew from Maradim, they had advised senior commanders that the enemy might be making a move along the coast in support of the Khafji incursion. The *Brazen's* Lynx, which was on patrol nearby, moved towards Maradim, but could not get a lock-on for its Sea Skua missiles, so the *Gloucester's* was called in to the attack. Its pilot, Lieutenant Commander David Livingstone, later recalled that he and his Observer, Lieutenant Martin 'Florrie' Ford 'picked the biggest one.'

> We fired at very short range from quite high up which was extremely uncomfortable because we felt very exposed being close to the enemy shoreline. We used the range of the missiles to our best advantage. [20]

The missile hit the water close to the Iraqi vessel, spraying it with shrapnel. The convoy of boats scattered, *Brazen's* Lynx firing a Sea Skua and RAF Jaguars diving in to the attack. Over the next thirty-six hours, more Iraqi vessels came out, either attempting to go down the coast to Khafji or make an escape bid towards Iran. The Royal Navy's Lynxes played the leading role in carving up the Iraqi Navy, with *Gloucester's* and *Cardiff's* aircraft carrying out the majority of the attacks. RAF Nimrod and US Navy P3 Orion maritime patrol aircraft together with Seahawk helicopters from American warships used their powerful sensors to feed a comprehensive picture of potential targets to the Lynxes. Intruder bombers, Cobra

**One of the Iraqi naval vessels destroyed by marauding Allied helicopters
and strike jets.** Toby Elliott Collection.

attack helicopters and Jaguars pitched in. Kiowa Warriors were also on the prowl,
but at night using their powerful sensors and weapons. It was found that visual ID
of targets was necessary to avoid killing an Iranian naval vessel, for a number of
them were sniffing around the battle zone as well as attack craft from the Gulf states.
It was a wild, confused fight, the enemy vessels twisting and turning among oil rigs
and suddenly darting out of the haze, or playing dead in the hope of avoiding
destruction. Most were left as burning hulks.

The Iraqis put up little fight, due to poor crew training and weapons systems not
capable of handling fast moving targets. On 30 January the *Cardiff*'s Lynx managed
to destroy an Iraqi vessel inside the Shatt al Arab Waterway, not far from Umm Qasr.
On hearing of this engagement *Gloucester*'s Lynx was launched and flew north on
the hunt for more enemy craft. In the channel leading up to Umm Qasr, Lieutenant
Ford and Lieutenant Commander Livingstone spotted an Exocet-armed TNC45 fast
attack craft that had belonged to the Kuwaiti Navy but was now being operated by
the Iraqis. After a quick identification check *Gloucester*'s Lynx attacked:

> *We watched the missile hit home. The TNC45 subsequently sank...* [21]

Next Lieutenant Commander Livingstone and Lieutenant Ford took on an Iraqi
minesweeper that had strayed into their line of vision. The enemy vessel took no
evasive action and was soon a blazing hulk. Taking the aircraft back to the
Gloucester for a missile reload Lieutenant Commander Livingstone heard that
Cardiff's Lynx had achieved another kill. On flying north again, the *Gloucester*'s

team picked up some suspicious contacts, one of them another TNC45.

> *We asked for permission to fire which was duly given and away went two missiles. One hit the bridge area of the TNC45 and the next one went into the mid superstructure.* [22]

The following day, while trying to help find a US Navy helicopter crew whose aircraft had crashed, *Gloucester*'s Lynx came across yet another TNC45. Lieutenant Commander Livingstone asked for permission to open fire and on receiving it...

> *...we delivered two missiles at it. We didn't see the first explosion, the second missile most certainly went in.* [23]

Accepting an invitation to visit the USS *Nicholas*, the two British naval aviators were congratulated on their hunting skills by the frigate's CO and, after picking up some steak and chips to eat as they flew home, headed back to the *Gloucester*. [24]

During the Battle of Bubiyan, as it became known, twenty-five Sea Skuas were fired and eighteen hit home, with at least seven Iraqi vessels sunk. Kiowa Warriors destroyed half-a-dozen more and the US Navy's attack aircraft finished off a number that were dead in the water.

Towards the end of January, the US-based *Navy Times* reported that the Pentagon had received nearly sixty letters from prisoners in various penitentiaries, offering to take part in behind-the-lines missions in the Gulf, if it would gain them a pardon. One eager inmate declared that he was more than willing to join some kind of 'government action team...maybe behind Iraq's lines?' He suggested the fact that he had been jailed for 'killing a man in the desert and taking his money' qualified him for playing a key part in liberating Kuwait. A number of prisoners were Vietnam War veterans and the *Navy Times* reported that several had suggested they would even be willing to return to jail after fighting for their country. [25]

Around this time, Saddam chose to give his first interview with the media since the beginning of the Allied air offensive. On satellite TV, the Iraqi dictator said that he would use chemical, nuclear and biological weapons against the coalition, if he needed to. While it treated the prospect of chemical and biological weapons seriously, the White House was sceptical that Saddam could field a nuclear weapon. White House spokesman Marlin Fitzwater told a press conference:

> *We don't believe he has a nuclear warhead right now but we do think he's close to developing one.* [26]

Meanwhile, on 29 January, Tehran had assured the USA that the eighty to ninety Iraqi aircraft that had, by that time, flown to Iran would be kept on the ground during hostilities. The Iranians turned out to be as good as their word, for the Iraqi aircraft were still in their possession in the late 1990s.[27] British warship numbers rose in late January, with the Type 42 destroyers *Exeter* and *Manchester* arriving, together with the Type 22 frigates *Brave* and *Brilliant*. The British mine-hunter force was also boosted with two more Hunts and the survey vessel *Hecla*. It had been decided that another Type 42 was needed in the Gulf, and so the *Manchester* had been replaced as *Ark Royal* escort by the Sea Wolf Leander class frigate HMS *Charybdis*. Like many of his shipmates, Lieutenant Thomas was not sorry to have left the *Ark*'s company:

The prospect of being held in the Med was worse, almost, than being back in the UK and not involved at all. We conducted continuation training as we passaged down the Red Sea towards the Strait of Hormuz and everyone was extremely focussed, as we realized it would soon be for real. The Manchester was, I believe, a professional ship that had acquitted herself well during her training cycle, but there were moments when I, and I believe many others, questioned whether we as individuals would be 'up to it'; whether we would be able to fulfil our role in the co-ordinated teamwork required to execute our mission. Thankfully, the excellent training from the Flag Officer Sea Training teams had prepared each and every one of us to play his professional part to the letter.

The *Manchester*'s CO, Captain Nigel Essenhigh, who normally sported an impressive black beard, had been forced to shave it off on deploying from the UK, in order to ensure his NBC suit gas mask would achieve an effective seal around his face. A decade later, when he was First Sea Lord, he remarked:

When my crew saw me shave off the beard they knew it was serious and we really were going to war. [28]

The *Brilliant*, meanwhile, made history, as the first British warship to carry women as part of her sea-going complement. Having female sailors in his crew was not something that gave *Brilliant*'s CO, Captain Toby Elliot, any qualms.

After a three-day shakedown at Portland we headed for the Middle East, with Operational Sea Training people still aboard to conduct NBC drills. At the time I thought that it was a long way to the Gulf and it might all be over by the time we got there. In any event, we were determined to make sure that we would be ready for whatever the Iraqis might throw at us. The most serious threat was from their air force and we had plenty of air defence exercises on the way to the Gulf. There were our own training jets and all through the Mediterranean, French, Spanish and Italian aircraft available to act as the 'enemy'. The air-defence activity tailed off as we reached the eastern Med, as we were moving into

HMS Brilliant *after arriving in the war zone.* Toby Elliott Collection.

what was considered to be the area of operations where we passed through the Ark Royal *task group. As we went through the Suez Canal, the Egyptian Army appeared to be very alert against potential terrorist attacks. All the way down to the Gulf I think everyone took preparation very seriously. The thing that focussed our minds more than anything else was the Chemical and Biological threat.* Brilliant *was unique in that she was the first British naval vessel to carry women sailors to war as part of a crew. The particular group of women we had aboard for the Gulf were all very talented and contributed a lot to the fighting efficiency of the ship, without a shadow of a doubt. Those that worked in the Ops Room, for example, were all first class. The only way you could tell the difference between a man and a woman working in an Ops Room, with all their flash gear on, was obviously when they spoke. After entering the Strait of Hormuz we started to notice a growing Coalition naval presence. There was such a large presence, in fact, that wherever you were in the Gulf; you were always in sight of one or two other naval vessels. Our main job was to stay with the supply vessels of the fleet train in the central Gulf. This meant staying off Bahrain but from time-to-time we did escort the supply ships up north to replenish the other warships.*

As January gave way to early February, more small craft were detected making runs down the coast and destroyed by helicopters from *Manchester* and *Cardiff*. These vessels appeared to be part of a mass exodus to Iran, following the same pattern as Saddam's air force.

A group of Iraqi prisoners of war captured this week after their ships were sunk by allied naval action said that they had been ordered by their superiors to defect to Iran and stay there until the Gulf war was over. Prisoners told their Kuwaiti interrogator that Iraq's navy had been told to head for the Iranian port of Bandar Khomeini... [29]

Now the USS *Missouri*, which had already been contributing TLAMs to the conflict, made headlines when she used her 16-inch guns to pulverize some bunkers being built by Iraqi army engineers in Kuwait. It was the first time she had fired her big guns in anger since the Korean War and they were in heavy demand.

... For a second day, the US battleship Missouri *slammed the Iraqis with shells from its 16-inch guns. Six rounds silenced a long-range artillery battery as it fired on allied troops. Another 28 rounds wiped out an Iraqi radar site. At midday, the huge guns on the big ship still were firing at targets on the coastline of occupied Kuwait.* [30]

Not long after, the *Wisconsin* was also in a good position to add the weight of her 16-inch guns to the bombardment. Whereas in the Second World War, battleships relied mainly upon teams of forward observers to zero in their guns on land targets, in 1991 they could put aloft their own set of eyes in the form of Remotely-Piloted Vehicles (RPVs) that transmitted back live television pictures. This allowed instant correction of fire solutions.

When the US battleship Wisconsin *began pounding a marina on the Kuwaiti coast, its first 1,900-pound shells landed wide of the target. But infrared pictures from a small aircraft circling the beach allowed the battleship's gunners to adjust their aim. The correction proved devastating. When the 30-round barrage from the* Wisconsin's *thundering 16-inch guns ended, the water was littered with the remains of 15 boats that Iraq could have used for raids against the Saudi coastline.* [31]

The Iraqis were not powerless to hit back and fired a Silkworm missile at an American frigate, which missed its target only by a few hundred yards. Shrapnel hit the US warship but there were no casualties among her sailors.

Back in America, the US Marines were lobbying hard for an amphibious landing to take place. They were so keen that they enlisted the help of newspaper reporters to air their case. Melissa Healey, one of the *Los Angeles Times'* Washington DC correspondents, was summoned to the headquarters of the US Marine Corps for a briefing. Official USMC spokesman Lieutenant Colonel Fred Peck, one day 'unloaded a spectacular amount of detail about amphibious landings', in fact so much information that after the war the reporter speculated that it might all have been part of some elaborate deception plan.

He even waxed poetic: 'The darker the moon and the higher the tide, the better it is for Marines to ride,' he intoned. Knowing that many analysts believed any amphibious landing to be a feint, I asked Peck how likely a landing really was. 'Oh, 95% certain,' he assured me. 'The only thing that could stop it would be if (Iraqi President) Saddam Hussein capitulates before we get there.'... I think Peck believed almost all of what he told me that day, but the incident reminded me that in the military, there are wheels working within wheels. [32]

Deception or not, by the middle of February there were at least 18,000 US Marines poised aboard assault ships in the Gulf. In fact, the Amphibious Task Force (ATF) that would be tasked with any assault had a total of 24,000 US Marines in 31 ships, some of them yet to enter the Gulf. [33]

To back them up twenty Harrier AV-8B strike jets were loaded onto the USS *Nassau*, which was more than three times the number of jets the assault carrier would normally carry. Although they would conduct missions in support of the anticipated amphibious landings, they were involved in the air campaign as well and two of the ship's jets were lost, one to enemy ground fire and the other in an accident. As part of the on going amphibious landing lobbying, a senior US Marine Corps officer told *Newsweek* magazine:

We need a victory. Beirut was a disaster. In Panama, we were overshadowed by the Army. We need a chance to show a new generation of the American people what the Marines can do.

But, the cost could be high, for, aside from the waters offshore being mined, the beach defences themselves were formidable.

On likely landing beaches Iraqi combat engineers had emplaced anti boat and anti personnel mines, thickets of stakes called 'hedgehogs,' underwater electric cables, barbed wire entanglements, and other obstacles meant to sink or ensnare landing craft and kill marines trying to reach the shore. To cover the beach, the enemy had erected Silkworm batteries, dug trenches, and built bunkers. [34]

There were fortified apartment blocks and other reinforced buildings overlooking the beaches, anti-tank ditches, and tanks dug in at strategic points. Four Iraqi divisions were devoted to defending the coast of Kuwait, with one in reserve. The Royal Navy, whose mine-hunters could be expected to clear the mines right under the noses of the Iraqi defenders, and would therefore be in great danger, was not consulted during the early planning. In fact, not even the US Navy's own MCM officers were fully informed and some other elements of the American fleet were not properly briefed. There had been an amphibious planning meeting in late December, chaired by Vice Admiral Stan Arthur, who had replaced Mauz in early December, with nearly all USMC and US Navy senior flag officers present. [35]

A plan called Operation Desert Saber was formulated, with landings to secure the port of Ash Shuaybah, to support the advance of the I MEF. The British were eventually brought into the loop to plan the MCM strategy, with Commodore Craig invited to a meeting aboard the USS *Tripoli* on 26 January. The British task group CO took his MCM boss, Commander John Scoles and they were briefed on US plans that astounded them. They envisaged battleships, destroyers, frigates and MCMs going into the northern Gulf in early February. Heavily supported and covered, the US Navy planners estimated mine clearance would take three weeks. Commodore Craig was astounded by how unrealistic the plans were. They struck him as being 'so ill-conceived and immature that I could not believe the US Navy had been their architect.'

> *Around me the mood changed rapidly to one of similar incredulity, not least among senior USN officers. We were apparently to move north in a combined group as early as 4 February, with my minehunters leading the way. We were then to advance through Iraqi minefields, whose position and density were frankly unknown...to within 4 miles of enemy gun, missile and rocket-launcher positions. There the mine hunters were to commence their clearance operations at dead slow speed in full daylight under the admiring gaze of the enemy. When sufficient water had been cleared, the battleships would come close in behind the hunters, commencing bombardment of enemy positions prior to 'possible' full-scale amphibious assault.* [36]

The crunch meeting came on 2 February, when General Schwarzkopf and I MEF CO, General Walt Boomer, went to the USS *Blue Ridge* for a conference with Admiral Arthur.

It became clear that a major amphibious assault would lay waste to vast sections of the Kuwait coast, but destroying the emirate to liberate it was not on the agenda. Then there was the question of massive casualties among coalition forces, either preparing for the assault by clearing the minefields, or when they attacked across the beach. Still determined to show what amphibious forces could do, the US Navy suggested taking Faylakah Island, which guards the approaches to Kuwait City harbour itself, and where there was believed to be a 2,500-strong Iraqi brigade. [37] Schwarzkopf assented, as it provided a classic diversionary move for his swing out deep into the western desert of Iraq. Some form of major naval advance north, and clearance of mines, would be needed in any event, to allow the battleships to support any ground offensive with their 16-inch guns. Mines also had to be cleared off

Kuwait, as, with or without a major amphibious assault, Ash Shuaybah would have to be opened to bring in humanitarian aid and military supplies.

When Commodore Craig met with American planners again on 4 February, aboard the US Navy flagship *La Salle*, he received the minimum reassurance he needed to commit British naval forces to operations in the northern Gulf.

By early February, sightings of floating mines had become more frequent, but the Allies were fairly sure they knew the limits of the Iraqi minefields off Kuwait. The naval command felt the lead elements of the task force could go forward and begin clearing paths through them with some confidence. However, on 8 February, for example, HMS *Gloucester*'s lookouts spotted a mine drifting by only fifteen feet away on her starboard beam. On 14 February, *London* led the British task group forward in company with the USS *Tripoli*, plus the *Wisconsin* and *Missouri*, the air-defence cruiser USS *Princeton* and some old wooden-hulled American minesweepers. The same day, General de la Billière made a morale-boosting visit to HMS *London* for talks with Commodore Craig, ahead of the move north into the most dangerous waters. The British Middle East Commander-in-Chief spoke to the flagship's crew about what risks remained. He told the sailors assembled on *London*'s upper deck:

> *The air battle has effectively been won, although Saddam Hussein does possess some aerial capability, which he could use in a suicidal and surprise manner.* [38]

Almost the entire British naval force was by now tightly integrated with the US Navy for this hazardous phase - of thirty-four vessels, half were British, but the whole

The two American battleships, with the Missouri leading, and the assault carrier Tripoli following on immediately behind, sail north on 14 February. McCaig Collection.

group was under the tactical command of the Americans, with the *Tripoli* acting as flagship. The *Brazen* and *Cardiff* - long overdue for relief - had by then sailed for home, but Commodore Craig felt he could not allow his flagship or *Gloucester* to leave at that point. The *London* and *Gloucester* were fully worked up, providing close cover for the Hunt class minehunters and *Herald*, the latter retained until sister ship *Hecla* was ready to take over her duties. It would be foolish in the middle of a full-scale war to let these three ships go, but, with the war dragging on into its fourth week, the crew of *London* had not been ashore for six weeks and a newspaper correspondent embarked in the frigate noted the sailors' mood:

There have been times when the war seems to be a collective figment of the imagination. Cruising through the blue waters of the Gulf, there are often hours when the horizon sweeps away without the companionable sight of another ship, compounding the sense of isolation from the broader war. [39]

However, despite the possibility of death or serious injury, many of the sailors in *London* were very disappointed that the frigate had not been directly involved in the action. Such was the nature of modern warships, and the NBC threat still remaining, even if Saddam's air force had been knocked out, that few of *London*'s sailors were managing to get some fresh air on the upper decks. According to the correspondent a good number of them had begun to lose interest in the conflict and were desperately counting down the days to their mid-March homecoming at Devonport.

Officers and ratings have been tuning in less and less to the BBC World Service and the arrival of newspapers is not as eagerly awaited as it was. Cable News Network, which the ship has only recently managed to receive is hardly watched. One Royal Navy commander puts talk of going home down to boredom. [40]

Petty Officer Burton's motivation had not diminished, but there again he knew what was going on in the war at large.

Those of us that were seconded to the Flag Staff certainly knew more than the average sailor. You might go down to the mess for a meal and pick up on a vibe that people were feeling left out of the loop on something. You couldn't tell them yourself, but you could go to the officers and suggest that they should give out some info.

On 15 February, as the task group came into the northern Gulf, a Royal Navy helicopter spotted a mine, which was destroyed by a team of divers dropped into the water by a helicopter from the USS *Curts*. British and Australian ordnance disposal divers carried out the same dangerous task, again by placing charges against mines to blow them up.

As part of the amphibious landing deception, sources at the Pentagon attributed the entry of a fourth aircraft carrier - the *America* - into the Gulf to the build-up for an assault across the beaches of Kuwait. In reality, the additional carrier meant that the other three could take it in turns to stand-down for maintenance, which they badly needed.

In response to receiving his final warning to leave Kuwait, Saddam issued a list of pre-conditions that subsequently proved not only to be his manifesto for the Arab world against the West, but also, partially, Osama bin Laden's. Saddam promised

115

A coalition diver in the water with a mine that he is about to destroy. C. Craig Collection.

compliance with Security Council Resolution 660, set in August 1990, but, in addition to lifting the embargo imposed following the invasion, the dictator demanded a raising of the ban on importation of nuclear weapons technology to Iraq. Saddam also demanded Israel's withdrawal from Gaza, the West Bank, Golan Heights and Lebanon, and that the Gulf should be free of foreign military bases, indeed any foreign military presence at all on land, at sea or in the air. Saddam told the coalition it should reconstruct Iraq's damaged infrastructure, but not Kuwait's, and that the ruling al-Sabah family must not be returned to power. He also proposed an Iran-Iraq security organization to defend the Gulf.

Saddam's ludicrously defiant statement was made in mid-February and coincided with concerted efforts by the Soviet Union to save its old arms client from further destruction. Needless to say, Saddam's demands were rejected by the coalition and President Bush called again for Iraq to stage an unconditional withdrawal from Kuwait.

The burden of keeping the Allied troops supplied with the rockets and bombs they needed occasionally fell on the shoulders of unlikely 'recruits', some of whom were old enough to have fought in the Second World War. One such was seventy-five year-old Guy Lipane, a merchant seaman who had retired to Florida to enjoy the sun in his twilight years, but found himself called back into service as the Chief Engineer of a gigantic cargo ship, the *Cape Farewell*. In mid-February, this ship was tasked with taking military supplies from freezing Bremerhaven in Germany to the Gulf, and Chief Engineer Lipane, dressed in a thin jumper, was missing the sun. 'This is the warmest thing I've got,' he observed sourly, shortly before the vessel set sail on a long journey, unarmed into the most dangerous waters in the world, usually carrying enough explosives to blow a fair-sized city to smithereens.

Floating mines, Exocet missiles and chemical warfare attacks are their nemeses. As they enter the Gulf, the seamen hold tight to their gas masks and lower the lifeboats in preparation for abandoning ship ... [41]

On 17 February active Silkworm batteries were detected trying to lock onto the US-

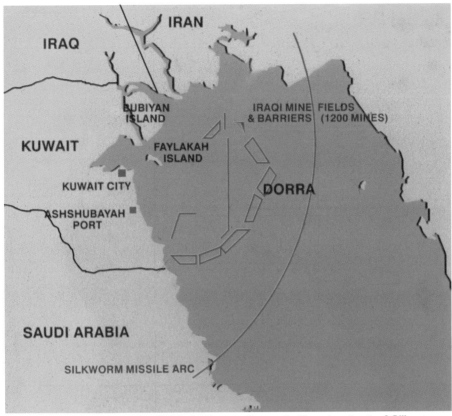

The position of Iraqi minefields in the northern Gulf and extent of Silkworm missile range. C. Craig Collection.

UK naval force, so the Americans ordered a withdrawal.

The task force moved back in towards the coast when it looked like the threat had receded, but, just before 2.00 a.m. on 18 February, an explosion rocked the USS *Tripoli*. She had fallen victim to a tethered mine, which meant the Iraqi fields extended further than expected, but the *Tripoli* was lucky. She suffered a thirty feet by thirty feet hole in her bow, below the waterline on her starboard side, parts of her filling with vaporized fuel and paint to form 'volatile fumes which, had they ignited, could have destroyed the bow.' [42]

The ship's communications were knocked out, compartments were flooded, but only four sailors were injured and none were killed. Royal Navy divers from the RFA *Diligence* played a key role in assessing the damage and helping to plug the massive hole. The coalition ships stayed where they were, until British mine warfare vessels could lead them out of danger. HMS *Herald* coordinated the tricky operation, with her sailors at full alert - Leading Medical Assistant Shore was well aware that, if his ship hit a mine, she could not expect to stay afloat.

It was what we called 'Mine Danger Red'. Everybody had to put his or her helmet on and no one was allowed below the waterline in the ship. Most people were therefore on the upper deck and I recall the ocean was bathed in

117

brilliant sunshine, which was great for the sun tan - except we are all wearing buttoned up overalls, anti-flash hoods and gloves, so not a lot of us was visible for bronzing. We heard on the BBC World Service that the IRA had set off some bombs in London, which was a bit surreal, what with us also under threat from being blown to bits.

To fix the field, they needed to find another mine and while HMS *Brave* had spotted mines drifting perilously close to her hull, they were untethered floaters. However, two-and-a-half hours after the first explosion, the USS *Princeton* detonated another mine. The cruiser had crept over a line of Manta influence mines, one of them detonating her stern.

The first explosion set off another mine 350 yards off *Princeton*'s starboard bow[43] and the ship almost had her back broken. In both incidents there were surprisingly few casualties and no deaths, but the *Princeton* was so badly damaged she had to be towed to a dockyard in the southern Gulf, while *Tripoli* withdrew for repairs under her own steam a few days later. Behind them, the two American warships left a new sense of vulnerability and Commodore Craig was all too aware that a similar catastrophe might well sink *London*.

...I reflected upon the loss of life if a similar explosion were to rip through my flagship, whose hull was but a fraction of Tripoli's *half-inch steel skin.* [44]

A Pentagon spokesman confirmed the *Princeton* had detonated influence mines as 'surprisingly there is no hole'.[45] In both ships damage control teams worked valiantly. The coalition task force was lucky - not only had the incompetent Iraqis failed to activate some of the mines a number of the ships had sailed over, they also didn't integrate the minefields with their air defence, artillery or missiles. The ships

The assault carrier USS Tripoli **in a dry-dock in the southern Gulf, the huge hole in her bow clearly visible.** H.M. Steele.

of the coalition naval force had been sitting ducks: 'More expertly laid and defended mines would have sunk ships and killed sailors and marines.' [46]

Not long after, a mine came to within twenty yards of *Brave*, with the USS *Fife* sending a team of divers into the water to destroy it, the British frigate's helicopter hovering overhead to show where it was located. Just prior to this sighting, British MCMVs had destroyed ten Iraqi mines.

Despite the mine strikes, the true nature of war could be remote from the naval forces, but sometimes evidence of the cost drifted past coalition warships.

Crewmen from a British destroyer recovered the remains of Iraqi marines floating in the Persian Gulf and buried them at sea with full military honors. The Iraqis were thought to have been killed by allied attacks on Iraqi patrol boats. [47]

Two days earlier the British minehunter HMS *Atherstone* had pulled a dead Iraqi soldier from the water. From his papers it was assessed that he was twenty-two years-old and a conscript. The *Atherstone*'s crew gave him a proper burial at sea. To guard against any last gasp desperate acts by the Iraqis, surface search was still a major task and the Royal Navy's aircrews continued to fly their Lynx helicopters on the limit, often pushing them to 150 knots, sometimes with the wheels of their aircraft only twenty feet above the waves.

The pilot of *Brave*'s helicopter was Lieutenant Steve Solleveld, who, together with his flight commander and observer, Lieutenant Ralph Dodds, found that sometimes it was necessary to fly even lower, to avoid being shot down by Iraqi anti-aircraft weapons on the Kuwaiti coast. As Lieutenant Dodds explained, it was a do or die situation:

> If their fire control radar had got a firm lock-on, the Iraqis would have fired a radar-homing missile at us. When our sensors warned us what was happening, Steve immediately started jinking the helicopter and dropped us to around 10ft and we were then too low for their radar to pick us up. [48]

Laden with Sea Skua missiles, at that height and speed the slightest mistake would have caused obliteration of the fragile flying machine. On one of its patrols the *Brave*'s Lynx was ordered to fly into Kuwait City harbour to check out, and possibly destroy, a fast moving radar contact that it was feared might be the Iraqis' last remaining fast attack craft. As he brought the Lynx in low over the water, Lieutenant Solleveld was pumped up for action but was sadly disappointed.

> When we got in there, we discovered it was a large buoy, but luckily we didn't get shot at.

As the Lynx made a swift exit, right under the noses of dozy Iraqi defenders, to avoid being detected due to the aircraft's emissions, everything unnecessary, including the Identification Friend or Foe (IFF) system was switched off. However, this made the Lynx potentially vulnerable to so-called 'friendly fire', as Lieutenant Dodds later explained:

> We ran the risk of being shot down by our own side. The Americans often took a while to respond to our radio voice transmissions telling them we were friend and not foe.

On 22 February, finally realizing they would not be able to hang onto Kuwait, the Iraqis began torching the emirate's oil wells, with 150 out of 950 ablaze by the

The British task group flagship HMS London *off Kuwait (nearest), with an* **American battleship (behind) and four British mine-hunters coming up** **(right).** C. Craig Collection.

following morning. To the south of HMS *London*, a couple of Silkworms were fired at *Wisconsin* but they missed. As Allied soldiers began to pour across the border from Saudi Arabia on 24 February, the US Marines played their part in the big deception that tied down five divisions of Iraqi troops along the Kuwait coast. Thirteen vessels of Amphib Group 3, carrying the 13th Marine Expeditionary Unit (13th MEU), hovered close to the coast.

> *At 0100 on 25 February, amphibious ships* Okinawa *and* Portland *broadcast over their radios recordings of amphibious operations.* [49]

The USS *Missouri* began bombarding the area around Ash Shuaybah, 16-inch shells being fired every five seconds. Three hours later helicopters from the 13th MEU launched from *Okinawa* and headed for a town north of the port.

As dawn broke, the helicopters came within sight of the Iraqis, but turned around off-shore. The trick worked, as Saddam's soldiers remained where they were, waiting with trepidation for a massive amphibious assault. The contribution from the sea also included a reinforcement into Saudi Arabia, with the assault carrier USS *Tarawa* and other Amphib Group 3 ships putting ashore a battalion of marines by helicopter, while hovercraft landed more marines and heavy equipment. They were to act as I MEF reserve, the 7,400 of the 5th Marine Expeditionary Brigade (5th MEB) on hand to help with mopping up enemy positions and handling of prisoners. Just under twenty miles off shore, on the gun line alongside the *Missouri* were *London, Jarrett, Gloucester* and, in shore of them clearing mines, five British MCMVs - *Cattistock, Hurworth, Atherstone, Dulverton* and *Ledbury* - plus *Herald*. All were well within range of Silkworm and shore gun batteries. The British mine-hunters, which came under fire more than once while carrying out their very dangerous task, were commanded by Commander Richard Ibbotson, in HMS *Hurworth*, who later reflected:

> *Often the mine-hunters were the closest Allied vessels to the Kuwait coast.* *It was a strange feeling being between the battleship and the Iraqis with huge* *shells curving over us.* [50]

The *London*'s sailors marveled at the terrible majesty of the battlewagon letting rip with her big guns, to destroy enemy positions blocking the coalition advance. Even

120

CPO Cunningham managed to escape from the Sound Room to do a little sightseeing.

> *The first couple of weeks we were too busy for me to get out on the upper deck to see what was happening, but, as the war went on, there were less aircraft flying around and the Iraqi threat at sea diminished, so I got more opportunities. It was incredible watching the flashes of the battleship guns ripping the night air apart and feeling the shock wave wash over me.*

In the ad-Dorra oil fields the *Brave* was acting as guard vessel for the support ships *Olna*, *Diligence* and *Argus*. The *Brave's* CO, Captain Bob Williams, used the PA system to tell his crew to stay sharp for any enemy moves to seaward.

> *We know the Iraqis have threatened to use chemical weapons and this is the right opportunity for them to do so, particularly as they are being driven back on land.* [51]

It came within minutes of the feint helicopters turning around, with two Iraqi Silkworms fired at the *Missouri* group, one of which malfunctioned and splashed into the sea soon after launch. The other missile kept a steady course towards the American battleship, at 605 knots and 375 feet up. [52]

The MCMVs saw a ball of fire coming towards them and nearby warships fired off counter-measures including chaff, flares and other decoys. One of the escort ships tried to shoot down the missile with her Phalanx anti-air cannon but, unfortunately, hit the well-armoured *Missouri* instead.

As the missiles were in-bound, HMS *Herald's* Sub Lieutenant Jeremy Churcher was on the ship's starboard bridge wing taking photographs of the nearby American battleship.

> *To be honest, we didn't really know what had happened until it was all over. Suddenly there was this flash of light, and something which could even have been an aircraft was chased across the sky by a Sea Dart missile from*

One of the American battleships fires another salvo at Iraqi troops in Kuwait.
Toby Elliott Collection.

one of our destroyers.[53]

People manning cannons and machine guns on the upper deck of naval vessels, including *Herald* and *Atherstone*, fired at the incoming missile to little effect. The contact that appeared on radar displays in *London*'s Ops Room could easily have been one of the many Allied aircraft that frequently transited through the combat area, unannounced. But *Gloucester*'s Ops Room decided this was something different, so two Sea Darts leapt off the destroyer's launcher rails and sped away at Mach 3. Below decks in the British destroyer, Lieutenant Commander Livingstone leapt out of his bunk.

> *I heard the hydraulics pump of the Sea Dart system start up with its high-pitched whine from the bowels of the ship. I jumped out of bed and was pulling on my boots when I heard the bang and whoosh from the Sea Dart, then repeated.* [54]

Sailors in the *Missouri* could not quite believe what they were seeing.

> *As the enemy weapon hurtled past* Missouri *and her escorts, Petty Officer John Roberts, RN, launched two of* Gloucester's *Sea Dart surface-to-air missiles. They destroyed the Silkworm in a spectacular explosion. For a terrifying moment,* Missouri's *after lookout thought that* Gloucester *had blown up.* [55]

Only three minutes passed between the Silkworm being launched and *Gloucester*'s Sea Darts destroying it. It was the first, and so far only, combat interception of a missile by a warship-launched missile in the history of naval warfare.

In the immediate aftermath of the Silkworm attack the task group was on edge and Commodore Craig ordered the Hunts and their mother ship to stage a careful withdrawal until the threat had been neutralized. One of *Herald*'s sailors, Steward Tom Crocker, reflected:

> *We wondered what was coming next.* [56]

An RPV from the *Missouri* went back along the path of the Silkworm and found the launchers and the control truck. The battleship fired thirty 16-inch shells, achieving another first - it was the first time a battleship had carried out counter-battery fire on an ASM shore battery that had fired on her. If any kind of amphibious operation was to be launched against Faylakah Island, it was tentatively scheduled for four days after the beginning of the ground attack. However, senior USMC and US Navy commanders suspected that Schwarzkopf's '...refusal to authorize certain operations to prepare for a landing suggested that he really had no intention of ordering an amphibious assault.' [57] Schwarzkopf's reasoning, that merely poising the marines off the Kuwait coast could be as effective as using them, had proved correct. The man who would have been in direct charge of the assault, Admiral John B. La Plante, based in the USS *Nassau*, gave vent to the frustration of those who did not go:

> *The kids were disappointed...* [58]

On 26 February the 1st Marine Division began the final push on Kuwait's International airport, which had been bombarded comprehensively the previous day and evening by *Wisconsin*'s guns. In the fierce fight that ended on 27 February, 320 Iraqi tanks, armoured fighting vehicles and other equipment had been destroyed by the marines and by the battleship's shells. The US Marines began mopping up further pockets of resistance around the edge of the city, which itself was liberated by Arab forces. The battle for Kuwait was turning into a rout, as the Iraqi Army fled from the coalition onslaught. A large convoy snaked along the highway, north-east towards Basra - military lorries, tanks, armoured personnel carriers mixed in with cars and trucks, hijacked from the Kuwaitis and all loaded down with the booty of war. They did not get very far, for the US Navy's strike jets soon descended to reap a terrible revenge on the Iraqis for their rape of Kuwait. Aboard the USS *Ranger* the traditional soundtrack to a combat launch cycle blared across the flight-deck from loudspeakers - Rossini's 'William Tell Overture', also the theme for the television series *The Lone Ranger*. Initially, fired up on adrenalin, the strike jet crews were thrilled by such a large target opportunity. Returning to load up his aircraft with more bombs, pilot Lieutenant Brian Kasperbauer said:

> This morning it was bumper-to-bumper. It was the road to Daytona Beach at spring break. Just bumper-to-bumper. Spring break's over.

Intruder bombardier Lieutenant Armando Segarra exclaimed:

> We hit the jackpot!

The higher command told the *Ranger*'s CO, Captain Ernest Christensen, to pile on the death and destruction. The Captain told his crew:

> It looks like the Iraqis are moving out, and we're hitting them hard...It's not going to take too many more days until there's nothing left of them.[59]

The front and rear of the convoy had been bombed, with more than 1,400 vehicles trapped, but most of the occupants had escaped, leaving behind 200 - 300 charred and bloated corpses. The bombs still rained down but soon the elation of seeing the enemy's army in headlong retreat and the taking of revenge paled and the aircrews became sickened by what they were doing. Their action reports questioned the wisdom of what had become, certainly with regard to that short stretch of Basra highway, a senseless slaughter. President Bush, having seen horrific television pictures of the coalition-inflicted carnage on the Basra highway, decided, in consultation with generals Powell and Schwarzkopf, that it was time to call a cease-fire. At 08.00 on 28 February the coalition forces ceased operations.

Some naval officers, including Admiral Arthur, thought the war should have ended twelve hours earlier. It was estimated that, between 24 and 28 February, 34,000 Iraqi troops were killed, 2,000 tanks destroyed and 86,000 Iraqi troops taken prisoner. Thirty-three Iraqi divisions were destroyed but the Republican Guard escaped largely intact. However, it was not the coalition's intention to chase them to destruction and overthrow Saddam Hussein.

> ...the UN mandate authorised Coalition forces to eject the Iraqis from Kuwait; it did not call for the occupation of Iraq or the overthrow of the Iraqi regime...[60]

At sea the Royal Navy task group received a signal containing congratulations from Her Majesty the Queen.

> The British forces have made a crucial contribution by sea, land and in the air to the successful completion of the Allied campaign. My

congratulations...upon a job well done. Elizabeth R.

For the *London*, *Gloucester* and the *Herald* it was time to head home amid the usual boisterous farewells. As the *Herald* passed *Hecla*, a joyous barrage of condoms containing yellow and red food colouring, rotten oranges, decomposing cauliflowers and rock-hard currant buns was sent across from the former to the latter. It was all liberally washed down by water from four fire hoses, aimed by *Herald* matelots delirious to be leaving the war zone finally. Unfortunately it was all a bit over the top and resulted in a rebuke the next day via signal from *Hecla*.

> WHILST YOUR ENTHUSIASM ON DEPARTURE IS UNDERSTOOD YOUR BEHAVIOUR WAS NOT 'IN THE TRADITIONS OF THE SERVICE' AND MARRED YOUR REPUTATION.

On hearing of this telling-off, one of *Herald*'s war-weary sailors caustically remarked:

> *If they can't take a joke, they should not have joined up...*

On 2 September 1945 in Tokyo Bay, the USS *Missouri* was the scene of the formal surrender of Japan, so ending the Second World War. In 1991 General Schwarzkopf also considered the *Missouri* for another grand finale.

> *Powell and I had discussed using the deck of the battleship* Missouri *as the site for the cease-fire talks. Douglas MacArthur had accepted the surrender of the Japanese on that deck in 1945 and I wanted to make it obvious that this meeting was a surrender ceremony in everything but name. But in the end the idea turned out to be impractical: the president had given us only forty-eight hours...in which to start the talks. Bringing the Iraqi delegation to a warship in the middle of the gulf - not to mention transporting military representatives from every coalition nation and the scores of reporters we wanted to witness the scene - would be a complicated if not impossible undertaking on such short notice.* [61]

The ceasefire talks took place instead in southern Iraq and the Royal Navy was there, as it had a presence ashore at the heart of decision-making via officers from the Royal Marines and the Royal Navy, seconded to General de la Billière's headquarters in Riyadh. One of them was Commander Colin Ferbrache, a former Commanding Officer of the frigate HMS *Alacrity*. Commander Ferbrache accompanied General de la Billière and General Schwarzkopf to Safwan airfield on 3 March for the surrender negotiations, an event that made a lasting impression on the naval officer.

> *It was an amazing moment in history. I'll never forget the exhilarating feeling as we flew from Saudi to Iraq in a posse of helicopters, with Apache gunships riding shotgun. We were on our way to the concluding act of the war.*

After landing, Commander Ferbrache and other coalition staff officers accompanied their generals into a tent where the ceasefire would be agreed.

> *Although it was hot and sticky, the air froze when the Iraqis finally arrived. It is hard to describe how chilly the atmosphere suddenly became. I suppose*

it was a bit like that moment in a Disney film when the wicked witch enters. There we were, face-to-face with the enemy. [62]

Within a few days of the ceasefire terms being agreed, the Iraqis handed over charts of their sea mines. Commander John Scoles, by then based in HMS *Hecla*, was eager to get to grips with planning the massive clear-up operation, particularly clearing routes into Ash Shuaybah, so that the humanitarian aid could flow into the devastated emirate. He was grateful that the Iraqis appeared to be cooperating positively.

The charts appear to be correct and so far our estimates of where the mines are match up with them. The threat of war has receded but that from mines has not gone away and is very serious. [63]

Of the more than 1,000 mines sewn by the Iraqis in the waters, where *Hecla* and thirteen coalition minehunters were operating under British control by the end of the first week in March, 300 had been cleared.

With the end of hostilities some aspects of the routine aboard ships in the task group could be relaxed, including the return of facial hair.

Traditional Senior Service beards are back in style aboard HMS Hecla *now that the threat of gas attack has lifted. All British service personnel in the Middle East were banned from having beards because facial hair prevents a protective mask from forming a seal against gas. Those heading for the war zone who had beards were ordered to shave them off. Today in Daily Orders aboard HMS* Hecla, *Lieutenant Commander Trevor Horne notified the crew they can grow beards again. He said: 'For those with beards, we still have the collective protection of a gas, chemical and biological sanctuary aboard the ship in the highly unlikely event of us being attacked.' In time-honoured tradition those of the crew proposing beards must formally give notice of their intention - just so no-one thinks they may be trying to get away with not shaving.* [64]

The coalition forces were aghast at the sheer wanton vandalism of the Iraqis, who had detonated a further 350 wellheads as they fled and during their occupation had looted, pillaged and raped with abandon. The vista that stretched before the coalition warships was a scene from Hell and it made a lasting impression on one newspaper correspondent who flew into Kuwait from the Royal Navy task group.

Apocalypse now. A sickly, mournful shroud of smog permanently masks the sun, plunging war-torn Kuwait into perpetual twilight. It has been estimated the temperature of the northern Gulf has been permanently lowered by five degrees. The oil fires will burn for years - Saddam's poisonous legacy to the world. Black rain pours down from the sky and the once calm, beautifully clear, blue waters of the Arabian Gulf are ruined by the lifeblood of the world's economy - oil. The coastal landscape is like an obscene vision from Dante's Inferno, with leaping flames from hundreds of burning oil wells flaring up in the gloom. A great scar of trenches, and barbed wire entanglements has been gouged into the coastline. The razor wire on the beaches may have been meant to stop marines wading ashore, but it proves no defence against the oil slicks. They continue to smear the beaches with black slime, killing sea birds and fish by the thousand. Birds attempting to escape the oil set off the hair triggers of land mines, causing eruptions of sand and feathers on the beaches. Once plush villas are blackened after being sacked by Saddam's vandals - still unoccupied because rich owners have no desire to return.

Kuwait is a desolate country where there is still very little food, no electricity and precious little drinking water. When one millionaire returns to his mansion he will be aghast at the effectiveness of the Allied precision bombing campaign. The Iraqis built a command bunker under the millionaire's magnificent landscaped lawn, bordered on four sides by his stately mansion. An American aircraft destroyed the bunker with a single 'smart' bomb, gouging out the lawn and the command bunker like a huge ice cream scoop. The buildings were left unharmed.

Very few venture into the ruined Kuwait City landscape lest they become victims of murder squads carrying out revenge attacks. Rusting Iraqi tankers are tied up at oil installations where storage tanks are still an inferno weeks after the Iraqis blew them up, belching pitch black smoke into the sky. The storage tanks have collapsed in the tremendous heat like ill-fated souffles.

Divers from the Royal Navy are moving up and down the ports of Kuwait, and British mine-hunting ships are off the coast. The mine-hunters are led by the survey ship HMS Hecla and guarded by the frigates Brilliant and Brave. Defusing booby traps on jetties and mines under

One of the Royal Navy clearance divers takes a leap into the unknown.

Iain Ballantyne.

A team of Royal Navy clearance divers goes about its grim work at Ash Shuaybah.

Iain Ballantyne.

water, the divers constantly breathe in oil fumes, clogging their lungs, contaminating the taste of food and water. The weather is so badly affected there can be four seasonal extremes in as many days. Sometimes it is so cold, wet and miserable, the Royal Navy ships off the Kuwaiti coast send ashore steaming hot cauldrons of beef stew for the divers. They sit huddled around a huge oil drum which spews forth fire, more like road workers reviving themselves in an English winter. There are gales and driving rain where there were once calm winds and sand storms. Veterans of past service with the Royal Navy's Gulf patrol are disturbed by the severe changes in the weather. It is not the Gulf they remember - something evil hangs in the air and chills the bones. Taking down their masks for a moment, the divers eagerly tuck into the stew. Any white clothing is covered in black soot within seconds. A warming cup of coffee is soon covered with a black scum. The oil sludge in the waters of the Kuwait ports is so thick the divers cannot see more than a few inches. One found an Iraqi corpse, when he put his hand through it. They grope like blind men for the mines. All the divers have to wear white disposable overalls on top of their diving gear when plunging into the sludge. They work around the clock, with American and Australian colleagues, in appalling condition, so the ports can be cleared to bring food to the stricken emirate. It is a depressing situation, but unlike most Kuwaitis, the servicemen at least have food, warmth and protection from marauders. In a warehouse on one port waterfront, some American soldiers found a lot of blood and the gutted remains of cats and dogs - the pets of absent millionaires preyed on by desperate humans. [65]

The Royal Navy divers at Ash Shuaybah were working with colleagues from the US Navy and Royal Australian Navy not only in clearing the waters of mines and unexploded bombs, but also checking oil supply platforms were not rigged with booby traps.

It was very dangerous work.

...the port reverberated to the bass drum boom of three booby trap explosives going off on an oil platform jetty. A huge orange inferno erupted from split pipes and a massive new black oil slick spread across the port's waters. Royal Navy diving team leader Lieutenant Steve Marshall explained: 'Some Australian divers have been working on the jetty. Luckily they weren't

A US Marine Corps CH-53 drops off supplies and troops at Ash Shuaybah, shortly after an oil terminal jetty (background) has exploded, due to an Iraqi booby-trap being triggered. Iain Ballantyne.

killed but were cut off from shore because the explosion destroyed part of the structure.' Shortly afterwards some of his men set off to rescue the trapped Australians. [66]

The coalition divers knew each other very well through working together during peacetime, as US Navy diver Christopher Bryant, who was normally based at Subic Bay in the Philippines, explained:

It has been a real reunion. We have all been appalled by what the Iraqis have done - if they couldn't take something, they trashed it. [67]

The Allied armies continued to occupy a good proportion of southern Iraq for some weeks, their line of advance stretching from al-Samawah to just short of Nasiriyah, and almost encircling Basra. The US Marine Corps' 2nd Division was to the north-east of Kuwait City, with the USMC 1st Division in and around Kuwait City itself and the 5th MEB guarding the main route south to Saudi Arabia.

Beyond the American lines the rebel uprising among the Shias of the south had effectively removed the Ba'ath regime from power. It

As coalition divers work hard to clear Ash Shuaybah, an American soldier patrols the port on a motorcycle, purchased from a canny local trader who somehow stayed in business despite the devastation. Iain Ballantyne.

was a revolt explicitly encouraged by President Bush in a speech, but he refused to authorize his army to provide the rebels with heavyweight support they needed to destroy the Saddam regime for good. When the Allied forces withdrew, the rebels knew that the Republican Guard, which had escaped the coalition campaign largely unscathed, would descend on them with utter ferocity. Everyone realized that Saddam was biding his time. A rebel asked US soldiers at a checkpoint:

Where is the help? [68]

One American senior officer told a reporter that, after the imminent US withdrawal to Kuwait and Saudi Arabia, Saddam would 'come down and slaughter these people...and they know it'.[69] Even as early as 3 March it was clear that a crushing defeat did not necessarily mean the end for the Iraqi dictator. The failure to annihilate the Republican Guard, and also the granting of permission to use helicopters as part of the ceasefire agreement, would prove decisive in enabling Saddam to hang onto power, despite the regular army being shattered, and rebellions in both the north and south of the country.

Little has been written about the activities of British submarines in the Gulf during the 1991 war. Despite official confirmation of their presence never being provided by the UK Ministry of Defence, enough has been detailed in open sources to say with certainty that two boats were deployed and carried out very risky missions in the northern Gulf, inserting Special Forces.

> About 27 January it was reported that U.S. aircraft had sunk an Iraqi tanker under which a British submarine was hiding, endangering twenty-two special forces men trying to return to her. [70]

The deliberate releasing of oil into the Gulf by the Iraqis at the same time, combined with accidental releases caused by the sinking of tankers, allegedly made 'submarine special operations nearly impossible'. [71]

HMS *Opossum* and HMS *Otus* were both Oberon class diesel-electric boats and the same source suggests that one of them was operating inside the Gulf from August. This was *Otus*, for, when Saddam invaded Kuwait, *Opossum*, which was commanded by Lieutenant Commander Steve Upright, was well East of Suez, visiting South Pacific islands, including Pitcairn where his sailors were greeted enthusiastically by descendants of the *Bounty* mutineers.

Under Saddam's blanket of suffocating smog, a British Type 22 frigate moves carefully through Kuwaiti coastal waters.
Toby Elliott Collection.

After a Christmas break in Singapore, *Opossum* entered the Indian Ocean and, to all intents and purposes, disappeared, until, in the spring of 1991, she passed through the Suez Canal. On 4 April *Opossum* briefly called in at Plymouth before going on to her home base at Portsmouth.

At neither naval port did she fly a Jolly Roger to indicate what she had been up to, but she did wear a distinctive camouflage pattern - pale tiger stripes over her matt black hull. Lieutenant Commander Upright later remarked rather cryptically:

> All I can say by way of explanation is that we didn't leave Portsmouth with the stripes. [72]

On 5 April, however, HMS *Otus* gave the game away by returning to Portsmouth wearing the same camouflage pattern and flying a Jolly Roger flag with a dagger on it, clearly indicating Special Forces missions.

For *Herald*'s Commanding Officer, Commander Peter Jones, the ship's homecoming on 10 April meant he could finally relax.

> *From the moment we left Plymouth it was my aim to get the ship and the crew home in one piece. We expected to go to war at any time from our arrival in the Gulf last October, so we were living on adrenalin. And I think there are many people in Plymouth who endured the constant strain of the city's Blitz period during the Second World War, who will understand what we went through during the war itself, during the weeks of waiting for attacks amid the gunfire and the bombing.* [73]

But the last British warship home from the Gulf was HMS *Brave*, coming alongside to an ecstatic welcome at Devonport Naval Base on 15 July. It had not been easy on her crew, continuing with the ship's deployment for almost a further five months after the war had ended. Some of the *Brave*'s crew considered themselves forgotten by an ungrateful public and were bitter and angry, although most of the frigate's sailors were simply glad to be home. Captain Williams paid tribute to his men:

> *The* Brave's *crew showed that today's Royal Navy sailors are capable of amazing tenacity and resilience. They worked their guts out under incredible stress in combat conditions.* [74]

But the most ignored players in the war were probably the little ships most at risk from the Iraqis, the MCMVs, led by Commander Richard Ibbotson in the *Hurworth* who summed up their war with typical Royal Navy understatement.

> *The war went, dare I say, like a text book operation for us. Obviously being in live minefields for weeks at a time, sometimes being shot at, had its novel moments and its stresses and strains.* [75]

CHAPTER SEVEN

KEEPING SADDAM CAGED

Dawn in the northern Gulf, and to starboard of the British carrier HMS *Invincible* was the fleet tanker RFA *Brambleleaf*. Cumbersome hoses linked the two ships together as they carried out the delicate process of a refuelling at sea. More oil for the *Invincible*'s thirsty engines was pumped over from the RFA, along with aviation fuel for her Sea Harrier FA2 fighters, to ensure they had the juice they needed to get airborne for Iraq. Astern was the Type 42 air-defence destroyer HMS *Newcastle*, riding shotgun to protect the task group flagship and the auxiliary as they performed their vulnerable replenishment. The *Newcastle*'s radars turned and burned, straining to detect any signs of a potential attack materializing from Iraq - her long-range Sea Dart missiles were ready to fire.

A couple of hours later, the *Invincible* parted company with the RFA tanker and

February 1999, and the RFA tanker Brambleleaf *(left)* replenishes the Invincible *with fuel for her Sea Harriers.* Nigel Andrews.

131

A Sea Harrier FA2 fighter, armed with AMRAAM missiles, is launched from
Invincible for another patrol in the skies over southern Iraq. Iain Ballantyne

addressed herself to the serious business of getting her FA2s airborne for a fighter
cover mission, as part of a thirty ship package alongside American F-14 Tomcats, F-
18 Hornets and EA-6 Prowlers. Four Sea Harriers would conduct the patrol,
carrying powerful Advanced Medium Range Anti-Air Missiles (AMRAAMs) which,
combined with the Blue Vixen 'look-down, shoot-down' radar, were said to make
the UK's jump jets the most deadly birds of prey over Iraq. Mission briefings
finished, the pilots walked to their planes and climbed aboard. Soon the tranquillity
of the morning was blown away with the howl, whine and roar of engines powering
the Sea Harriers one-by-one down the flight deck.

As silence descended again, a Hawkeye Airborne Early Warning (AEW) aircraft
from the US Navy carrier USS *Carl Vinson*, which was sailing some miles south, did
a low, slow pass, dipping its wings in salute on the way to take up station off Iraq
as a flying radar station. Next, *Invincible*'s AEW helicopters took off to fly their own
patrol patterns. Up on the British carrier's bridge, the man in command, Captain
James Burnell-Nugent, gave the opinion that his crew were realistic enough to know
they could not provide an antidote to Saddam all by themselves.

> *People understand that this campaign has, even though bombs and missiles
> are going off every day, reached a plateau. The diplomatic arena is where the
> solution to this problem will be found and we are only backing that up.* [1]

Eight years after the Desert Storm ceasefire, a war was still being waged in the
northern Gulf, as the warships and aircraft of the American and British fleets sought
to keep the Iraqi dictator caged.

At sea the embargo imposed as punishment for Iraq's invasion of Kuwait was still
in force, as Saddam had refused to comply fully with the ceasefire requirements with
regard to disarmament. Had the war progressed for a further forty-eight-hours,
giving the coalition ground troops and air forces time to completely destroy the
Republican Guard, then perhaps the regime would have fallen, for there would have
been no brutal shock troops to put down the rebellions that followed the conflict.

But, even a year on from the end of the war, it was clear that many believed a huge blunder had been committed in Washington DC, when the US administration, alarmed by the television images of horrific carnage on the road to Basra, ordered a cessation of hostilities.

> ...the Navy pilots' briefing reports were quickly forwarded to Schwarzkopf's headquarters...and on to Washington. Those who now criticize the cease-fire decision think these early reports were given too much emphasis...Today many senior U.S. military officers and civilian officials believe that decision was a mistake. The primary reason is obvious: Saddam Hussein, defying every expectation, has survived a catastrophic military reversal and now seems to be as firmly in control of Iraq as ever. [2]

One US military officer suggested:

> ...we're going to be back...doing this again in three to five years. [3]

Another observed:

> If they didn't like slaughtering the Iraqis pouring out of Kuwait City, all they had to do was stop it. They could have called off those air strikes but left the ground campaign to run. But they panicked. [4]

In fact the naval bombardment of Iraq resumed far quicker than anyone could have imagined. On 17 January 1993, the second anniversary of the beginning of Desert Storm, American warships launched cruise missiles at Iraqi military sites, while carrier aircraft joined the attack. One of the picket ships, helping to compile a

The No Fly Zones established to protect the people of Iraq from further genocide. US DoD.

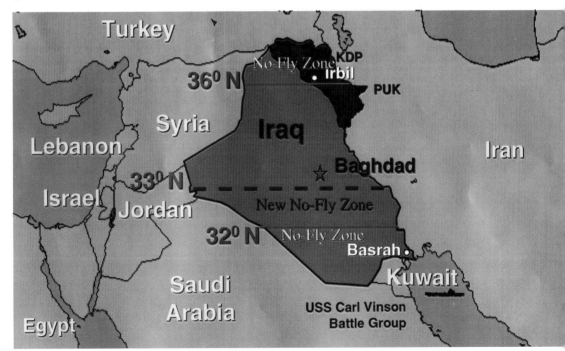

133

surveillance picture of the northern Gulf, was HMS *London*, called back into theatre while taking a break from the Armilla Patrol by visiting ports in Bangladesh and Sri Lanka.

By the end of 1992 the Iraqis had moved SAMs and AA guns into southern Iraq, ignoring US demands for their removal. Therefore, a few weeks later, US, UK and French planes bombed targets south of the 32nd Parallel in a so-called southern No-Fly Zone. Saddam ordered his forces to challenge the allies, losing several fighter jets. As well as destroying Iraqi military positions in the far south, cruise missiles were launched at a factory making nuclear weapon components outside Baghdad.

The No Fly Zones that US Navy and other Allied jets enforced by late 1992 covered much of northern and southern Iraq. Their aim was to prevent the Ba'athist regime in Baghdad from pursuing a campaign of genocide against the Kurds and Shia Arabs. From the start there were frequent exchanges of fire between coalition aircraft and Iraqi air defence systems. The northern No Fly Zone was set up in 1991, in what became known as Operation Northern Watch, and it had been established in the wake of a successful intervention on the ground by coalition forces. With the Gulf War barely over, UK Prime Minister John Major had been outraged by the slaughter of rebellious Kurds and called for military intervention to set up safe havens. On 16 April 1991, the Ministry of Defence told 3 Commando Brigade that it was to embark on Operation Safe Haven, during which as many Kurds as possible would be escorted to safety. On 13 May, Iraqi troops at one of Saddam's palaces opened fire on marines from 45 Commando but two of the assailants were killed when their fire was returned. In fact, Saddam's troops clashed with the Royal Marines in several firefights and came off worse each time.

The operation was labelled Provide Comfort by the US military, which contributed marines alongside troops from Canada, Holland, France, Italy and Spain and support at sea included the assault carrier USS *Guadalcanal*.

Royal Marines of 40 Commando clustered on top of an M113 armoured personnel carrier, as a column of Kuwaiti tanks passes by during Exercise Blue Falcon, May 1992. Iain Ballantyne.

Some of Saddam's ill-fated navy was dragged out into the Kuwaiti desert to act as a memorial to the recent war. Iain Ballantyne.

By the beginning of June, the situation was secure enough for the coalition troops to leave, with the safe havens guarded by airpower.

The Royal Marines returned to the Middle East in May 1992, when part of 40 Commando deployed to the Kuwaiti desert for Exercise Blue Falcon. This was a confidence building mission, to show the Kuwaitis the Allies would defend them if Iraq threatened their borders again. During their time in the desert, some of the Royal Marines visited the Kuwait National Exhibition Centre, a vast arena in the middle of nowhere that had been turned into a memorial to the recent war.

> *There are row upon row of Iraqi tanks, some split open and blackened. A hot wind blows in across the desert from Iraq, swirling sand around the ruptured armour. It flutters the pages of a diary resting on one tank hull among the bloodstained, ragged remains of an Iraqi soldier's uniform. The diary's flickering pages momentarily rest on the date 17 January 1991 - the day the Allies unleashed Desert Storm. Alongside the tanks are hundreds of trucks, armoured personnel carriers and the Kuwaitis have even dragged some of Saddam's makeshift patrol boats in from the sea, speedboats with ludicrously large quadruple anti-aircraft guns mounted on them. The massive assembly of redundant military hardware is the Kuwaitis' testament to Saddam Hussein's brutal occupation and rape of their homeland. It is the parking lot of the dead. [5]*

The British marines embarked in the frigate HMS *Beaver* for a short period, to rehearse boarding techniques during a patrol close to Iraqi territorial waters. As he watched the marines rapid-roping down onto *Beaver's* forecastle, her CO, Commander Charles Montgomery, discussed why his ship was up-threat.

> *One of the principal aims of our being here is to underpin the defence of Kuwait. Preventing anything getting through that could be used to re-arm Iraq is one way of doing that. We are also here to reassure British merchant ships that they will be protected if need be. There are various levels of risk in the Gulf, with the ship at her highest alert state up here in the north near Iraq, but there is a certain degree of wariness along the whole length of the Gulf about Iran. [6]*

As the Royal Marines exercised in the desert close to the border with Iraq, Saddam was continuing his campaign of genocide against the rebellious Shia Arabs, napalming their towns and villages and destroying marshlands that had supported them for centuries. Tension had increased, as Iranian F-4 strike jets had carried out bombing raids in support of the rebels. The UN had also recently extended the Kuwaiti border, enclosing an oilfield that previously belonged to Iraq and also part of its Umm Qasr naval base. To try and keep the peace, in late August 1992 the USA, UK and France agreed to police a No Fly Zone over southern Iraq, south of the 32nd Parallel. US Navy combat aircraft were in the vanguard of this new mission, which was called Operation Southern Watch. In January 1993 the Iraqis twice sent soldiers across the border into the Kuwait portion of Umm Qasr:

> ...to retrieve four Silkworm anti-shipping missiles that the United Nations Special Commission on Iraq (UNSCOM) had ear-marked for destruction. [7]

But this aggressive defiance of the UN was nothing new. It had been going on almost from the end of the 1991 war.

On 11 April 1991 the UN had declared a formal ceasefire to the Gulf War and formed the United Nations Special Commission (UNSCOM), which, on 9 May, sent chemical weapons inspectors into Iraq to hunt for weapons of mass destruction (WMD). Under UN Resolution 687, Iraq was required to submit to the destruction of WMD and long-range missiles. However, Iraq's response to the UNSCOM inspections was characterized by reluctance to cooperate and a pattern of 'hide and seek' soon became established, via a sophisticated programme of WMD concealment. This was allied with intimidation of inspection teams.

In April 1993, an attempt was made to kill former President George Bush, who was due to visit Kuwait to receive tribute for his part in its liberation. The assassination bid was foiled when a truck packed with explosives was intercepted on the Iraqi border, after a tip-off that it was heading for Kuwait City, and interrogations revealed a direct link to Saddam's intelligence service. The US response came on 26 June, when twenty-three cruise missiles were fired at the intelligence service headquarters in Baghdad by the destroyer *Petersen* and the cruiser *Chancellorsville*.

Saddam had anticipated the weapons inspections would be abandoned by 1992, and that UN sanctions against Iraq would be lifted. But as 1994 dawned, sanctions were still firmly in place and beginning to erode Iraq's economy and continued to hamper attempts to rebuild its military power.

Desperate to have the sanctions lifted when the UN formally reviewed the situation in early October 1994, a substantial Iraqi force took up a threatening position close to Kuwait border. It was a blatant attempt to bully the international community. With a reinforced British combat group, centred on 45 Commando RMs, immediately ordered to Kuwait, to hold the line alongside the US Marines, at sea American and British naval forces also gathered.

While the Kuwaiti Army had been re-equipped with Croat-manufactured M84 tanks and fortifications had been constructed along the border, the 80,000-strong Iraqi formation, spearheaded by 20,000 Republican Guard with 300 tanks, would easily have swept them aside. The lightly-armed US and UK ground forces would have found it a tough fight, but there again the strike jets of the *George Washington* were a powerful deterrent, as was the TLAM capability of her escort group, which included the cruiser *San Jacinto*.

A major concern was that Saddam might order small boats to mine the northern Gulf and the British frigate HMS *Cornwall* was tasked with spotting any such attempts. With her was the nuclear-powered attack submarine HMS *Splendid*, the UK having operated SSNs in the Gulf since 1993, while the destroyer *Cardiff* was on her way back to the region to provide air-defence.

In the face of this determined response, on 13 October Iraq decided to abide by an explicit request from the UN to move its troops away from the border area.

Maritime forces had become so important to containing Saddam because, by the mid-1990s, the resolve of the West was fragmenting. France withdrew its planes from policing the No Fly Zones and would eventually call for an end to sanctions, in line with much of the Arab world and others, including the Russians and Chinese. But the British and American navies showed no sign of relaxing their vigilance, and in early January 1995 the Maritime Interception Force, which included the destroyers HMS *Liverpool* and HMS *Exeter*, caught a tanker called the *Al Marousa* attempting to leave Iraqi waters, with a cargo of illegal oil. She was diverted to a Kuwait port where her cargo was sold by the UN for an estimated £250,000.

For America, the importance of maintaining the sanctions against Iraq, and guarding against Iran, was such that, in June 1995, the US Navy established the 5th Fleet specifically to oversee naval operations in the Red Sea, Arabian Sea and the Gulf. With no vessels permanently assigned, its combat power was drawn from the Pacific and Atlantic fleets via rotational deployments. Having lost the *La Salle* command ship to the 6th Fleet in 1993, the 5th Fleet's commander was based ashore in Bahrain.

Meanwhile in Iraq itself, persistent pressure by the UN weapons inspectors had forced an admission from Baghdad, in July 1995, that the regime had indeed possessed alarming quantities of biological weapons.

In June 1996 Saddam's security forces in the north seized key members of dissident groups and agents acting for the CIA, shattering the organizations and foiling plans to overthrow the regime. Two months later three armoured divisions rolled into northern Iraq. The Anglo-US response to this violation was moving the edge of the southern No-Fly Zone further north, to the 33rd Parallel, just south of Baghdad and, on 3 September 1996, American warships in the Gulf, including the cruiser USS *Shiloh*, launched fourteen TLAMs against targets in southern Iraq, to deliver a short, sharp shock. The following day, US Navy warships fired a second salvo of thirty missiles. By November 1996 Saddam was forced to discuss an oil-for-food deal with the United Nations, wherein Iraq was allowed to sell enough oil to feed its people and also to obtain essential medicines.

However, such humanitarian supplies, thought destined for the long-suffering Iraqi population, often ended up on the black market, sold at extortionate prices to provide more cash for the regime's coffers.

A Tomahawk cruise missile launches from the forward vertical launch system of the cruiser USS Shiloh *on 3 September 1996.* US DoD.

On 11 December, off Muscat, the Type 42 destroyer HMS *Edinburgh* handed over Armilla Patrol duties to sister ship HMS *Southampton*, which closed up in defence watches for passage through the Strait of Hormuz. At the time the UK was maintaining two warships on Armilla, so *Edinburgh* would be back after a break 'out of area'. In January 1997, the *Southampton* began Maritime Interception Operations (MIOPS) alongside not only ships from the US Navy, but also from Canada and Holland. As the British destroyer headed north, she took on fuel from the USNS *Rainier* and sailed for a time in company with the carrier USS *Kitty Hawk*. Her deployment book later explained how MIOPS patrols were conducted:

> *The patrol areas are positioned such that any ship in International Waters and on passage to or from Iraq must pass through at least one of them. There is generally one warship in each area and our normal patrol pattern, conducted in Defence Watches, would be to visit every corner of our 'box' as often as possible and monitor the course and speed of all surface radar contacts very carefully. The Khawr Abd Allah and the Shatt Al Arab are the two navigable waterways which feed Iraq and any radar contact tracking directly towards us or away from one of these would be labelled a 'Contact of Interest' (COI). We commenced our patrol on the morning of 8 January and more by luck than judgement, found our first COI within an hour.* [8]

Interrogation by radio of the small cargo dhow revealed that it was heading for Umm Qasr, allegedly carrying foodstuffs. A boarding revealed this to be true - its holds contained flour and sugar - and so the dhow was allowed to go.

With even some friendly Arab states reluctant, or hostile, to act as launch pads for any extra military pressure on Saddam Hussein to comply with UN arms

138

inspections, by the late 1990s the only option available to US and UK governments was the deployment of carrier task groups in international waters. When the *Invincible* sailed from Portsmouth on 2 September 1997, her sailors had no idea that soon their ship would be on the brink of launching air strikes against Iraqi targets. The ship's autumn programme originally included a three-month extended deployment to the western Atlantic for exercises with the US Navy. However, before her transatlantic passage, *Invincible* embarked Harrier GR7 strike jets as well as her usual FA2 fighters, the first time a Carrier Air Group (CAG) had included the RAF aircraft. Experience in the Adriatic in the mid-1990s, where a Sea Harrier was shot down while bombing targets around Gorazde in Bosnia, had shown that, while the naval variant of the aircraft might still be a superb fighter, it lacked the ability to be more than a token strike aircraft. After a brief NATO exercise involving the Spanish Navy's Harrier AV8 MK2s, the GR7s returned to the UK while the carrier sailed west. However, events in the Gulf , where Iraq was again obstructing UN inspectors, led to *Invincible* being diverted from Barbados to Gibraltar, arriving there on 19 November, after covering 3,500 miles in a week. To achieve that the carrier maintained an average speed throughout the crossing of between 26 and 29 knots. The ship's CO, Captain Roy Clare, was mightily impressed with *Invincible*'s performance and his sailors' endurance.

> There have been very high speeds to sustain, which is very impressive from an engineering point of view. The speeds also made it uncomfortable - it's very noisy in the after decks, so I'm very impressed by the stoicism of the crew.[9]

At Gibraltar *Invincible* re-embarked her RAF air component, which meant she now carried eight FA2s, seven GR7s, four Sea King AEW helicopters and two ASW Sea Kings, with a further five Sea King ASWs in the RFA *Fort Victoria*. With Iraq continuing to impede unrestricted access by UN inspectors to sixty-three sites, the UK Government made it clear that sending *Invincible* to the Gulf was a serious option, to carry out air strikes if need be. The UK title for the operation, which also included a boosted RAF presence in Kuwait, was Operation Bolton and Defence Secretary George Robertson explained that a credible threat of force was needed to overcome Saddam's obstruction.

> These inspectors have already found substantial production capabilities, weapons and equipment, including 690 tonnes of chemical agents. We know he still has more chemical and biological capabilities in hiding. Iraq still represents a real threat to its neighbourhood and to the wider Middle East.[10]

Now under the command of Captain James Burnell-Nugent, *Invincible* made a brief detour to the Adriatic where her Harriers helped provide cover for NATO peace stabilization forces in Bosnia. The carrier was back at Gibraltar by 12 December, with her sailors hoping the Iraq crisis would swiftly subside, allowing them to spend Christmas at home with their families. With the Iraqis still refusing unfettered access, the *Invincible* headed for Cyprus, so she could be re-supplied and pass swiftly through the Suez Canal if need be. When the situation again cooled off a little, with great efforts being made on the diplomatic front, *Invincible* headed west across the Mediterranean to celebrate the New Year in Palermo, Sicily. Leading Airman

(Photographer) Neil Hall had just months to go before he left the Royal Navy and, as a veteran of the Armilla Patrol, anticipated his final posting, to the Type 22 frigate HMS *Coventry* in the Gulf, in December 1997, would turn out to be uneventful despite the latest stand-off with Saddam.

> *The ship was half way through a seven month patrol and, although there were some problems in the region, the deployment was not seen as a particularly tense one anymore. Talk around the ship was of the fast approaching stand-off in Thailand, which was eagerly anticipated by me and everyone else, after taking part in endless boarding operations that never seemed to achieve much. Come January, however, rumours started to fly around that Thailand might be called off because of the stand-off between the UN and Iraq. Rumours soon turned to fact and we found ourselves facing a lot of uncertainty as to what would happen. The increased activity was given the name Operation Bolton and at this point we all realized that something more serious was brewing, as HMS* Coventry *turned northwards and made her way up threat in the Gulf.*

The *Invincible*, meanwhile steaming east again, made a transit through the Suez Canal and, on 25 January, was heading north through the Strait of Hormuz, escorted by the *Coventry*. Shortly thereafter both FA2s and GR7s flew their first night sorties over Iraq, helping to enforce Southern Watch alongside aircraft from the USS *Nimitz* and USS *George Washington*. US Navy carrier numbers soon rose to three with the arrival of the USS *Independence*. The *Invincible*'s air group CO, Commander David Swain, explained how the patrol routine had bedded down:

> *The requirement was a day and night mission over Iraq every 24 hours, with* Invincible *contributing in each mission, four FA2s for force protection and four GR7s for interdiction. However, the desire to maximize the UK contribution to the coalition effort, as well as the degree of training and integration required, resulted in more than double that rate of flying.* [11]

A mighty Anglo-US naval force was assembled in the northern Gulf, in early 1998, for possible action against Iraq. Here, sailors aboard the US Navy aircraft carrier USS George Washington watch as the Royal Navy aircraft carrier HMS Invincible comes alongside. US Navy.

Each Anglo-US 'package' consisted of up to thirty aircraft and, in such crowded skies accidents could easily happen. Lieutenant Commander Mark Hart, embarked in the carrier on the staff of Commander UK Task Group (COMUKTG), Rear Admiral Ian Forbes, recalled one such tragedy:

> *There was a mid-air collision between two US Navy F-18s, after which the body of one pilot was recovered by a Sea King from* Invincible, *which heightened everyone's awareness of the situation; we all now knew that this was a real crisis and lives were at risk.* [12]

In the northern Gulf *Invincible* was joined by a mine-hunting task group consisting of three Sandown class MCMVs, with HMS *Herald* as the tasking vessel and RFA *Diligence* in support. The attack submarine HMS *Spartan* was also in theatre and the air-defence destroyer HMS *Nottingham* was on a planned Gulf deployment. By the first week of February, when UN Secretary General Kofi Annan announced he would visit Iraq to negotiate with Saddam in person, the Anglo-US team was worked up to full fighting pitch. Like other warships, the *Coventry* returned to port to collect her war load of ammunition, with Leading Airman Hall awestruck by the sheer scale of the preparations for combat that he witnessed.

> *As the sole Royal Navy photographer in the Gulf at the time, I swiftly realized that I had 'access-all-areas' to feed the increasingly hungry international media with images of the Royal Navy on the front line. However, even with my knowledge of the scope of things, it wasn't until we arrived in Bahrain in mid-February, that the true seriousness of the situation hit home. The amount of ammunition being poured into UK and US ships was formidable - missile containers and ammunition crates, all under armed guard, lined the length of the harbour, ready to be loaded onto dozens of*

The day before Kofi Annan's last-ditch talks with Saddam, in the Gulf, aboard the George Washington, Aviation Ordnancemen load an AIM-9 Sidewinder air-to-air missile onto a Hornet strike-fighter. US Navy.

waiting vessels. When we left Bahrain on the Friday we were told that we would be at war by Monday, unless Kofi Annan could finally persuade Saddam to let the UN weapons inspectors do their job in Iraq. There didn't seem much hope of that and I sat down in a quiet corner of the mess to write my final letter to my daughter, Laura, resigned to the fact that we were going to be at war within a couple of days.

In *Invincible*, Commander Swain noted that, as Kofi Annan landed in Baghdad on 20 February, '...*Invincible* was fully prepared for a very short notice offensive military action.'

FA2 and GR7 pilots were fully tuned for their tactics and techniques by day and night, and despite the overcrowding of a 22 aircraft CAG, the flight deck was 'on song'. This was a definitive post-Cold War aircraft carrier operation. In full public gaze it provided a clear demonstration of the diplomatic signalling power of maritime forces. [13]

The focus of the world was on the Gulf, and in particular on *Invincible* and the US Navy's carriers, as they would provide the principal military response if diplomacy finally failed to yield Iraqi compliance. The Chaplain of *Invincible*, Martin Poll, 'found himself caught up in a tense waiting game...' in which he witnessed a change in the atmosphere of the ship as people began to think, 'This could be for real'...

Young sailors on their first sea draft and those with young children at home found this a very challenging time as their thoughts turned to the consequences of going to war. There was no desire for action, but there was a determined professionalism that if it was required, then all should be carried out efficiently and effectively...Everything seemed to be moving inexorably towards some sort of conflict...

The Chaplain found that his ability to provide reassurance was in great demand.

...the quiet word spoken to a young sailor clearly concerned at the prospect of going into action, or listening as a father expresses his concerns for his family at home. By 20 February Invincible *was in all respects ready for any required action against Iraq. In all the messdecks and cabins, everyone was glued to live satellite TV reports about these final crucial stages of negotiation.* [14]

However, a solution was found and Saddam backed away from the brink, allowing Kofi Annan to announce to jubilant workers at the UN headquarters in New York that he had avoided war and achieved access for the arms inspectors.

Aboard the British carrier Chaplain Poll reflected:

Thank God that this time Invincible *did not have to go into action...* [15]

In HMS *Coventry* there was initially a strange sense of anti-climax, as Leading Airman Hall later recalled:

It was late on Sunday when we were told that Annan had brokered a peaceful settlement with the Iraqi leadership and that we would be diverting to Dubai. I remember that my first reaction was disappointment, having experienced such a long and tense build up to war, but all too soon I experienced intense relief. I was heading back to the UK safe and sound, and looking forward to being with my family.

Even though Saddam appeared to back down, a heavy naval presence was maintained to ensure his compliance. A survey of US fleet dispositions on 9 March 1998 revealed that the *Independence* was on a port visit to the UAE while the *George Washington* was again enforcing Southern Watch in the northern Gulf. The *Nimitz* had returned to the USA and the USS *John C. Stennis* was in transit across the Atlantic. The USS *Guam* ARG was carrying the 24th MEU through the Suez Canal, headed north having just completed a Gulf deployment, while the USS *Tarawa* ARG, carrying the 11th MEU, was in transit across the Indian Ocean towards Arabia. American ships assigned to MIOPS in the Gulf were the destroyers *John Young* and *John S. McCain* and the cruiser *Normandy*. At the time US military personnel deployed to the Gulf region were beginning to receive vaccines against the biological warfare agent anthrax, which had recently been assessed to be present in huge quantities in Iraq. On 17 March the *Tarawa* ARG arrived in the Gulf and Vice Admiral Tom Fargo, Commander, US 5th Fleet greeted the newly arrived sailors and marines with a morale-boosting message:

> *Your timely arrival will support a US presence that tempers potential adversaries, helps maintain peace and stability in a potentially volatile region and protects our vital national interest.*

American naval forces in the Gulf reached a peak in mid-March 1998 when the *John C. Stennis* arrived to take over from the *George Washington*. Those two CBGs, together with *Independence*, represented 30,000 sailors and marines and more than 150 combat planes afloat off Iraq. For a short time there were also two British carriers in the northern Gulf, with *Illustrious* having arrived to take over from *Invincible*. During the summer of 1998, the British government released its Strategic Defence Review (SDR), in which it announced that all three of the Royal Navy's Invincible class carriers would receive substantial modifications to enhance their ability to support GR7s at sea. After decades of looking towards central Europe as the decisive theatre of any future war, the UK's defence strategy was clearly now maritime-based and SDR stated that, by 2015, the Royal Navy should have two new 60,000 tonnes super-carriers capable of carrying up to fifty supersonic strike aircraft. Less than thirty years after deciding to axe the Royal Navy's last big carriers, and withdraw from a role East of Suez, the new Labour government was committing Britain's security to both.

The *Illustrious* was the first of the ships to enter dockyard hands for modification after her return from deployment in the late summer of 1998, while, following her own post-Gulf maintenance period, *Invincible* was fleet flagship again.

Saddam Hussein had meanwhile returned to his game of brinkmanship, and, after months of tweaking the UN's nose and getting away with it, finally brought down yet another cruise missile storm on his cursed country. On 17 December US Navy cruisers and destroyers in the Gulf, plus B-52 bombers flying from the Anglo-US island base of Diego Garcia in the Indian Ocean, unleashed an intensive barrage of TLAMs. More than 200 missiles were launched by warships in the first wave. By day two of the offensive the Pentagon revealed the total number of air-launched and ship-launched cruise missiles fired so far, in what was dubbed Operation Desert Fox,

Flight deck crew aboard the USS Enterprise crouch low as the third wave of strikes against Iraq goes in during Operation Desert Fox. US Navy.

had exceeded the total expended during all of Desert Storm. Aircraft from the USS *Enterprise* and British land-based GR1 Tornado bombers also attacked targets in Iraq. Saddam's military machine and its potential to create WMD was 'seriously degraded' according to the Pentagon. Admiral Thomas R. Wilson, Director of Intelligence for the US Joint Staff, told one briefing that the Republican Guard was also high on the target list. Defense Secretary William Cohen outlined the motivation behind the air assault:

> We're diminishing his ability to attack his neighbors, either conventionally or with Weapons of Mass Destruction. And since Iraq has now prevented the United Nations inspectors from doing their job, we have to resort to military action to continue to contain him. We are not attacking the people of Iraq and we have no desire to increase the suffering that Saddam Hussein has imposed on his people.

Secretary Cohen said targets included Iraq's air defence system, its command and control infrastructure, airfields and other military facilities. The Defense Secretary outlined what he believed were Saddam's motives for defying the international community.

> One objective is to get rid of the inspectors. The second objective is to get rid of the sanctions. He has felt all along that he could frustrate, deny, obstruct, in any way deprive the inspectors from carrying out their obligations, and also seek support in changing their effectiveness. We intend to keep the sanctions in place. We intend to keep our forces on the ready. In the event he seeks to reconstitute again or threaten his neighbors, we will be prepared to take military action once again. So we intend to continue the containment policy.

With the campaign only a few hours old, General Henry Shelton, Chairman of the US Joint Chiefs of Staff, revealed that a second CBG led by the *Carl Vinson* was joining 5th Fleet units in the Gulf. General Shelton was quizzed about whether or not Saddam Hussein himself was a target and replied:

144

We have not been tracking Saddam Hussein and he was not an objective established for this operation.

The military action by the USA and UK was not welcomed in some quarters. Russia objected strongly, withdrawing its ambassadors from Washington and London and allegedly going as far as putting its navy and air force on alert. The British naval presence in the Gulf at the beginning of the attack on Iraq was spearheaded by the Type 22 frigate HMS *Boxer*, enforcing the UN trade embargo against Iraq with the RFA *Brambleaf* in support. At the helm of *Boxer*, and therefore CO of British maritime assets in the Gulf, was Captain Richard Ibbotson, who had commanded the Royal Navy's mine-hunters off Kuwait at the end of the 1991 Gulf War.

Among US Navy vessels committed to the operation were the cruiser *Gettysburg*,

Bomb damage assessment photos of the Baghdad Directorate of Military Intelligence Headquarters, Iraq, used by Chairman of the Joint Chiefs of Staff General Henry H. Shelton, US Army, in a Pentagon press briefing on 17 December 1998. US DoD.

destroyers *Paul Hamilton*, *Hopper* and *Stout*, all equipped with TLAM. The Tomahawk-equipped attack submarine USS *Miami* also took part. The assault carrier USS *Belleau Wood*, assault ships USS *Germantown* and USS *Dubuque* were in the Gulf carrying 1,400 combat marines of the 31st MEU, plus Cobra attack helicopters and Harrier strike jets. The US Marines were already on the ground in the Kuwaiti desert when the first missiles were launched against Baghdad, providing a protective shield for Kuwait. The overall commander of Operation Desert Fox, General Anthony C. Zinni, of the US Marines, revealed during a mid-January briefing at the Pentagon, that the United States had contingency plans to counter any Iraqi move towards Kuwait, launch of missiles against neighbouring countries or any other possibilities. He told reporters:

We have plans for everything.

Operation Desert Fox, which saw 415 cruise missiles fired at Iraq in just four days, marked the turning point in the confrontation between the Anglo-US axis and Saddam - now the slide to full-scale war began. With the inspectors withdrawn as a precursor to the attack, the maritime embargo and the No Fly Zones remained the only means of trying to force Saddam to comply with the cease-fire conditions. While the world's attention was being drawn away by the evolving crisis in the Balkans, where the Serbs were committing genocide in Kosovo, a forgotten conflict was waged in the northern Gulf. Almost on a daily basis British and American jets bombed Iraqi air-defence systems and other military sites while at sea the oil smugglers became ever more determined to break through the ring of coalition warships. To underline the UK's determination to contain Saddam, HMS *Invincible* was, in the New Year of 1999, ordered back to the Gulf at the head of a naval task group, this time carrying only FA2 fighters.

Within hours of Desert Fox ending, Prime Minister Tony Blair had declared that Saddam could best be caged by the threat of force, stating that the US and UK remained 'ready to strike if necessary' and labelling the more muscular military approach 'the first stirrings of a new global reality.'

Mr Blair added:

The sooner and quicker you act, the easier it is to act and the less costly it is in terms of life, expense and diplomacy. [16]

However, others were not convinced, with Gulf War UK commander-in-chief Sir Peter de la Billière among those questioning the viability of a bombing campaign.

You cannot bomb people into submission; it tends to make them defiant. I think there is a considerable risk this will happen, not just in Iraq but across the Islamic world. [17]

For HMS *Invincible*, by February on the front line of the so-called new 'global reality' in the northern Gulf, every day saw FA2s launched into dangerous skies. With help from the Serbians and Russians, who supplied weapons technology despite the UN embargo, formidable air-defences still existed in southern Iraq. As they waited for the fighters to return from each mission, the carrier's flight deck team anxiously scanned the skies to count all the aircraft back safely.

Dots are now visible in the sky astern of Invincible - *they gradually get*

Sea Harriers recover to the flight deck of Invincible after a Combat Air Patrol. Nigel Andrews.

closer and closer, stacked up behind each other like airliners making the final approach to Heathrow. Matching its speed to that of the carrier, a Sea Harrier hovers parallel to the ship, hanging in the air like a gigantic insect and then sliding over the flight-deck. Crewmen bustle around the jet, tying it down and securing it to the deck. The remaining three Sea Harriers are recovered in very quick succession, the noise, heat and downwash is terrific, the superheated blast mixing in with severe buffeting caused by Mother Nature. The jets have all made it back safely with missiles still slung under them, indicating they didn't have to shoot down any Iraqis. The pilots climb down and swiftly march across the flight-deck and into the ship, heading for the 800 Naval Air Squadron debriefing room, where they will discuss how the mission went. Debriefing concluded, one of the Sea Harrier pilots explains what it is like to go up against Saddam's air defences: 'The superiority of our planes and weapons system, plus those of the Americans, are the reason the Iraqis are reluctant to really mix it with us in air-to-air combat. A favourite trick of the Iraqi warplanes is to try and lure us over anti-aircraft guns or SAMs, by running away over them. They also try and tempt us into giving chase at the end of a mission in the hope that we'll run out of fuel and drop out of the sky. Keeping your wits about you and concentrating the whole time is therefore essential. That's why we are totally drained mentally and physically when we climb out of that cockpit at the end of a mission. But, despite the dangers, being a Sea Harrier pilot is a superb job. If a flight is cancelled due to bad weather over southern Iraq, you are disappointed - you're all keyed up, the

147

A Sea Harrier pilot waits on HMS Invincible's upper deck, to climb into his jet for another Combat Air Patrol in the face of Saddam's SAMs. Nigel Andrews.

adrenalin is pumping, but you've got nowhere to go. Adrenalin and danger is all part and parcel of it'. [18]

Shore batteries of ASMs still posed a potent threat to Allied naval forces in the Gulf for, while his navy was destroyed during the 1991 Gulf War, Saddam had managed to preserve significant numbers of Silkworms.

Ensuring they kept their radars inactive to avoid attracting Allied air strikes was a key objective for the Iraqis. Questioned aboard *Invincible*, UK task group commander, Commodore Anthony Dymock was under no illusions about the residual Iraqi threat.

We cannot afford to let our guard down for a moment. While the Silkworm is a primitive weapon, with not much in the way of targeting, it does have a long range and can create a big bang at the end of its reach, which will make a mess of any vessel it hits. Saddam's task is not to sweep the Coalition forces from the sea - he wants to score a big propaganda victory by downing an aircraft or badly damaging a warship. [19]

The potential small boat threat was also treated very seriously, but senior naval commanders visualized hard-core Ba'athists, armed with RPGs, making a nuisance of themselves in the tightly packed shipping lanes of the northern Gulf, rather than suicide bombers. Small craft smuggling oil were a serious preoccupation for HMS *Cumberland*.

A suspect vessel is detected by the Type 22 frigate - first by radar in her Ops Room and then by the 'number one eyeball' of an upper-deck lookout.

Apparently the smaller the vessels are the more they might have to hide - a large proportion of the oil being smuggled out of Iraq to provide funds for Saddam's weapons programmes is carried in tiny, ramshackle Arab dhows or rusting tugboats.

'People imagine that we target the big tankers,' explains Lieutenant Mike Dineen, on Cumberland's bridge, as he reaches for a radio handset to interrogate the small vessel on the horizon. 'But vessels like this one are more likely to be trying to break UN sanctions.'

Lieutenant Dineen uses a standard quiz to assess the likelihood of it being

HMS Cumberland *rides shotgun on* Invincible *as the British carrier launches Sea Harriers for another patrol over southern Iraq.* Nigel Andrews.

up to no good: *'This is British warship* Cumberland *five miles on your starboard.'*

A crackly reply comes back.

'Good afternoon sir,' responds Lieutenant Dineen.

'We are operating in support of UN Security Resolutions and we request you answer some questions with regard to your cargo, destination and other details.' As Lieutenant Dineen proceeds, info is signalled to an American intelligence centre in the region. If any facts don't add up, the vessel will be visited by a boarding party dropped from the frigate's Lynx helicopter.

Lieutenant Dineen has a well-developed instinct for interrogation because he was once a boarding team leader. This time the suspect appears to be innocent of any violation and is allowed to proceed. However, just a few days before this harmless interception, Cumberland *managed to stop a blatant sanctions-busting tugboat. 'She had so much oil aboard, her upper decks were awash,' Lieutenant Dineen recalls, still astonished by the cheek of it.'It was incredible - 300 tonnes of contraband oil on a 190 tonnes tugboat'.*[20]

Over a cup of tea in the wardroom, the Commanding Officer of HMS *Cumberland*, Captain Alan Richards, explained that his warship's interceptions of smugglers were an essential part of international pressure on Saddam.

If there were no attempts to smuggle oil out we would not be here. Why more oil is not being exchanged for food is a question only the Iraqi regime can answer. Neither myself or my sailors want to see the Iraqi people failing to benefit from a system designed to ensure they are provided for. [21]

As the sun went down over the Gulf the frigate set course for a patrol area further up threat. By the following morning she would be the closest Allied warship to Iraqi shore-based missile batteries.

As the British task group had begun its deployment in the northern Gulf, in Washington DC senior American military officials were being questioned about the worth of warships conducting recent cruise missile strikes on targets in Afghanistan, following Al-Qaeda attacks on US embassies in east Africa of the previous August. Captain Mike Doubleday, of the US Navy, told reporters:

> At the time the attack took place, we knew that there was going to be a meeting of Osama bin-Laden's organization...The attack was not against any specific individual, and I think most of you are aware that we have long said that military forces are not an effective tool to be used against individuals.

In fact, even as Desert Fox had been in full swing, Secretary of Defense Cohen had been asked for his opinion in the likely threat from Osama bin Laden's organization. He had responded:

> ...the threat of terrorism has been with us for some time. It is increasing. As a result of Osama bin-Laden and some of his associates, there have been plans...to attack US facilities. We have been aware of these plans, we have tried to verify those plans, we have tried to assess their credibility... It is our anticipation that attempts will be made, as attempts have been made in the past. We have been somewhat successful, quite successful, as a matter of fact, in frustrating several ...

But, as subsequent events in the port of Aden and in the USA would show, not successful enough.

CHAPTER EIGHT

NO TOUGHER FIGHT

United States Marine Corps Gunnery Sergeant Matthew T. Olivolo was driving to Staten Island from Brooklyn, on the Verrazano bridge, when, over his car radio he heard that the World Trade Center had been hit by an aircraft. Realizing that, with such a massive accident, the traffic chaos would be huge, Sergeant Olivolo pulled over at Staten Island Harbour and, being a keen photographer, could not help getting his camera out to capture the scene across the water, where smoke was clearly visible pouring from one of the towers. The Gunnery Sergeant would later recall:

> *When I saw the second impact, I knew something was wrong and realized that it had to be intentional.* [1]

News of the hit on the Pentagon came over the radio and Sergeant Olivolo began to feel that something truly dreadful was happening to his country. But any contemplation of the incident in Washington DC was banished when, across the water, the first tower of the WTC began to collapse.

> *I was thinking, 'how are they going to put out those fires?' At that point, the first building collapsed and I knew it was only a matter of time before the second tower went too. When I got to the recruiting station where I was working, everybody was watching television. All of them seemed to be in shock, but we knew we had to do something.*

Not knowing what else to do, Sergeant Olivolo and his fellow marines helped set up a casualty station that, sadly, had no customers.

> *...we could see the smoke from the two towers from the recruiting station...it was only four blocks away.*

The World Trade Center burns on 11 September 2001, in a photograph taken by US Marine Corps Sergeant Matthew T. Olivolo.

Over the coming days the marine NCO, like many other traumatized New Yorkers, went to the scene of devastation at Ground Zero to see what he could do to help. Taking his camera with him, Olivolo recorded the aftermath, capturing images that have become seared in the memories of people across the globe. That September morning had been the defining moment of the new century. It was a day that tore away the illusion that the post-Cold War world was a safer place. However, an incident in southern Arabia less than a year earlier had provided ample warning that the emerging terrorist threat was formidable and its shock troops were prepared to do anything to strike down the symbols of American imperium.

More than thirty years after Britain withdrew from Aden, America had established a presence in the southern Arabian port that was an open invitation for Al-Qaeda terrorists to make an attempt to destroy a US Navy warship.

The Clinton administration's response to the bombing of two US embassies in east Africa in 1998 had been weak, reinforcing the perception in Osama bin Laden's mind that the US military was morally timid, and afraid to put troops on the ground, despite its technological supremacy. Filled with a burning desire to deliver another serious blow against 'the Great Satan', the terrorists assigned to the task of attacking an American warship were not the most competent, but they did at least learn from their mistakes.

The Al-Qaeda cell in Aden decided their weapon should be a small boat packed with munitions, eventually obtaining waterproof C4 explosives, probably manufactured in the USA.[2] Aden's harbour teemed with dozens of small fishing vessels and the bombers were easily able to carry out dry runs of how they might approach an American warship. Renting a house overlooking the harbour, the terrorists constructed a tall fence around the property so they could turn their boat into a massive bomb without being scrutinized by prying eyes. On 3 January 2000, the would-be bombers launched the boat from a nearby beach, their target being the destroyer USS *The Sullivans*. However, the explosives had not been distributed around the vessel properly and it sank.[3] Nine months later the bombers would get the C4 distribution right. For, on 12 October, the USS *Cole* called at Aden's US CENTCOM Defense Fuel Support Point. An American naval vessel had first used the facility in December 1999, with two dozen more refueling without incident. The *Cole*, which was part of the *George Washington* CBG, was making her way south to the Gulf, having come through the Suez Canal and Red Sea. The Arleigh Burke class guided-missile destroyer, commissioned in 1996, was carrying a crew of twenty-six officers and 315 sailors and lookouts on her upper decks spotted the Al-Qaeda boat, but mistook it for part of the local refuelling team. The bombers reportedly stood to attention as it rammed the American destroyer, detonating 400 - 600lbs of explosives, which ripped open the port side of the ship at the waterline, killing seventeen American sailors and injuring forty-two. Petty Officer Chris Regal would never forget the terror of that moment.

It was the loudest sound you could remember...people were hysterical...it was chaos, and blood, and injuries and just horrible.[4]

The explosion was later estimated to have involved the same force as a Second

World War-era torpedo.

Imagine a 40-foot gash in the side of a ship at the waterline, yet the ship is steady with only a 4-degree list! Titanic sank by striking a stationery iceberg.

A single torpedo with less explosive power than the sophisticated terrorist bomb has sunk many a ship. Yet, Cole absorbed devastating damage and stayed steady....the captain obviously trained his crew to survive and thrive in the chaos that ensued at the very instant that powerful bomb exploded. There is no higher praise for a captain. There is no tougher fight and there is no tougher crew than the one which saves a ship.[5]

The main damaged areas were the forward engine room, the auxiliary machinery space and spaces above, including mess halls. But, most serious of all, there was progressive flooding. In short, the *Cole* was mortally wounded and came close to sinking. Both power and severed communications were difficult to restore quickly and the back-up systems had to be isolated from circuits going through the damaged areas. To make matters worse the ventilation system would not have been isolated quickly enough, so smoke spread swiftly throughout the vessel. It is likely there was no light except emergency lighting, until auxiliary generators could be isolated and started up and light provided by batteries would have been exhausted before that happened. The heroic damage control effort that saved the ship therefore took place

A port side view of the USS Cole, showing the hole created by the explosion. US DoD.

in the dark, hot, wet, fire-filled spaces and initially without communication. Training was the crucial factor in saving the ship, as each damage control team was on its own for the first few minutes that determined if the ship died or lived to fight another day. That the *Cole* was able to survive such damage was not only a tribute to the prompt and effective actions of her crew but also to her sturdy construction. Most modern warships are not armoured. In fact, many of today's smaller warships, like mine counter-measure vessels, are built of glass-reinforced plastic while larger ones, such as the *Cole*, are constructed of only thin, mild steel plate. However, the most sensitive parts of the ship were protected with light Kevlar armour, largely to protect personnel from splinters. The *Cole* was not only mortally wounded, she was also operating without the mutual support of other American warships. The first friendly warship on scene was the British Type 23 frigate HMS *Marlborough*, which was on her way back to the UK from a deployment in the Gulf. She immediately offered the assistance of her doctor. A French military plane was used to help transport injured sailors from hospital in Aden to military medical facilities in nearby Djibouti, while an American C-9 Nightingale air ambulance was sent from Germany. Fifteen US Navy medical personnel were flown to Aden from Bahrain. Investigators from the Federal Bureau of Investigation (FBI), Naval Criminal Investigation Service and the State Department headed for the Middle East. In the Gulf any vessels of the 5th Fleet not at sea immediately left harbour and, on 13 October, a US Marine Corps Fleet Anti-Terrorism Security Team was deployed to Aden to prevent further terrorist attacks. In the USA, Admiral Robert J. Natter, Commander-in-Chief, US Atlantic Fleet, to which the *Cole* belonged, told a press conference:

> *This senseless act of apparent terrorism is not one that we will take lightly.*
> *I will tell you that USS* Cole *is a ship that was built to fight. The ship and its crew fought this tragedy very professionally.*

But some were questioning the logic behind sending a warship to refuel at the Yemeni port in the first place. One US-based naval officer fumed:

> *Aden is, and always has been, a very dangerous and unstable place.*[6]

However, Admiral Natter observed:

> *Port security is a responsibility of the host nation and the port authority.*

Some sources were saying that the *Cole* had enough fuel in her tanks to make it to the Gulf without needing to stop at Aden, but warships customarily top up their fuel tanks when they get to a certain level anyway, rather than let them run dry. However, a decline in the number of US Navy auxiliary oil tankers in recent years meant that an alternative source of fuel might not have been available during the final leg of her journey. Accurate advice on threat assessments was meant to be provided to warship Commanding Officers before they took their ships into any port and there was speculation that this may not have been so in *Cole*'s case. [7]

On 13 October the frigate USS *Hawes* and destroyer USS *Donald Cook* arrived, but stayed out of the harbour while sending teams of sailors across to assist the *Cole*. A sailor from the *Hawes* later wrote home:

> *The pictures on the news, do absolutely no justice to the damage caused to*
> *the ship...the collateral damage to surrounding compartments is pretty*

extensive...The deck (floor) of the mess decks, just above the affected compartments, is now a part of the overhead (ceiling) of the mess decks. What used to be a distance of about 10 feet, is now a matter of inches, or fractions thereof... [8]

Another sailor sent across to help was deeply shocked and also full of admiration for the way the crew saved their ship:

The Number One engine room is flooded solid...The Messdecks deck is now pressed against the overhead. The entire galley was pushed to the starboard side and the equipment is unrecognizable. This is where many crew members died. The ship was very nearly lost. They are truly heroes. [9]

On 16 October the USS *Tarawa* ARG arrived and FBI investigators, living in hotels ashore, moved to one of the US Navy ships to ensure their safety. On 17 October Yemeni police investigators discovered bomb-making material in the house overlooking the harbour, but there was no sign of the occupants whom local residents described as Arabs 'from beyond Yemen'. Meanwhile many of the *Cole's* injured had been flown to medical facilities in the USA and the US Navy announced it had hired the Norwegian-owned *Blue Marlin* heavy lift ship. She was close at hand, having just transported two US Navy mine-hunters to the Gulf. US Defence Secretary William Cohen announced that refuelling operations in Yemen had been suspended pending a thorough review while, on 18 October, Admiral Vern Clark, the US Navy's Chief of Naval Operations, revealed the contents of an e-mail, which one of the *Cole's* dead sailors sent home before the blast. It said:

Mom, we're in dangerous waters, but I'm OK.

The admiral said the message told him the *Cole's* sailors knew they were in harm's way, but they accepted the risk, for the mission was one that helped protect the USA. 'Freedom and the values we cherish sometimes come at a high price,' Admiral Clark

In the Gulf of Aden, October 2000, the badly damaged destroyer USS Cole *is towed out to be lifted aboard the Norwegian heavy transport ship MV* Blue Marlin, *for transportation back to the USA.* US Marine Corps.

observed. Wary of further attacks, on 24 October US Central Command officials declared Threat Condition Delta, the highest level. A Pentagon spokesman said:

> Vessels in the US 5th Fleet will remain at sea for the foreseeable future. We are not universally welcomed in a lot of places overseas, and some people there have shown their objections to US military presence in a variety of ways, unfortunately, some of them very violent.

Five days later the USS *Cole* was towed out of Aden harbor to deeper water by the Military Sealift Command fleet ocean tug USNS *Cataba* and the following morning the process of loading her onto *Blue Marlin* began.

Riding shotgun on the damaged destroyer during her marathon piggyback ride home, was her sister ship, the *Donald Cook*. An engineering assessment team from the US Navy's Naval Sea Systems Command was aboard the *Cole*, to keep her ticking over safely and complete an assessment of the viability of restoring her to full fighting order.

Meanwhile, the US Department of Defense (DoD) had formed a special review body, the Cole Panel, to carry out an investigation, which was independent of, but working in coordination with, the FBI-led effort to bring the terrorists to book. By mid-November at least sixty suspects had been taken into custody for questioning by the Yemeni authorities, but the FBI was not allowed to sit in on interrogations and the transcripts forwarded to its agents were 'poorly translated and heavily edited'. [10]

The future use of Aden as a refuelling stop was unlikely for US Navy warships and even passage through the Suez Canal was ruled out from the beginning of November. However, the Royal Navy continued to use the waterway for its vessels sailing to and from the Gulf. The *Cole* reached home waters in mid-December and was taken to the shipyard that had constructed her - Ingalls Shipbuilding at Pascagoula, Mississippi - where she would be for a year under-going repairs costing $240 million. By late December, the Cole Panel's findings had been passed to the Navy Staff in the Pentagon for review but the FBI had not yet concluded its investigation.

The Cole *arrives at the Ingalls Shipyard, Mississippi aboard the MV* Blue Marlin, *mid-December 2000.* US Navy.

As the tenth anniversary of Desert Storm passed in January 2001, the USA found itself with a new President - George W. Bush, son of the man who led the coalition to war in 1991. In the ten years between the Bush presidencies UN sanctions had, of course, prevented Saddam from rebuilding his military might. But they had also been used as a weapon against the Iraqi people, to destroy society and increase their enslavement through impoverishment. Sanctions created resentment of the West that was now almost as strong as the Iraqi peoples' secretly nurtured hatred of Saddam and his bestial regime. Beyond Iraq's borders Saddam was seen as a hero by many in the Arab world for defying the West, which his formidable propaganda machine portrayed as cruel and weak.

A thriving black market, including a lucrative illegal oil trade that continued despite the efforts of Allied warships in the Gulf, enriched the regime's ruling family and also kept loyal Ba'ath party members comfortable.

The destruction of the regular Iraqi Army during the Gulf War, and subsequent murders by Saddam's executioners of many senior officers who dared to plot against the regime, had also served the Ba'athist cause well.

A new 'peoples' army' consisted of tens of thousands of loyal militia troops, including the fanatical Fedayeen Saddam. The troops of the Republican Guard had also been kept bound to Saddam via better pay and conditions for its six, comparatively well-equipped, divisions while a 15,000-strong formation called the Special Republican Guard was even more loyal and tightly integrated into the regime. With no arms inspectors in Iraq it was difficult to tell the exact status of Saddam's WMD ambitions, and whether or not the Desert Fox campaign had achieved what the previous eight years of inspections had not.

By early 2001 it was clear that caging Saddam with sanctions, that he deliberately flouted or circumvented, was not the answer. The new American administration was convinced that regime change was needed to eradicate the WMD threat, actual or latent, and bring stability to the region. Just over a year before he became president, George W. Bush told a journalist:

...it's time to finish the task.[11]

To wrest the initiative from Saddam, the USA and UK proposed so-called 'smart sanctions', which entailed removing controls on civilian goods, while enhancing those on items for dual-use (ie: civilian and/or military) by increasing border controls. Also, by reducing Saddam's illegal income from smuggling while continuing to control his legitimate earnings through an escrow account at the UN, the USA and UK hoped to inflict personal pain on Saddam, by decreasing his ability to accrue wealth. Bans on military equipment would be maintained. However, it was unlikely that the 'smart sanctions' proposals would be passed by the UN Security Council, as France, China and Russia enjoyed a lucrative trade partnership with Iraq that might be endangered. Total removal of all sanctions was their favoured position, but that would enable Saddam to rebuild both his conventional and WMD arsenals within a matter of a few years. The bid to impose the smart sanctions failed and so, the stalemate continued.

Having left an $88.5 million refit period in 2000, the 92,000 tons USS *Enterprise*

A pair of F-18 Hornets fly over the aircraft carrier USS Enterprise, after completing a mission in support of Operation Southern Watch, on 10 April 1999. Already a veteran of combat in Arabian waters, the Enterprise was destined, in late 2001, to unleash strike jets against Al-Qaeda bases in Afghanistan. US Navy.

departed for her seventeenth deployment on 25 April 2001. The *Big E*, as she was known, had always been where the action was. Her maiden voyage saw her enforcing a blockade during the Cuban Missile Crisis while, in the closing act of the Vietnam War, her F-14s covered the evacuation of Saigon. In the Tanker War in the Gulf and Operation Desert Fox her strike jets drew blood. Now she was returning to the Middle East to act as guardian of the eastern Mediterranean and the Gulf. As the *Enterprise* sailed across the Atlantic, nobody could have forecast that out of a clear blue sky, just over four months later, would come a daring terrorist attack that would require the carrier to launch retaliatory air strikes into Afghanistan. After visiting Portsmouth on the south coast of England, the *Enterprise* headed north with four of her battle group ships - the cruiser *Philippine Sea*, destroyer *McFaul*, attack submarine *Hampton* and fleet oiler *Arctic*. They participated in Joint Maritime Course 2001-2 (JMC 01-2), a Royal Navy-led multi-national joint and combined warfare training exercise. Among the fifteen Royal Navy vessels participating was the British fleet flagship, HMS *Illustrious*, which was using the exercise to work-up for leading a task group deployment to the Middle East that autumn. The JMC action was staged off the coast of northern Scotland and forty-six ships, five submarines, 1,400 marines, and over 100 aircraft participated.

Following the conclusion of the exercise, the *Big E* headed across the Mediterranean with her escort ships, preparing for a passage through the Suez Canal. Once in the Gulf she would take over from the USS *Carl Vinson*. There was no doubt in the minds of the *Big E*'s aviators that soon the radars of Iraqi SAM missiles and anti-aircraft guns would be locking onto their aircraft. Increasingly,

158

Saddam's forces were firing too, sometimes at Allied aircraft in Kuwaiti airspace.

In Portsmouth, planning for the Royal Navy's big Middle East deployment was well advanced. Playing a leading part in planning the joint Omani-UK Exercise Saif Sareea was Gulf War veteran Lieutenant Commander Richard Thomas. The former Signal Communications Officer of HMS *Manchester* had spent the late 1990s on an exchange appointment with the US Navy that culminated in him graduating from the Naval War College at Newport in 1998, with a post graduate diploma in National Security and Strategic Studies. Now Lieutenant Commander Thomas had been assigned to the UK Maritime Battlestaff. Given responsibility for the USA desk, he was also the lead planner for the maritime side of Saif Sareea.

> *Though by no means a Middle East expert, having participated in the Gulf War and operated in the Gulf in HMS* Sheffield *during 1995, I felt confident that I could progress planning to meet both Omani and UK requirements. Our Admiral would act as the Combined Joint Task Force Commander, embarked in HMS* Illustrious *for the exercise, so there were many 'moving parts' to orchestrate.*

On the other side of the Atlantic, as the first anniversary of the attack on the *Cole* approached, the US Navy was awaiting the results of its Judge Advocate General Manual (JAGMAN) investigation. The FBI had issued its own report into the *Cole* bombing on 26 January, less than a week after the inauguration of President Bush. Al-Qaeda was clearly the culprit, but the new Republican administration wanted to carefully consider various options for dealing with bin Laden and his fighters, rather than just launch a few cruise missiles against targets in Afghanistan, where the terror organization was an honoured guest of the fanatical anti-Western Taliban regime. President Bush was caustically dismissive of his predecessor's predilection for flinging TLAMs around.

> *The antiseptic notion of launching a cruise missile into some guy's, you know, tent, really is a joke. I mean, people viewed that as the impotent America...a flaccid, you know, kind of technologically competent but not very tough country that was willing to launch a cruise missile out of a submarine and that'd be it.* [12]

While a series of TLAM attacks was, therefore, not instantly forthcoming, the US Navy was, however, consolidating the lessons of the *Cole* attack, as Vice Admiral Michael Mullen explained.

> *Last year's attack on the USS* Cole *left an indelible mark, and the US Navy has rightfully placed a new emphasis on developing measures and procedures to better protect our ships and our sailors. In the days following the USS* Cole *bombing, we instituted sweeping changes to waterfront security along the US East Coast.* [13]

With military installations so well protected the terrorists had, of course, already decided to hit so-called 'soft targets' and via unexpected means.

Having seen what cruise missiles could do during Operation Desert Storm in 1991, the Royal Navy had decided it needed them for its own submarines. That acquisition was the keystone in the foundations for the Royal Navy's new ethos of Maritime

Contribution to Joint Operations (MCJO). This envisaged the UK fleet not only being able to strike deep inland with its TLAMs, but also acting as the prime enabler for operations by all three branches of the British armed forces, which would operate from its warships and auxiliaries.

Therefore, in the summer of 2001, as part of the process of increasing the Royal Navy's deep strike capability, the British attack submarine HMS *Trafalgar* conducted the first UK cruise missile test firing for three years. The third British hunter-killer submarine to achieve TLAM capability - the other two being HMS *Splendid* and HMS *Triumph* - the *Trafalgar* headed for waters off Florida for the test firing not long after completing a refit at Devonport Dockyard.

Back in the UK, in early September, HMS *Illustrious* was preparing to leave Portsmouth to head south for Saif Sareea.

It would be the biggest deployment of British naval power since the Falklands War of 1982. Thirty-five thousand British and Omani forces personnel were to be involved, with twenty-four British surface ships and two nuclear-powered attack submarines from the UK gathered in the Arabian Sea. Rear Admiral James Burnell-Nugent, who was the Commander UK Maritime Forces (COMUKMARFOR), commanded the British task force.

The *Illustrious* group was composed of the Type 22 frigate *Cornwall*; Type 23 frigates *Monmouth* and *Marlborough*; the Type 42 destroyers *Southampton* and *Nottingham*. The two SSNs were to be *Superb* and *Trafalgar*. Crucial support was provided by the RFA supply ships *Oakleaf*, *Fort Rosalie* (the renamed Gulf War veteran, *Fort Grange*) and *Fort Austin*. Leading the UK's own ARG was the veteran assault ship *Fearless*, elderly but packed with sophisticated command and control equipment. Also in the ARG, carrying Sea King and Lynx helicopters of the Commando aviation squadrons, was the new assault carrier *Ocean* while the RFA Landing Ships *Sir Bedivere*, *Sir Tristram*, *Sir Percivale* and *Sir Galahad* transported heavy equipment. A Mine Counter-Measures task group, headed by the *Diligence*, as HQ ship and with the survey vessel *Roebuck* providing further tasking facilities, was also deploying. The deployed mine-hunters were the Sandown class MCMVs *Inverness* and *Walney* and Hunt class *Quorn* and *Cattistock*.

As part of Saif Sareea, units from 3 Commando Brigade - by 2001 one of the UK's key rapid reaction formations - would be carrying out a mock amphibious assault on the shores of Oman.

The prominence of the commandos in Saif Sareea was a sign that the tide had turned for the Royal Marines. By the end of the 1990s the British had begun a massive regeneration of their amphibious warfare capability, by bringing *Ocean* into service and ordering construction of a whole range of landing ships. Much of the thinking behind MCJO was merely a reflection of some simple truths about the world in the twenty-first century. Most operations would inevitably be conducted within striking distance of naval-led joint forces, as much of the world's population, the majority of its capital cities, and nearly all major centres of international trade and military power, are found within 100 miles of the sea. Trade routes and sites of natural resources converge in the most intense areas of human activity in the coastal regions, the littorals. The UK Government document outlining SDR stated:

In future, littoral operations and force projection, for which maritime forces are well suited, will be our primary focus.

But then, a new form of warfare was unveiled in a terrifying terrorist spectacular.

It was the most profound shock to the American nation since the Imperial Japanese Navy launched its surprise attack on the US Pacific Fleet's main base at Pearl Harbor on 7 December 1941. Sixty years later, 11 September became a new date cursed with infamy. The blow delivered during this Pearl Harbor of the twenty-first century came from civilian airliners hijacked by fanatical Al-Qaeda terrorists. On one day in December 1941, the Japanese killed 2,400 servicemen in two hours, while on the morning of 11 September 2001, 2,752 civilians perished at the hands of Al-Qaeda, in the ruins of the Twin Towers in New York and many more died in the smoking rubble of the Pentagon. But still, a naval affairs magazine correspondent visiting the US military nerve-centre felt remote from the destruction.

The Pentagon complex is so huge and the unreality of it all so overwhelming that I stood talking calmly about with some Marine Corps officers. An admiral got on the Public Address system and informed everybody that all the planes used in the attacks had been hijacked and that staff and visitors would be clearing the building and sent home. But if the terrorists thought that we would be frightened by the first act of war in the eastern USA since 1865, they miscalculated. Most peoples' first

Fire and rescue workers unfurl a huge American flag over the side of the battered Pentagon. US Navy.

reaction was that they wanted to know how they could help. Driving out of the area, the traffic was smooth and polite, with everyone giving emergency vehicles a free lane. As I drove away from the Pentagon I was amazed at the sheer complexity of the attack. In pure military terms, it was a masterful assault. In moral terms, it was an outrage perpetrated by sick minds and it will require suitable vengeance. Those who made this attack will find, like the Japanese sixty years ago, that they have stirred a giant and filled him with a terrible resolve. This will be a long, hard war, but the USA and its allies will triumph because they are democracies.[14]

Aboard the British fleet flagship, HMS *Illustrious*, by 11 September at Malta, the staff officers busy preparing for Saif Sareea watched the dreadful events unfolding in

The hospital ship Comfort *passes the Statue of Liberty, as she moves in to anchor off Manhattan, to provide help in the aftermath of the 11 September terrorist attack on the World Trade Center.* US Navy.

Two days after the Al-Qaeda attack on the USA, the destroyer USS Winston S. Churchill is pictured steaming hard in the English Channel. US Navy.

the USA, where eighty-five Britons were among the dead. Lieutenant Commander Thomas realized that,

...something immense had just occurred that would probably change the world... I seem to recall being struck by the sheer scale of probable loss of life as the TV showed the towers crumble. The audacity of such attacks on the continental United States was also striking, as was the fact that it was so well co-ordinated.

The Gulf War of 1991 had been a perfect illustration of how not to wage war against the USA, for the militarily inept Saddam had gifted the Americans a conflict on their terms. In 2001 nobody, not even the Iraqi leader, would face the USA head-on, so that left asymmetric warfare. In asymmetric warfare, the goal is the absolute destruction of an enemy without having to seek open battle with his military. The target is society and its foundations and the weapons are symbols of a free and open society, which make for a devastating impact - airliners, cars, small boats and humans, all packed with explosives. As subsequent months would prove, the terrorists were not above using weapons such as shoulder-launched SAMs, but their targets were civilians not the military. In the immediate aftermath of 11 September, among the most instantly available forces to help deal with the casualties and defend America were the ships of the US Navy. The hospital ship USNS *Comfort* embarked naval medical personnel in New Jersey and headed for New York. The carrier USS *George Washington* set sail from Norfolk and mounted air patrols while preparing to send her helicopters in to New York to help airlift casualties to the *Comfort*. Other US Navy ships at sea off the east coast of America included five AEGIS-equipped cruisers, all tasked by the North American Aerospace Defense Command (NORAD) to provide air defence against further attacks by terrorists using civilian airliners. Meanwhile, US Navy warships were also defending the USA's west coast and Hawaii. In Europe the Arleigh Burke class destroyers *Gonzalez* and *Winston S. Churchill* were at sea off the south coast of England. The *Gonzalez* had been in port at Devonport, Plymouth, as part of NATO's Standing Naval Force Mediterranean and sailed immediately after the terrorist attacks. The *Winston S. Churchill* was already at sea, conducting a series of combat training exercises with the Royal Navy's Operational Sea Training organization. The powerful AEGIS combat systems of the two American destroyers provided additional protection for the UK and Europe.

As Al-Qaeda struck, the results of the US Navy's JAGMAN investigation into the attack on the *Cole* were being published. Chief of Naval Operations, Admiral Vern Clark, agreed with the findings of Admiral Natter, who concluded that the commanding officer of *Cole*, Commander Kirk Lippold, acted reasonably in adjusting his force protection posture, based on his assessment of the situation. 'I found Admiral Natter's analysis to be both well reasoned and convincing,' said Admiral Clark.

> *...and I therefore agreed with his determination that the facts do not warrant any punitive action against the commanding officer or other members of* Cole's *crew.*

Among the lessons learned from the attack was a need for additional training and equipment, as well as a heightened awareness of force protection that would enable ships to operate within a reasonable level of risk in a high-threat environment. The US Navy also noted shortcomings throughout the network of commands, departments and agencies that provided support to warships operating in foreign waters.

When planning for the UK's Saif Sareea deployment started in 1997, no one could have imagined kamikaze airliner attacks sparking a major war several hundred miles north of Oman. As it was, Saif Sareea took place without any disruption, with 3 Commando Brigade Royal Marines and the British Army's 4 Armoured Brigade conducting their desert war games alongside Omani troops and tanks, while British jets and aircraft from the host country flew support missions. Having not deployed in such strength to the Middle East since 1991, the UK commando brigade was based at the sprawling Camp Fairburn, about seventy miles inland from the Gulf of

Oman. In the early stages of the exercise the commando brigade's CO, Brigadier Roger Lane, was hedging his bets about whether or not his troops might be diverted to action in Afghanistan. Brigadier Lane agreed that the Royal Marines had experienced their fair share of terrorism - Northern Ireland in particular - but that the attacks on America were beyond anyone's experience.

Harriers are launched from the carrier HMS Illustrious *during Exercise Saif Sareea.* Jonathan Eastland/AJAX News & Feature Service.

> *We have been in the counter-terrorism game for many years and have seen some horrific incidents. But, of course, none of us has ever seen anything of the scale and audacity of the attack that was inflicted on the USA.*[15]

The most significant aspect of the exercise was the deployment of close to thirty British warships. Rear Admiral James Burnell-Nugent, who was of course, a veteran of two tense Gulf deployments as captain of *Invincible*, could see that naval forces would play a vital role in any forthcoming action.

> *Navies have a crucial contribution to make in shaping events on land. The Royal Navy no longer just roams the seas looking for fights with other navies.*[16]

The UK forces swung from mock combat to the real thing with ease. Both *Trafalgar* and *Superb* had diverted to active operations, even as Saif Sareea progressed, the former joining sister vessel HMS *Triumph* in unleashing TLAMs at targets in Afghanistan during the first wave of Anglo-US strikes on 7 October. Six days later both submarines fired more cruise missiles at a rapidly diminishing list of suitable targets. The *Triumph* had transited through the Suez Canal around ten days prior to the first TLAM strikes. On 11 September she had been engaged in stalking surface vessels as part of an ASW exercise of Iceland.

> *Re-tasked to the Gulf on 12 Sep 01...she arrived east of Suez, re-armed with Tomahawk Land Attack Missiles, ready to fire 17 days later, her third time east of Suez in two years.*[17]

The *Triumph*'s odyssey vindicated the Royal Navy's decision in the mid-1990s, when

defence cuts were severe, to concentrate on nuclear-propelled submarines, after discarding the last of its diesel-electric boats. Only nuclear power provided the sheer underwater speed - in excess of thirty knots - and endurance needed to achieve *Triumph*'s feat, bearing in mind she probably had to go to Diego Garcia first to pick up her TLAMs, before heading north to her firing position in the Arabian Sea.

Few, if any, regional allies felt able to allow British and American aircraft to participate in direct military action against Afghanistan by flying from their soil. With no substantial facilities on land in the Gulf, for either aircraft or ground troops to launch attacks from, maritime air power was the only option in the opening phase of the campaign.

By early October the US Navy's *Enterprise* and *Vinson* had been reinforced by the *Kitty Hawk*, which had embarked Special Forces troops. Cruise missile-armed, nuclear attack submarines, destroyers and cruisers were included in the escort groups of the three carriers. The CO of one, the destroyer USS *John Paul Jones*, later revealed that when the first Tomahawk left its launcher, no cheers were heard in the Combat Information Center of the warship. Because the ship conducted frequent missile drills, the crew knew exactly what to expect. 'It's hardly different from practicing because the training is so realistic,' explained the CO. 'The only difference is the missile actually leaves the ship.'

A surprisingly low number of aircraft were used to drop the bombs and launch missiles - for example, the Pentagon revealed that 9 October's strike involved 'five to eight land-based bombers and eight to ten naval strike aircraft'. This reflected the low number of strategic targets in Afghanistan and the great efforts made to ensure all strikes were conducted with utmost precision.

The *Theodore Roosevelt* CBG joined the air offensive in its second week, with a Stars and Stripes flag that had been raised by firefighters over the remains of the World Trade Center in New York flying from her island. The same flag was carried in the cockpit of one of her strike jets during a bombing run against terrorist targets. The *Roosevelt*, and her sixteen-strong battle group, had departed Norfolk in mid-September, sent on their way by the Acting Secretary of the Navy, Gordon England, who said:

> It is time for us to pick up the mantle to destroy terrorism and remove this cancer. [18]

Following the opening strikes, other key targets within Afghanistan were attacked by the coalition, to ensure it had total air superiority for the next phase - the insertion of Special Forces. On 19 October a raid was mounted against a Taliban compound near the southern city of Kandahar, in an attempt to gather intelligence that might lead to Osama bin Laden. Some of the troops were launched from the *Kitty Hawk*, using Black Hawk helicopters that extended their range by refuelling in Pakistan. To back up the Special Forces, two Special Operations-capable US Marine Corps ARGs were deployed, centred on the assault carriers *Kearsarge* and *Bataan*. On 26 October, the UK Government confirmed that a substantial portion of the Royal Navy task force sent to the Arabian Sea would be staying behind after the conclusion of Saif Sareea in mid-November. The full details of the British force being made available for action in Afghanistan were given by Armed Forces Minister Adam Ingram, in a House of Commons statement. He explained that 200 Royal Marines from 40 Commando would be based in the assault ship *Fearless* and the *Illustrious* would also stay. The carrier would land her Harrier jets to take aboard Commando helicopters and RAF Chinooks suitable for flying missions into Afghanistan carrying Special Forces. Also in the naval force would be *Southampton* and *Cornwall*, together with seven RFA support ships. Mr Ingram described the 40 Commando marines as 'the lead elements of an immediately available force to help support operations.' He went on,

> The House will recognize that the deployment of our Armed Forces is a grave step. We do it in the confident knowledge that by doing so we can depend upon them to make a difference. Our Armed Forces are special and

The British assault ship HMS Fearless *was retained in the Arabian Sea to act as a launch pad for the Royal Marines.* Iain Ballantyne.

we are deservedly proud of them. We ask a lot from them and they will not let us down.

In his speech Mr Ingram revealed that one of the TLAM-armed submarines would remain in the region, ready to fire again if need be. That boat was *Trafalgar*, as the *Triumph* had returned home. Like other key Royal Navy commanders in the region Commander Amphibious Task Group (COMATG), Commodore Jamie Miller, found himself switching from pretend warfare to preparing for the real thing. 'We always expect the unexpected,' he said, when interviewed aboard *Fearless*. 'UK armed forces are very highly trained and flexible. They are ready to do anything that is asked of them, from fighting to providing humanitarian aid.'[19]

Evidence of acceleration in the pace of operations was provided by the beginning of November, for on the first day of the month more than fifty strike aircraft were used in attacks, including approximately forty carrier-based jets.

Kabul fell to the coalition-supported Northern Alliance on 13 November, with around 100 Royal Marines swiftly inserted via RAF transport aircraft to secure nearby Bagram Airport. This move outraged the Northern Alliance, which had not been notified in advance and so ordered the British commandos confined to the airport.

However, in late November, the US Marines entered the battleground with the blessing of anti-Taliban forces, which needed help mopping up pockets of resistance. The initial waves of US Marines left the assault carriers *Peleliu* and *Bataan* - stationed close to the Pakistan coast in the Arabian Sea - aboard Sea Knights and Sea Stallions. The helicopters landed in Pakistan and the marines transferred to Chinooks and C-130 transport planes for the final leg of each insertion. Three hundred US Marines landed in the first wave on 25 November. The Leathernecks involved were from Combined Task Force 58 (CTF58), which was under the command of Brigadier General James N. Mattis. He had nearly 9,000 marines and sailors at his disposal to project American resolve and combat power ashore. Mattis told reporters aboard *Peleliu*, as the first marines went in:

We are going to support the Afghan people's effort to free themselves of the terrorists and the people who support terrorists.

Within hours of landing at Dolangi Airfield, the marines had destroyed a Taliban flying column headed their way, with help from US Navy F-14 Tomcat strike jets. By 27 November, more than 600 Marines from the 15th and 26th MEUs had arrived at the new forward operating base. In the meantime members of US Special Forces, together with the UK's SAS and SBS, were hunting for Osama bin Laden and his hardcore followers beyond Afghanistan's cities and towns.

To assist them, on 26 November alone, a quarter of more than 100 air strikes by US Navy and US Air Force jets had been against tunnel and cave complexes in the Tora Bora mountains of southern Afghanistan. Meanwhile, American and British warships in the Arabian Sea were mounting stop-and-search patrols to intercept attempts by Osama bin Laden, or any of his supporters, to escape from the tightening coalition noose.

By the beginning of 2002 the canvas of the war on terrorism was broad, with the

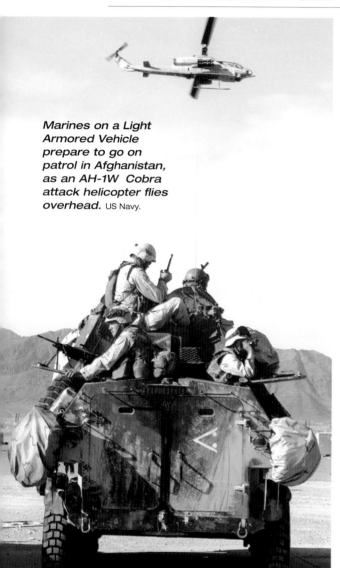

Marines on a Light Armored Vehicle prepare to go on patrol in Afghanistan, as an AH-1W Cobra attack helicopter flies overhead. US Navy.

USA preparing the ground to widen the conflict to Saddam's Iraq. The coalition's Maritime Interdiction Force (MIF) continued to maintain a presence from the northern Gulf to the Arabian Sea, its twin objectives being to clamp down on Iraqi oil smuggling and prevent terrorists from conveying arms, or themselves, by sea. In mid-February sailors from the cruiser USS *Vella Gulf* seized the *Lina*, a vessel 'of undetermined Registry', which had eluded previous efforts to prove she was involved in Iraqi oil smuggling. The suspect ship was stopped in the Gulf of Oman and a boarding party succeeded where previous efforts to find the evidence had failed. In the past a complex system of reinforced locks on hatches and holds prevented boarding parties from seizing control before the *Lina* re-entered territorial waters. A US Navy spokesman revealed how the Iraqi vessel had attempted an unwise course of action:

The boarding teams encountered the usual reinforced and welded entrances, as well as aggressive ship manoeuvring designed to hamper and delay the team's ability to board the ship. At one point during the operation, the Lina *manoeuvred threateningly and appeared intent on ramming*

Front and back of a wanted leaflet showing the Al-Qaeda leader and other top terrorists at large, despite the overthrow of the Taliban. US DoD.

The carriers of the US Navy supported operations to mop up the remnants of the Taliban and Al-Qaeda in Afghanistan. Here, aboard the USS *John C. Stennis* on Christmas Day 2001, a US Marine Corps NCO steadies a 2,000 pound bomb as it is loaded on the wing of an F-18 Hornet. US Navy.

> *Vella Gulf, closing to within 150 yards. Swift manoeuvring by Vella Gulf's bridge watch team quickly defused the threat of collision.*

The *Lina*'s crew was detained and she was towed to a holding area in the Gulf for full investigation.

At least two American CBGs remained committed to action in the Arabian Sea and the Gulf. In April they were led by the *John C. Stennis* and the *John F. Kennedy*, the latter having arrived in mid-March to replace the *Theodore Roosevelt*. Two ARGs remained committed, by then headed by the *Bataan* and *Bonhomme Richard*.

The Royal Navy maintained its substantial presence in the Gulf, Arabian Sea and Indian Ocean into the spring of 2002. The *Ocean* left the UK in mid-February to replace *Illustrious* and aboard the former were 250 Royal Marines from 45 Commando, who had replaced the RMs from 40 Commando as the rapid-reaction spearhead unit.

The *Fearless* returned to Portsmouth just ahead of the *Illustrious*, her extended deployment to the Middle East having exhausted her. It was announced that *Fearless* was finally to be decommissioned, after a career stretching across thirty-six years, as the MOD did not think it worthwhile spending a lot of money returning her to operational capability, especially as the brand new assault ship HMS *Albion* was due to enter service in 2003. The Type 22 frigate *Cornwall* had also headed home, replaced by sister ship *Campbeltown* on station, the latter's surveillance mission taking her deep into the Indian Ocean and close to the Horn of Africa, which had for long been a refuge for terrorist groups, including Al-Qaeda. She in turn was replaced in August by sister ship HMS *Cumberland*. Meanwhile, the newest British frigate in commission in the Royal Navy, HMS *Portland* had, in March 2002, just arrived in the Gulf to enforce UN sanctions against Iraq, taking over from sister ship HMS *Kent*.

A sign of the importance the USA placed on UK involvement in the war on terrorism was the fact that a British officer was second-in-command of the multi-national coalition naval force assembled in the Middle East.

The apparent success of the US-led action in Afghanistan had emboldened some European nations that were previously less than forthright with supplying active military support. Ships were sent by France, Spain, Greece and Holland among others. Even Germany, a country that always experiences political turmoil whenever it contemplates sending troops abroad, contributed Special Operations troops in Afghanistan and sent three frigates and a fast patrol craft group. The German naval vessels operated out of the French base at Djibouti from January 2002. When he switched from purely commanding UK forces to this important new role, as the boss of coalition naval forces, Rear Admiral Burnell-Nugent was accompanied by many of the staff officers who had planned and executed Saif Sareea. They included Lieutenant Commander Thomas, who later recalled:

> There was a tangible increase in the importance of the UK Maritime Battlestaff, as it was a key element of the UK's participation in the global war on terrorism. On completion of the exercise the Admiral and staff had re-located ashore to Bahrain to be alongside the US Navy's 5th Fleet headquarters.
>
> The Admiral was appointed as the Deputy Maritime Coalition Commander for forces in theatre and he was working for a USN three star admiral. The combined staffs were basically engaged with other nations developing the maritime plan to conduct the War on Terrorism.

In March, Rear Admiral Burnell-Nugent handed over to former Commandant General Royal Marines, Major General Rob Fry. Nothing could better illustrate the fact that the UK's Royal Marines were about to move centre stage, for Major General Fry's appointment as COMUKMARFOR came as the UK government decided to send a 1,700-strong Commando Battle Group to fight in Afghanistan. Referring to his other role, as deputy commander of coalition maritime forces, Major General Fry acknowledged:

> There are other nations that are qualified to do the job. But the UK was there early, it committed key elements to offensive operations and it has a well-established close working relationship not only with the USA, but also the other members of the Coalition.[20]

With the spearhead - 45 Commando's Headquarters Company plus its Whisky and Zulu companies - inserted into Afghanistan from HMS *Ocean* and other ARG ships in the Arabian Sea, the rest of the Commando Battle Group flew in by air from the

UK. The commando brigade's HQ commanded the battle group, which also included artillery, engineers and other important supporting units. The British commandos were expected by the middle of April to begin combat operations in Afghanistan, as the Allies stepped up pressure on remnants of Al-Qaeda and the Taliban. British Secretary of State for Defence, Geoff Hoon, had made it clear in March, when he announced the commitment of British ground troops to combat, that Al-Qaeda and its supporters 'continue to pose a direct threat to states outside Afghanistan, including to the United Kingdom'.

By May, a sober assessment of operations in Afghanistan, since the arrival of the Royal Marines' battle group, revealed steady, but unspectacular, progress, which was the norm in such campaigns. The key area of operations had been the badlands along the Afghan-Pakistan border where Special Forces from coalition countries had closed in on Al-Qaeda groups. Aside from backing up efforts by Pakistan's security forces to close down their operating bases, members of the SBS were among those said to have engaged terrorists in firefights. UK Special Forces worked closely with units from the USA's Delta Force and SEALS as well as the Australian and New Zealand SAS. During fighting near Gardez, in eastern Afghanistan, USMC Cobras, flying from assault carriers in the Arabian Sea provided airborne firepower for US Army troops engaged in heavy combat with the Taliban and Al-Qaeda. A SEAL was killed during the same clashes. The Royal Marines were withdrawn from Afghanistan before the summer was out, and while they undoubtedly denied terrorists use of the border territory to regroup and launch attacks, they did not engage in combat with any of the enemy.

During one interception in the Gulf, barbed wire barricades confronted HMS *Portland*'s Royal Marines, as did hatches that had been welded shut. After securing control of the Iraqi tanker *Vienna*, a search discovered 3,100 tons of contraband diesel fuel. Chief Petty Officer Gary Richardson, who was second-in-command of the *Portland*'s boarding team explained what it had been like to be up the sharp end of such an operation.

> *In each boarding we did in the Gulf, there was an initial team of Royal Marines sent onboard a target ship. In boardings the first stick and second sticks are responsible for securing the vessel while the third is the search team. There were two major takedowns during the deployment, the* Vienna *and another Iraqi vessel, both of them turning out to be illegal oil smugglers.*

The British frigate HMS Portland takes the oil smuggling ship Vienna under tow in the northern Gulf. US Navy.

A Royal Marine in one of *Portland's boarding parties provides protection during training exercises aboard the frigate.* US Navy.

Those two boardings were the experience of my life. The first one, which was the Vienna, *we got on there in the middle of the night. Then they had a problem with their engines and we had to get some of our engineers over to do a temporary fix. This all started about midnight. Then we came off about 6am, but by 6.30am we went back onboard because the engine had gone completely and we had to take the vessel under tow. All the boardings were done by rhibs and that gave you a real buzz, as you came up to the target ship and got ready to climb onboard. You didn't know how the contact vessel would react. The majority of the vessels we boarded were Iraqi and the oil would be secreted in hidden compartments. After putting up a show of trying to evade us, they were quite agreeable and co-operative. Some of them would offer us food and water, although we never took any of it. Even the ones we caught smuggling would be like that. They used to ask to do prayers and we said that was okay so long as they didn't mind having a guard and they were quite happy with that arrangement. There were aspects of the majority of the smuggling vessels that were a bit of a give-away, such as having only slits to see out of where you would expect bridge windows. They would also have a periscope to steer the ship by and I suppose the idea was that they would seal themselves up in there when we came aboard. With the* Vienna *and the other boarding there was a real sense of achievement in capturing illegal oil*

172

cargoes. They were extra exciting, I suppose because we did those two boardings on the move, while others were done in the holding area for merchant ships, while the vessels were at anchor.

As the deployment came to a close, with fifty-six boardings carried out, *Portland's* Commanding Officer, Commander Jonathan Handley, evaluated the risks confronting British boarding parties:

The hazards associated with boarding operations are certainly not to be underestimated. With the additional challenges imposed by the extreme temperatures prevailing in the Gulf, and the fact that boarding operations can take place at night, great care has to be taken at all times by all members of boarding parties. As far as the ship is concerned, good seamanship and predicting the move of the other vessel while not endangering your own is all-important. While it was not the prime focus of our activity we were certainly well aware of the possibility that Al-Qaeda operatives may be moving around by sea within our area of operations. We were therefore continuously vigilant in that regard.

In the summer of 2002, the Iraqis stepped up their embargo-busting efforts, for on 19 July, the Australian frigate HMAS *Arunta* detected sixteen cargo dhows attempting to break out of the Khaur Abdullah Waterway (KAA), between Kuwait and Iraq. Australian teams in the space of just ninety minutes boarded five vessels, that were clearly not complying with the UN sanctions. Four more boardings were carried out over a three-hour period, while other coalition warships took care of a further three. Seeing the warships in their path, the remaining four dhows turned back. Approximately 1,050 metric tonnes of oil was found as a result of the 19 July boardings. During an earlier incident four motor dhows tried to break through the embargo over a twenty-four-hour period but, again, were intercepted by MIF ships, including the British frigate HMS *Argyll*, which had taken over from *Portland*.

A search of one dhow by *Argyll's* boarding team revealed over 300 tonnes of illegal oil. A total of 1,350 tonnes of contraband oil, which was valued at approximately £210,000, was found on three of the dhows while the fourth evaded capture by returning to Iraqi territorial waters.

It was thought that the Iraqis covertly transported around 480,000 barrels of illegal oil a day by various routes, via land as well as sea. Despite the efforts of coalition warships, American defence sources estimated that only a quarter of the total amount smuggled out via sea routes was interdicted.

By the late summer of 2002 the Americans were pushing hard to maintain UN sanctions and get weapons inspectors admitted to Iraq again. But Saddam's spokesmen continued to deny their country was developing nuclear, biological or chemical weapons. By the autumn, with the pace of operations in Afghanistan declining, a single carrier battle group was deployed to the Middle East. In the late summer the *George Washington* had been relieved on station by the *Abraham Lincoln* CBG, which was tasked with operating in support of Operation Enduring Freedom and also enforcing Southern Watch. The *Lincoln* was carrying Carrier Air Wing 14, flying the new F/A-18 E/F Super Hornet strike fighter, which would soon

As she arrives in the Gulf, the USS Abraham Lincoln tells the world she is ready to strike at America's enemies. US Navy.

be in action against the Iraqis.

Dramatic developments still unfolded in the war on terrorism, reminding everyone that the threat remained serious. Earlier that summer, terrorist suspects were arrested in Morocco after their plot, to drive small boats packed with explosives at British and American naval vessels in the Strait of Gibraltar, was uncovered. They hoped the busy waters of the gateway to the Mediterranean would allow warships little room for manoeuvre. Ever since the *Cole's* misfortune, many navies had enhanced their training to counter such a threat and the events of 11 September 2001 had provided fresh impetus. British confidence in terrorist counter-measures was illustrated by the visit of the Royal Navy frigate *Campbeltown* to Aden at the end of June.

The decision to name one of the US Navy's new San Antonio assault ships after the city that suffered so grievously at the hands of Al-Qaeda, was revealed on the first anniversary of the terrorist attacks, by US Secretary of the Navy Gordon England. New York Governor George Pataki thanked Mr England for the decision:

The USS New York *will ensure that all New Yorkers and the world will never forget the evil attacks of September 11. She will also remind people of the courage and compassion New Yorkers showed in response to terror.*

174

CHAPTER NINE

INTO THE GATHERING STORM

I n the Italian naval base at La Spezia, two 680 tons corvettes were slowly rusting away. The *Moussa Ben Noussair* and *Tarek Ben Zaid* had been stranded there after their completion, for over a decade. They were part of a naval procurement order placed with the Fincantieri shipyard by Iraq but, following the invasion of Iran, it had been frozen and that situation remained after the occupation of Kuwait. The Italian government eventually disposed of most of the ships, with the Italian Navy taking delivery of four frigates and some other corvettes sold to Malaysia. However, Saddam had paid for the two stranded warships in 1986, so that, even in late 2002, they were still being kept ticking over by a handful of exiled Iraqi sailors.

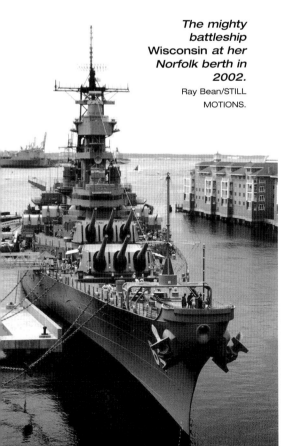

The mighty battleship Wisconsin *at her Norfolk berth in 2002.*

Ray Bean/STILL MOTIONS.

Over the years, Iraq has refused to sell the ships, and Italy isn't embarrassed about hosting their crews, who oil the cogs and polish the brass while patiently waiting to set sail... To save money, they do their own handwashing and hang up their boxer shorts to dry on deck, alongside the Iraqi flag.[1]

On the other side of the world, the 48,425 tons battleship USS *Missouri*, which had last fired her guns in anger at Iraqi troops in Kuwait, was in a different state of suspended animation. She had been removed from the US Navy's reserve fleet at the end of the 1990s and was now a memorial ship at Pearl Harbor, in remembrance of casualties of war. The *Wisconsin*,

175

The USS Constellation *leaves San Diego, bound for the Gulf.* US Navy.

too, had left front line service, but despite being a tourist attraction at Norfolk, Virginia, was, even in late 2002, still listed in the US Navy's Reserve Fleet. She was a 'mobilization asset', which meant the sixty-two-year-old battleship could be a candidate for reactivation and, while unlikely, it was not without precedent. *Wisconsin* had first seen action in the Second World War, in the Pacific, and was taken out of the Reserve Fleet for the Korean War of the 1950s. Decommissioned once more in 1958, *Wisconsin* had remained in mothballs until 1988, when she was reactivated again, as part of President Reagan's regeneration of the American fleet. After her part in the Gulf War, *Wisconsin* was deactivated and mothballed. Access to the battleship was restricted mainly to her exterior, for environmental control systems continued to preserve the interior spaces and equipment.

The likelihood of Wisconsin *being recalled to the active fleet for action against Saddam is, however, slim. Not only would it take too long to restore the ship herself to fighting efficiency, but the assembling of a full-trained new crew might prove problematical. But, still the* Wisconsin *lies in readiness. She is sleeping, but not gone.* [2]

Weapons inspectors had returned to Iraq by the middle of November 2002, following a unanimous vote by the UN Security Council in favour of Resolution 1441, requiring Saddam to prove beyond doubt that he had discarded his remaining WMD. It was the first time since 1998 that such teams had entered the rogue state and American naval units led a build-up in the Middle East to back up the inspectors' actions with a credible threat of force.

At the beginning a November the *Constellation* and her CBG had departed the west coast of the USA while, on the east coast, the *Harry S. Truman* CBG was reportedly also being made ready for action against Iraq. Other preparations included the chartering of two Australian high-speed catamarans by the US Department of Defense, to help transport troops and tanks. Already deployed in the Gulf, and contributing strike jets to the on going Anglo-American air campaign to degrade Iraqi air defences, was the *Abraham Lincoln*. In early November, the US Navy blooded the F/A-18E Super Hornet, in a raid launched from the *Lincoln* in response to hostile acts by Iraqi air-defences against US and UK aircraft. Precision-guided weapons were used to hit two SAM systems and a command bunker near Al-Kut, approximately 100 miles south of Baghdad. The assault carrier *Belleau Wood*, and her ARG, carrying the 11th MEU, was also up threat in the northern Gulf, with the marines using exercise areas on Faylakah Island, where they came under attack more than once from suspected Al-Qaeda terrorists. By autumn, some 800 US Marines were also deployed in the Horn of Africa, supported by the USS *Nassau* ARG and the command ship USS *Mount Whitney*, the latter carrying elements of the 2nd Marine Division and II Marine Expeditionary Force (II MEF), under Major General John F. Sattler. Meanwhile, across the Bab Al Mandab, the narrow stretch of water that separates the Horn of Africa from Arabia, a CIA-led operation employed an unmanned air vehicle armed with Hellfire missiles, to destroy a car allegedly carrying an Al-Qaeda terrorist suspected of organizing the attack on the *Cole*. This strike came a few weeks after a French oil tanker was badly holed off Aden, by terrorists using a small boat packed with explosives. In Afghanistan, attacks by residual elements of Al-Qaeda and the Taliban were on the rise. In mid-November, a US Marine Corps Harrier AV-8B strike jet provided air support after terrorists launched two 107mm rockets, mortar rounds and a rocket-propelled grenade at Allied troops. Paratroopers from the US Army's 82nd Airborne Division, who subsequently searched the area, came under fire and strike jets were again called in during sporadic firefights. Operations were being conducted within the framework of a new US strategy, recently outlined by President Bush, which advocated pre-emptive strikes against terrorists and rogue states. In late November, US Deputy Defense Secretary Paul D. Wolfowitz said that continuing to contain Saddam was not an attractive option.

> *The one risk that it seems to me to be highly exaggerated, is this risk that the removal of the Saddam Hussein regime would be a cause of instability in the region. To the contrary, that regime itself is a major cause of instability in the region.*

In early December, CENTCOM, which was now commanded by US Army General Tommy Franks, deployed a Tactical Operations Center (TOC) from its HQ in Tampa, Florida, to Qatar. Ostensibly a long-planned exercise aimed at testing the TOC's communications capabilities across the CENTCOM area of operations, it would, conveniently, place several hundred key personnel in theatre to oversee military action against Iraq, should the arms inspections fail to yield the desired results.

By early December 2002, the Iraqis were obliged to deliver to the United Nations

Spanish marines rapid-rope onto the deck of the So San, to search for weapons of mass destruction. Via US DoD.

a full declaration of WMD and measures taken to dispose of them. When it came, the document's many thousands of pages proved not to provide the necessary incontrovertible proof needed. In December, as the UN considered this incomplete declaration in New York, in the Indian Ocean the Spanish Navy chased a ship suspected of carrying WMD, which US intelligence agencies had been tracking since it departed a North Korean port in mid-November. At dawn on 7 December, the frigate SPS *Navarra* intercepted the freighter *So San*, 600 miles off the Horn of Africa. The captain of the ship, which had its name painted out, refused to comply with SPS *Navarra*'s radio request for a boarding and also ignored an order to reduce speed. This prompted the frigate to fire warning shots across *So San*'s bows and Spanish marines conducted a boarding from *Navarra*'s helicopter. A search by the marines and American teams revealed fifteen disassembled Scud missiles hidden under bags of cement. It turned out she was headed for the Yemen, but there were concerns the Scuds could later be taken to Libya or Iraq. However, the Yemeni government demanded their return and, as the North Koreans turned out to have sold them within international law, the ship and weapons were released.

As December drew to a close, the *Kitty Hawk* returned to her base in Japan from a seven week deployment, to give her sailors and marines some Christmas leave and enable the ship herself to receive maintenance. The US Navy's only permanently forward-deployed aircraft carrier, based at Yokosuka, *Kitty Hawk* was tasked with ensuring stability in the Asia-Pacific region through training and exercises with regional allies. The *Kitty Hawk* and her escort ships were also tasked as America's so-called '9-11 Battle Group', available to respond to any major threats to US security and that could include action against Iraq.

In early January 2003, the USS *Tarawa* ARG departed San Diego and headed across the Pacific towards Arabia.

There's a sense of something both important and urgent these days aboard

USS Tarawa. *As the amphibious assault ship steams westward through the Pacific Ocean... The flight deck is more active than usual, as embarked Marines from the 15th Marine Expeditionary Unit practice small arms fire. Meanwhile, almost daily, the crew trains at general quarters and fire-fighting drills. In the hangar bay, it's not uncommon to see mechanics working fervently to fix a broken item or replace a part. Gun mounts, where the 25mm chain guns sat quietly for a long time in port, now buzz with watches around the clock. The tempo of everything seems to have increased...Since departing San Diego Jan. 6, they have steamed for three straight weeks, underscoring the sense of importance behind this deployment. 'What this crew may face in the near future cannot be understated,' said Tarawa Commanding Officer Capt. Jay Bowling. 'They watch the news, they know what's going on. They sense the urgency and the importance of what's ahead'.*[3]

If it came to war, the 15th MEU's 2,000 marines, four Main Battle Tanks and support helicopters, including Cobra gunships, were destined to fight alongside Britain's 4,000-strong 3 Commando Brigade Royal Marines. In fact, part of the UK formation's 40 Commando had been on exercise with the USMC in California's Mojave desert in December. Aboard HMS *Ocean* at Devonport, in the south-west of England, as the helicopter carrier prepared to set sail in early January, 40 Commando's CO, Lieutenant Colonel Gordon Messenger, considered what might lie ahead.

There is no blood lust...everyone is aware that this is a contingency operation and we will probably return having done nothing. In terms of preparation, we are making sure our equipment could be used in anger if need be, while hoping that it won't be necessary. But we are prepared for every eventuality, which is our job as a Commando in the Royal Marines.

The 40 Commando marines were coming aboard *Ocean* barely a year after they had been on the front line in the war on terrorism, as Britain's first troops into Kabul. For, after the earlier debacle at Bagram Airport, the Northern Alliance had consented to allowing Royal Marines to police the streets of the Afghan capital. Now, with a full-scale war-fighting role potentially ahead, the 625-strong Commando was being augmented with artillery, engineer and logistics support assigned from within 3 Commando Brigade. Three hundred marines were to sail in *Ocean*, while the rest of the 40 Commando Group would go from Southampton in RFA landing ships. Lieutenant Colonel Messenger was asked how his elite troops would cope with being cooped up while diplomats and UN inspectors made one last effort to find a peaceful solution.

We are used to being at sea for fairly extended periods. So, it is not a problem. I have no doubt we will be able to keep our edge.

As he prepared to set sail, rather than trying to see into the future, *Ocean*'s CO, Captain Adrian Johns, preferred to concentrate on how he would get the carrier back up to full efficiency after a recent refit in Portsmouth.

My orders extend to the Mediterranean where we will participate in exercises. I am not going to speculate about anything East of Suez.

179

When pressed further about his feelings, Captain Johns observed:

> *The mood on the ship is positive and upbeat, but there is an undercurrent of sober reflection too... .*

Six Lynx helicopters fitted with anti-tank missile systems and machine guns, together with six Gazelle scout helicopters, both of 847 Naval Air Squadron (NAS), were embarked prior to departure from Devonport, while ten Sea King troop transport 'copters of 845 NAS flew on at sea. The *Ocean* left Plymouth just days after the *Ark Royal* had sailed out of Portsmouth. This time the *Ark* was destined to go all the way up-threat in the Gulf, rather than being held in the eastern Mediterranean, as had happened in 1991. The *Ark*'s departure was recorded by veteran maritime photo-journalist Jonathan Eastland, who had been there two decades earlier when other ships set sail into a gathering storm.

> *On a cold and bright winter's afternoon, the Royal Navy's Fleet Flagship set sail, gliding past thousands of well-wishers lining the Hot Wall ramparts of Old Portsmouth. Grid-lock had brought the Hampshire naval city to a standstill as saturation news coverage of HMS* Ark Royal's *imminent departure worked up a level of interest unprecedented in recent years. Those who had managed to make it to a vantage point stood stoically subdued for an hour or more - some had staked their positions before dawn - waiting patiently and uncertainly for another page in British maritime history to turn. This was not like the noisy send-off for the task force that sailed for the Falklands War twenty years previously. In 2003, a radio reporter failed to spark an enthusiastic 'three cheers' as the* Ark *cracked on speed through the harbour's narrow entrance channel. Mostly, people watched in silence. A few whistles here, a Union flag waver there, a plaintive question from a five-year-old - 'When is daddy coming back?' - to his mother who was sobbing quietly*

Aboard HMS Ocean, as she prepares to leave Devonport, a Lynx attack helicopter belonging to 847 NAS is taken up by lift onto the flight deck of the carrier. Nigel Andrews.

Upper decks filled with marines and sailors, the Ocean leaves Plymouth.
Tony Carney.

behind me. A young Liverpudlian Wren told reporters who visited the carrier the day before the ship set sail: 'Well, there might be a war...but there again, there might not.' You could almost hear the News Editor of the TV station yelling in frustration: 'Is that the best we can do!?' Beneath the surface of the nose-blowing, hanky-wringing, over-sentimental coverage provided by the media, it was clear that the sailors and marines of the Royal Navy were setting off on a deployment in which they would do their job - whether it was exercising with Asia-Pacific fleets or launching an amphibious assault on Iraq - with customary British professionalism and phlegmatism. Of little interest to a media voracious for matelot angst were hard facts, such as the Royal Navy being the only other fleet, aside from the mighty USN, able to field

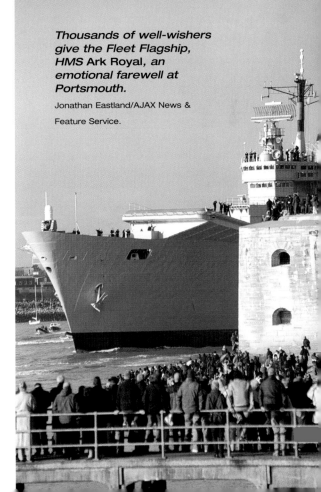

Thousands of well-wishers give the Fleet Flagship, HMS Ark Royal, an emotional farewell at Portsmouth.
Jonathan Eastland/AJAX News & Feature Service.

an Amphibious Ready Group at all... Another 'fact' hammered home relentlessly by the media was that this was Britain's biggest task force since the Falklands War of 1982. This was not strictly correct - a force of equal capability and size was already on its way to the Middle East in 2001 when Al-Qaeda struck New York and Washington D.C. None of us who were there on that bright morning in early September 2001, to witness a more low-key departure by the then Fleet Flagship, HMS Illustrious, could have guessed what a difference fourteen months would make.[4]

The *Ark Royal* had returned from an exercise in the Mediterranean in early November and, after a maintenance period in Portsmouth, was anyway due to leave for a timely Far East deployment called Naval Task Group 2003 (NTG 03). Already deployed to the Gulf was the destroyer HMS *Cardiff*, conducting UN sanctions enforcement operations against Iraq. A Royal Navy Mine Counter-Measures group composed of four ships - *Brocklesby*, *Sandown*, *Bangor* and *Blyth* - was exercising with Saudi Arabian naval units. The survey vessel HMS *Roebuck* was there too and could be expected to act as the MCMVs' tasking ship in any war.

In a House of Commons statement, delivered on 7 January, UK Secretary of State for Defence Geoff Hoon explained the rationale behind the substantial British naval deployment.

While we want Saddam Hussein to disarm voluntarily, it is evident that we will not achieve this unless we continue to present him with a clear and credible threat of force.... .

In addition to *Ark Royal*, the scheduled NTG 2003 deployment consisted of the destroyer *Liverpool*, frigate *Marlborough* and the RFA supply vessel *Fort Victoria*.

The attack submarine *Splendid*, armed with cruise missiles, was also believed to be part of the task group.

The RFA tankers *Orangeleaf* and *Oakleaf* were already in the Mediterranean. To ensure the Royal Navy could field a fully-formed amphibious force, and protect it, *Ocean* plus the destroyers *Edinburgh* and *York* had been added. Being sent as part of the ARG with *Ocean* were the Landing Ships Logistic *Sir Tristram*, *Sir Galahad*, and *Sir Percivale*. Another Middle East veteran, the supply ship *Fort Rosalie* and her sister ship, *Fort Austin*, were soon heading for the Gulf. Two further mine warfare ships - *Grimsby* and *Ledbury* - were also deployed from the UK in support of NTG 03.

Attached to the task force, while not being acknowledged as officially part of it, were the frigates *Cornwall*, sailing in support of NTG 03, probably to escort merchant vessels carrying military equipment, and *Northumberland*, which was to sail with it on her way to conducting counter-terror operations with NATO's Standing Naval Force Mediterranean (SNFM). The aviation training vessel *Argus* was deployed as a Primary Casualty Reception Ship, repeating the role she fulfilled off Kuwait in 1991. A further three RFA ships were already in the Gulf: The tanker *Bayleaf*, assigned on a permanent basis to support Royal Navy and allied patrol ships; the battle damage repair vessel *Diligence*; the modified landing ship *Sir Bedivere*, acting as a support ship for the MCMVs.

The frigate *Chatham* left Devonport around the same time as *Ocean*, heading out

182

The frigate Chatham *receives a patriotic send-off from Plymouth.*
Tony Carney.

to relieve sister ship, *Cumberland*, as part of the Spanish-led Task Force 150 counter-terrorist force in the Indian Ocean. If the shooting started, *Chatham* could easily be withdrawn and deployed into the Gulf.

It was significant that Rear Admiral David Snelson, the incumbent UK Maritime Component Commander (UKMCC), forward based at the US Navy headquarters in Bahrain, would command NTG 03. Rear Admiral Snelson's staff were already tightly integrated within the US command structure that would run any naval war and he was, like his predecessors, deputy coalition naval commander.

I was in on the planning from the beginning, and I was able to an extent to influence the American maritime plans. We worked together an awful lot with the Americans, and with the Australians, and so integrating with them was, I suspect, much easier than it was in the 1991 Gulf War.

It was anticipated that the primary mission of the British task force would be to act as a launch pad for an amphibious assault by units of 3 Commando Brigade and in his January statement to the House of Commons, Mr Hoon told MPs:

We plan to deploy amphibious forces in Ark Royal, Ocean *and associated shipping, including Headquarters 3 Commando Brigade, 40 Commando Royal Marines and 42 Commando Royal Marines with supporting elements...None of this means that the use of force is inevitable. And despite the speculation that will arise as a result of these announcements today, it remains the case that no decision has been taken to commit these forces to action. But, as I said on the 18th of December, as long as Saddam's compliance with UNSCR 1441 is in doubt, as it continues to be at present,*

183

the threat of force must remain and it must be a real one.

The decision not to deploy Sea Harrier FA2 fighters or Harrier GR7 strike jets in *Ark* caused considerable dismay in some circles. Sharkey Ward, who knew both the capabilities of the Sea Harrier and the threats posed in the Gulf, was among the critics.

> *In the particular scenario likely to confront the Allies in 2003, the Royal Navy should be able to rely on the US Navy for air-defence for most of the time, but it will have left behind its own dedicated 'eyes' and 'teeth'. Having to rely on allies for major capabilities, even friends as well-trained and equipped as the Americans, still represents a big gamble. It is easy to understand, however, that, with the Navy budget getting squeezed more each day, and probably not enough sailors available to send a second carrier devoted to fixed-wing fighters, the top brass of the Royal Navy had to cross its fingers and put its trust in the US Navy.*

Some defence pundits expressed concerns that the British task force would be far too exposed to the considerable air threat still posed by Saddam's air force and sea-skimming missiles, both of which could be eliminated by the FA2. However, the UK had no realistic short-term alternative to leaving the Harriers behind. The British ARG lacked an additional major assault platform from which to launch helicopters carrying troops. The brand new assault ships *Bulwark* and *Albion* had not yet entered service and therefore the answer was to use one of the Invincible class carriers in her secondary role. The *Ark Royal* was the only suitable ship currently available. The *Illustrious*, which had performed the helicopter carrier role in the Arabian Sea in 2001, had just entered another major refit at Rosyth Dockyard in Scotland, while the third Royal Navy carrier, *Invincible*, had completed a refit, but was on sea trials and would not return to the front line until the spring of 2003. However, the US Navy and US Marine Corps had more than enough strike jets and fighters to handle air-defence and ground attack. So, although both the FA2 and GR7 were extremely capable, they would not bring anything to the party that the coalition's lead force could not provide. What the USA valued and needed, above all else, was the amphibious assault experience of the Royal Navy and its high quality Royal Marines.

On arriving in the Gulf, where she immediately became part of the US Navy's 5th Fleet, the *Constellation* - 'America's Flagship' - had received a visit from the straight-talking senior officer who would control her in any campaign to depose Saddam Hussein. Vice Admiral Timothy J. Keating, Commander, US Naval Forces Central Command and 5th Fleet, addressed all hands at a meeting held in *Constellation's* Hangar Bay 1.

> *You're trained, aggressive, willing and ready...Now let's go out and do what it is we came to do.*

Within days of arriving in the Gulf, the *Constellation's* jets carried out air strikes on targets in southern Iraq. Other ships assigned to the *Constellation* CBG in early January included the cruiser *Valley Forge*; guided-missile destroyers, *Milius* and *Higgins*; destroyer, *Kinkaid*; frigate *Thach* and the attack submarine *Columbia*. The

Kinkaid was ordered home in the second week of January to decommission, but her crew was due to make an immediate return to the theatre of operations. Instead of being dispersed throughout the fleet, the *Kinkaid*'s sailors were flown to Perth, Australia, to carry out a sea swap with the crew of another Spruance class destroyer, the *Fletcher*. The *Fletcher* had just stood-down from the Gulf, where she had been up-threat, leading the MIF during which she carried its CO, Captain Peter Jones of the Royal Australian Navy.

Also in Australia was the *Abraham Lincoln*, originally due to head back to the USA in mid-January. However, with the real possibility of combat, the *Lincoln*'s deployment was extended and so she pulled into Perth instead of heading home. An Australian Defence Ministry source revealed that the US Navy carrier would conduct 'routine repairs' and her flight deck would be resurfaced.

A number of the carrier's embarked aircraft were sent to an airbase and from there conducted bombing practice on a nearby range. Back in the USA, the USS *Boxer* ARG left for the Gulf while the USS *Iwo Jima* ARG completed pre-deployment work-up and would be available to carry the 26th MEU, in early February.

As all this military hardware was sailing, or being readied to set sail, UN inspectors were continuing their fruitless search for WMD, but hopes of a peaceful settlement were fading fast. The declaration documents provided by Iraq had been a massive miscalculation by the ruling regime, which

The destroyer USS Fletcher, *which for a time led the coalition naval force that kept the lid on Saddam's oil smuggling activities.* US Navy.

tried once too often to bluff its way out of a tight corner. Saddam's prime objective appeared to be providing the minimum amount of cooperation needed to enable the UN inspection process to delay military action indefinitely. However, the USA, which considered the flawed arms declaration documentation to have been a material breach of Resolution 1441, was probably not going to wait much longer before setting a military campaign in motion. In addition to CBGs and ARGs, the hospital ship *Comfort* had been sent to the Gulf, an ominous sign. The US Marine

Corps' I Marine Expeditionary Force's (I MEF's) HQ element had been ordered to Kuwait at the end of 2002 to begin planning and, in the second week of January, the rest of the I MEF began moving to the Middle East. Senior military sources estimated that a total of 75,000 US Marines would be involved in any action against Iraq, out of an overall total of at least 150,000 US sailors, soldiers, airmen and marines.

It was expected that the first wave of attacks would involve precision-strikes by US Navy warships and submarines (plus Royal Navy boats) launching TLAMs from the Gulf and Red Sea, and possibly even the eastern Mediterranean. At least 250 cruise missiles were thought to be in the US Navy's Middle East arsenal by mid-January. As the time for talking ran out, the US Navy's Chief of Naval Operations, Admiral Vern Clark, visited the *Constellation* to give her sailors a boost with a strident pep talk. 'Remember, the American people are watching you,' the CNO told his sailors.

> *Be ready to go write some history...If the call comes and if the President says do this...then do it. Hit fast, hit hard, hit with precision.*

Prior to heading through the Suez Canal, the British task force had only paused in waters off Cyprus, to allow its Royal Marines to carry out amphibious assaults using beaches and training areas in UK Sovereign Bases on the island. As marines from 40 Commando completed their training, the CO of the unit's Alpha Company, Major Justin Holt, observed:

> *We are as ready as anyone. We have prepared for the worst and hope for the best.*[5]

Liaison teams from the US Marine Corps had been training hard with UK commando units both on Cyprus and in the UK. By this time the Tomahawk-armed attack submarine HMS *Turbulent* had been diverted to join the task group.

Having deployed East of Suez in the summer of 2002, in support of the war on terrorism, *Turbulent* now found herself required to prepare for possible cruise missile firings. 'Having spent the Christmas holiday in Singapore, we went to Diego Garcia to top up our numbers of TLAMs,' explained *Turbulent*'s CO, Commander Andrew McKendrick.

> *Going into the Gulf in mid-February,* Turbulent *went alongside in Bahrain, where security was extremely tight, for general briefings about the situation. Exactly where we would end up and what we would be doing was not known.*

Meanwhile, at Pearl Harbor, the American TLAM-armed attack submarine USS *Key West* had sailed out past the *Missouri* on 24 January, also, ostensibly, on a deployment in support of the war on terrorism but available for 'possible contingencies elsewhere in the world'. [6]

The *Key West* had been one of the first American naval units ready for action in the Arabian Sea after the terrorist attacks of 11 September 2001 and now she was destined to be in the vanguard of the war to remove Saddam from power. The *Key West*'s CO, Commander Chuck Merkel, said, as his boat prepared to leave:

> *The crew is ready and excited to go out again and complete anything our nation requires.*

The assault carrier USS Bataan, her flight deck packed with aircraft, makes an impressive sight as she steams at high speed across the Mediterranean, to make her passage south through the Suez Canal. US Navy.

Meanwhile, the steady flow of Allied naval hardware through the Suez Canal showed no sign of stopping. Trailing astern of the Royal Navy ships was another TLAM-armed US Navy attack submarine, the *Montpelier*.

And, as February began, America's ATF East, composed of seven ships carrying more than 4,750 sailors and 7,000 marines from the 2nd Marine Expeditionary Brigade (2nd MEB), took its turn to go through the canal. The assault carriers *Kearsarge*, *Bataan* and *Saipan* spearheaded ATF East and on guard aboard the *Bataan* was marine Corporal Chris Coger. 'Any time we get into a choke point, the ship becomes an easy target,' he said, as he watched the desert landscape beyond, his M16 rifle at the ready. To his left and right sailors manned .50 cal and M-60 machine guns. Everyone in the ATF's ships was at full alert despite the Canal Zone being heavily guarded by the Egyptian Army. 'I know I'm in an uncertain environment,' said Corporal Coger.

I saw a guy on the shore pointing his thumbs down at us. It makes me feel unwelcome.

The morning after the ATF East ships exited the canal, US Secretary of State Colin Powell went to the UN in New York, to make his case for tough action against Iraq. Secretary Powell wasted no time in providing what he felt was compelling evidence. A few minutes into his presentation, he played a tape alleged to be a recording of a conversation between two senior Republican Guard officers about removal of weapons, the day before UN inspectors resumed their activities. 'We evacuated everything,' one officer reassured the other. In another taped conversation Secretary Powell played, one Iraqi officer told another to make sure he had cleaned out all the ammunition and scrap storage areas and then destroyed his written instructions.

187

'This effort to hide things from inspectors is not one or two isolated events,' Secretary Powell told the UN.

> Quite the contrary. This is part and parcel of a policy of evasion and deception that goes back 12 years, a policy set at the highest levels of the Iraqi regime.

After outlining what the USA believed to be the terrifying scale of WMD amassed in secret, and the Iraqi dictator's continuing ambition to acquire nuclear capability, Secretary Powell closed his presentation in dramatic style.

> For more than twenty years, by word and by deed, Saddam Hussein has pursued his ambition to dominate Iraq and the broader Middle East using the only means he knows - intimidation, coercion and annihilation of all those who might stand in his way. For Saddam Hussein, possession of the world's most deadly weapons is the ultimate trump card, the one he must hold to fulfil his ambition.

The former US Army general concluded:

> We must not shrink from whatever is ahead of us. We must not fail in our duty and our responsibility for the citizens of the countries that are represented by this body.

During a visit to Mayport Naval Base in Florida, President Bush told American sailors: 'In this challenging period for our country, great tasks lie ahead for the Navy and for our entire military. And I know we can depend on you, because this United States military is second to none.'

The President told the sailors that the USA and her allies were being called on to defeat a new kind of enemy.

> This enemy reaches across oceans. It targets the innocent. There are no rules of war for these cold-blooded killers. They seek biological and chemical and nuclear weapons to commit murder on a massive scale. This enemy will not be restrained by mercy or by conscience, but this enemy will be stopped.

President Bush said he believed the gravest danger America and the world faced was the threat from 'outlaw regimes' that seek or possess WMD.

However, the majority of the international community favoured multi-lateral action through the UN, with war avoided at all costs. Around the world there were massive anti-war demonstrations and, with news coverage pumped into their ships, the sailors and marines could not ignore them. Aboard HMS *Ocean*, the Royal Marines watched the TV news and tried to put any misgivings it created to the backs of their minds. Sergeant Pete Baldwin of 40 Commando's Bravo Company was of the opinion that what would matter most in the days to come would be not letting his brother marines down.

> There are concerns among the lads that people are not fully supportive back home. But the rights and wrongs of things is not something that people discuss here very much. It's not very helpful. What we care about is doing what we are paid to do to the very best of our ability and not letting our mates down when it really counts.

Although France was doing its best on the diplomatic front to slow down the Anglo-

US momentum towards war, in early March it had ordered its *Charles de Gaulle* CBG to the eastern Mediterranean, where it called in at a NATO naval base on the Greek island of Crete. France justified a naval presence within striking distance of the war zone by declaring that it might order a military intervention if Saddam used WMD against coalition troops.

Meanwhile Russia, another major international player with huge business interests in Iraq, but similarly against military action, abandoned its plans to send warships on an observation mission into the Gulf. As time for diplomacy ran out, Russia joined Germany and France in trying to seize control of the crisis agenda, by putting forward propositions to increase UN weapons inspectors inside Iraq, and providing reconnaissance planes to try and detect WMD.

But, America's National Security Adviser Condoleeza Rice called time on Saddam and, during a tough-talking interview, stated:

> *What we need now ...is for the world to unify and to stop talking about whether we should go to war, whether we shouldn't go to war, and to say to Saddam Hussein, "It is time"....People have a right to protest; people can say what they think. The fact of the matter is that they're not saying what they think in Baghdad, because that's a regime that cuts people's tongues out if they say what they think. It would be worthwhile to step back to remember the true nature of the Iraqi regime...how they rape and torture...kill women in front of their families to make a point...to remember that Saddam is acquiring and has acquired Weapons of Mass Destruction...that he's used chemical weapons on his own population and his neighbours. And ask yourself: 'Do you really want this regime to go unchallenged for the next 12 years, as we've done for the past 12 years?'.*

During a visit to the USA to discuss war plans, UK Secretary of State for Defence Geoff Hoon told a Pentagon news conference:

> *I certainly think we have understood the threat in Iraq for longer, in a more detailed way, than many of our European allies have done.*

With its destroyer and frigate force cut back by successive governments to thirty-two warships, there were barely enough major Royal Navy surface combatants available for protecting the task force, its auxiliaries and the more than sixty merchant ships that were chartered to take the UK's 1st Armoured Division to the Gulf. The assistance of allies, some of whom were not officially in the coalition, was therefore vital.

Spain and Italy, which supported military action against Saddam overtly on the political stage, maintained a low-profile naval presence. The Spanish deployed two frigates to patrol waters around the vital choke point of the Strait of Gibraltar, to guard against possible suicide boat attacks by extremists sympathetic to Iraq. NATO's own Standing Naval Force Atlantic (SNFL) would play its part too, commencing escort work through the same choke point in early 2003, supported by not only the Spanish forces but also US Navy and Portuguese units.

> *We have to maintain security in the area and to secure the safe transit of designated ships. The Strait of Gibraltar operation is a purely escort task. We*

are meeting merchant ships in deep water and taking them through a potential danger area prior to releasing them in the Mediterranean or the Atlantic Ocean.[7]

A Spanish warship also joined naval vessels from Italy and France in the Red Sea, again to guard lines of communication. The Canadian and German navies maintained a strong presence in the Indian Ocean as part of the war on terrorism, but would not be involved in coalition action against Iraq as their governments were opposed to it. However, with careful management of resources, the Royal Navy had still managed to boost its activities around Gibraltar and Cyprus where patrol craft policed territorial waters and surface warships made their presence felt from time-to-time.

A close watching brief had been kept on Iraqi Silkworm and Seersucker ASM launchers situated in the al-Faw Peninsula. This was essential to protect the coalition Maritime Interdiction Force (MIF) ships that operated close in to the Iraqi coast and, for example, in early February 1999, in the wake of Operation Desert Fox, precision-guided munitions had been used to destroy a Silkworm battery. Another ASM site had been hit on 7 September 2002 '...after its radar reportedly tried to lock onto a US warship off Kuwait.'[8]

The remaining Iraqi ASM launchers were now being hit hard by coalition air strikes because, in the words of a CENTCOM spokesman, they were 'threatening coalition maritime forces.' The decision to start eliminating this threat was seen as

Aboard the guided-missile destroyer USS *Higgins* in the northern Gulf, bridge team sailors man the helm while conducting general quarters drills. US Navy.

a necessary precaution, ahead of deployment into the Gulf of the main body of the armada assembled by America and Britain. The MIF's activities close in to Iraq, and even up the Shatt al-Arab and Khawr Abd Allah waterways, helped ensure that the Iraqi maritime forces stood little chance of causing serious problems for the coalition. Having recently been based in the destroyer USS *Milius*, the MIF's commander had moved to the Australian assault ship HMAS *Kanimbla* once she arrived in the Gulf. The force under Captain Jones' command by then included a naval vessel from Poland, the logistics support ship ORP *Kontradmiral Xawery Czernicki*, as well as the usual contributions from the Royal Australian Navy, US Navy and Royal Navy. With combat operations likely in the near future, Captain Jones explained how the MIF had kept a very tight lid on the northern Gulf.

> *The aim of the MIF is to have ships stationed at both the mouth of the Khawr Ab'd Allah waterway, or KAA, and in a UN Inspection Area, 24 hours a day, seven days a week. In addition we will have ships in the midfield to provide a tiered capability. Over the last year the constant pressure exerted by the MIF on smugglers has resulted in the virtual drying up of the illegal tanker trade coming out of the KAA. As a result most of the illegal traffic is cargo dhows. Typically 20 or 30 dhows will attempt a night escape, but a 70-dhow breakout is not unusual.* [9]

Observing from the UK, Gulf War Royal Navy commander Chris Craig had been relieved by the pursuance of this strategy.

> *There will be no field of 1,800 sea mines laid unobserved over five months.*

He thought the prospects for success were good:

> *... provided the Alliance deploys an appropriate force-level, retains some Security Council legitimacy, sidesteps wimpish 'allies' and continues to strive for some form of international consensus, then Saddam and his super weapon ambitions can be swiftly removed and a semi-democratic regime established. It is a big task to contemplate, even with the most favourable conditions. But if, in the process, the West gains a more secure oil supply for its greedy economies, then I for one will be illiberally delighted...but, it is possible to say that only one thing is certain: Events, when they finally unfold, will serve to prove that retired military men often make lousy forecasters.* [10]

But others back in the UK, with far less experience of the reality of combat operations in Arabia, sought to criticize the Royal Navy for even contemplating sending its carriers into the northern Gulf. They considered the Silkworms and Seersuckers, mines and the suicide boat danger precluded such a deployment. A letter in the *Daily Telegraph* newspaper even labelled the decision to send *Ark Royal* into the Gulf a decision by men who knew nothing about war. Having lost his ship, HMS *Ardent*, to air attack during the 1982 Falklands War, the incumbent First Sea Lord, Admiral Sir Alan West, was obviously not guilty of such a patently ridiculous accusation.

> *I know all about risk. If you are talking about air threats, the loss of my ship in the Falklands is a good example of a situation where we deployed warships ill-equipped for the dangers they would face. However, the Government and the senior Admirals of the day decided it was a risk worth*

taking. I know very well that taking risks in a war situation can mean dead people. There is always an element of risk. It is the game we are in. Carriers can operate in the Gulf. Two Invincible class ships carried out deployments in the northern Gulf in the late 1990s and the US Navy operates much bigger carriers than ours in there. A latent mine risk exists...Iraq still has residual anti-shipping missile capability and an air force that might try to exert itself over the sea. The threat of suicide boat attack is present beyond the Gulf, never mind in it, as we saw when the USS Cole was attacked in Aden. HMS Campbeltown visited Aden last year because the risk assessment was such that we decided it could happen. It is all about balancing risk with the capabilities you can deploy to reduce it - air-defence destroyers that can shoot down missiles and planes, mine warfare ships, measures to counter suicide boat attack. In the case of the Gulf in 2003, you also look at what the US Navy will have in terms of layered defence. The secret to our success in the Gulf War of 1991, where we faced the same range of threats, was our experience in the Falklands, where the RN learned some hard lessons. That still applies today. [11]

With no progress being made via the United Nations route by the second week of March, it was clear that the coalition's awesome military power would have to be unleashed.

Incredibly, even at this late stage there were, at the highest level of government in the UK, those who suggested it might be possible to support the USA politically, while holding back a military contribution until after the fighting, when peace-keeping forces would be needed.

This uncertainty percolated down to the troops on the ground in the Gulf, including the CO of 3 Commando Brigade, Brigadier Jim Dutton.

But the possibility that the Americans might go it alone militarily receded during the last fortnight and it became clear then that a full Anglo-American operation was about to be launched.

While the amphibious ships and carriers of the US Navy and Royal Navy took up their assault positions in the Gulf, the *Harry S. Truman* and *Theodore Roosevelt* CBGs were held in the eastern Mediterranean. Their aircraft were supposed to use Turkish airspace to reach targets in Iraq once the attack order had been given. However, Turkey's government was reluctant to provide help to the coalition. Having barred the US Army's 4th Infantry Division from landing at its ports, to assemble for an invasion of Iraq from the north, permission to use Turkish airspace for fighter jets and cruise missiles had also been refused by Ankara. The *Truman* and the *Roosevelt*, therefore, stood ready to transfer to the Red Sea. Pressure was maintained on Turkey, which was being awkward because it feared war could seriously damage its economy. Also, some NATO allies who were against any military action had blocked the sending of extra air-defence missiles to protect Turkey from Saddam's Scuds.

While the forty ships carrying the 4th Infantry Division's heavy equipment continued to hover in the eastern Mediterranean, in case the northern front could be opened after all, the *Roosevelt* and *Truman* kept themselves at combat pitch. The *Truman*'s sailors and aircrews worked intensive shifts of between twelve and eighteen hours, while her chaplains and an embarked psychologist were busy providing advice on stress and anger management.

Aboard the *Roosevelt*, pilots and most of the crew were ordered to rest during the day, so they would be fresh for night operations against Iraq. Elsewhere in the warship, senior officers including Rear Admiral John Harvey, Commander of Cruiser-Destroyer Group Eight, worked on their contingency plans.

> *You have a Navy to support the diplomacy. If it works, then fine, we leave and go somewhere else.*

But if war was necessary, Rear Admiral Harvey was confident his ships and sailors were ready and willing. The admiral's confidence was boosted by the fact that the majority of the sailors aboard the *Roosevelt* and other ships under his command were veterans of the air campaign against the Taliban and Al-Qaeda. The massive anti-war demonstrations against military action, that had been held around the world, did not bother him and he was not worried about his sailors' morale.

> *I get around the ship quite a bit and I would say morale is just fine. One of the unique things about the American sailor is that they will talk directly to you no matter who you are, so I think I get a lot of honest feedback. You have got to understand one thing when dealing with American sailors or servicemen - they grow up in a society where people march and carry signs over all kinds of things - it comes with democracy. It's OK. Those are rights guaranteed under our freedom of speech and assembly. We have all taken an oath of office to the US; we'll do the right thing for the US today.*

And, with huge advances in military technology achieved in the years since the 1991 Gulf War, Rear Admiral Harvey was sure that his men and women had the best tools for the job.

> *We have great confidence - not arrogance - in the ability of our ships to do exactly whatever is needed.* [12]

Riding shotgun on the *Roosevelt* was the destroyer USS *Winston S. Churchill*, which, from her launch in 1999, had been a symbol of the so-called special

The USS Harry S. Truman *departs Suda Bay, Crete, in early 2003.* US Navy.

relationship forged between the USA and UK during two world wars and other military campaigns. A Royal Navy officer had plotted the *Churchill*'s course to the Mediterranean, for it was traditional for the vessel to carry a UK officer in the post of Navigator, at the time Lieutenant Stuart Yates, who reflected:

> To have been chosen to navigate another nation's warship and be the RN's 'ambassador' is a humbling thought. I never imagined serving onboard a USN warship but my contribution and role is no different than if I was serving onboard a Royal Navy warship. Throughout my naval career I have continuously trained for the eventuality of going to war, knowing that when I got the call, I would be ready both mentally and professionally.'

In the *Roosevelt*, Hornet pilot Lieutenant Jonathan Biehl considered that going to war would be the pinnacle of his career.

> I feel confident that I am ready to do whatever I am asked to do. This will be my first time flying in actual combat and so I am a bit anxious because I haven't done it before and, obviously, I don't want to mess it up. But from the experience I have had in training, I think I will be so busy, and I will be concentrating so hard, that I won't have time to think about the fear factor or not being able to perform. [13]

While it might only have a few ramshackle attack craft and auxiliaries left, the Iraqi Navy could still cause problems, as happened around three days before the Allies opened operations against Iraq. There was a clash between a Kuwaiti patrol craft and an Iraqi boat that refused to answer requests to stop, and an apparent attempt by another vessel to menace the *Sir Bedivere*. A correspondent from the UK's *Daily Mail* newspaper embarked in HMS *Chatham*, which had, as predicted, been redirected into the Gulf from the Indian Ocean, reported that a helicopter from the frigate came across two small patrol boats as they sped towards the edge of Iraqi territorial waters. After being circled by the helicopter, which was armed with a heavy machine gun, the Iraqi boats raced back towards the coastline.

Tension was rising across the Gulf region and also further afield, even in India, which feared an upsurge in terrorist attacks by Islamic militants as a result of military action against Saddam. Rear Admiral Joseph Krol, Assistant Deputy Chief of Naval Operations in the Pentagon, told an international naval conference in Delhi that the carrier *Abraham Lincoln* had been continuously at sea for nine months, apart from her R&R and maintenance break in Australia. He felt confident enough about the ability of the US Navy to achieve its objectives swiftly that he told conference delegates he was sure the *Lincoln* would be returning home from the Gulf in about six weeks time.[14] No one expected the US and UK forces to fail in their conventional war against Iraq, but many worried that, by seeking to depose Saddam, pressure would be taken off the campaign against global terrorism. As if to confirm the seriousness of that threat, during the conference there was a terrorist attack on Mumbai railway station and an assault on a police station in Kashmir.

In the Gulf a massive out-pouring of US Marines from ships into Kuwait was taking place. After their marines, tanks and other equipment had been sent ashore the *Bonhomme Richard* and *Bataan* switched to a new role as Harrier carriers. More than twenty Harriers were put aboard each ship, with, for example, the *Bataan*'s normal complement of twenty-plus helicopters reduced to two, to make room for the extra attack jets. Using the *Bataan* and *Bonhomme Richard* as such would ensure the maximum amount of air power could be projected forward over Iraq. Having spent some time in the southern Gulf on training exercises, *Ocean* and the ARG arrived in waters off Kuwait to join *Ark Royal* in mid-March. One of the young commandos aboard *Ocean*, Marine Grant Slaney, expressed everyone's desire to get on with the job.

> *We are definitely ready and the sooner it's finished, the sooner we can get home...*

As the time for the majority of 40 Commando to join the rest of the brigade ashore in Kuwait approached, the unit's chaplain, Ron Martin, did the rounds aboard *Ocean*, offering words of comfort to anyone anxious about what might lie ahead, much as his predecessor must have off Port Said more than forty years earlier, in the previous HMS *Ocean*. The chaplain later revealed that he had given out more than 300 silver crosses to the commandos.

> *When the lads are facing the reality of putting themselves in harm's way, it obviously makes them think about the important things in life. It's not as if they're all converting en-masse, but most people have some sort of spiritual sense in them whether they believe in God or not...It's my job to be with the lads if they need me, but I am not there to tell them that God's on their side or tell them they are fighting a holy battle.*

Throughout the British naval task force it was becoming clear that war would soon be a reality. Captain Johns, in *Ocean* had, like many, hoped the threat of force would be enough.

> *I think we all felt that the application of military pressure might drive a diplomatic solution. However, at the end of the day, I knew, and I think everybody else on board knew, that things might come to the crunch and we needed to be prepared to act ... My focus at that time was really making sure that we'd gone through all the 'what ifs' that we'd thought of every eventuality, every contingency and that people and everything on board was prepared both physically and, I think, psychologically for what we might have to face...*

In London and Washington DC the decision for war was taken and now the armed forces would be asked to achieve what diplomacy had so utterly failed to bring

Leaflets printed aboard US Navy warships in the Gulf were dropped on southern Iraq, advising the locals not to aid regime officials trying to flee the country. US DoD.

Do not aid Iraqi military and regime leadership attempting to escape.

ATTENTION!
The Coalition is here to block the escape of Iraqi leaders attempting to flee. If you harbor, aid, or assist these individuals you risk confiscation of your vessel and endanger yourself and your crew. If you observe defectors, report it to Coalition forces.
DO NOT LET SADDAM'S REGIME ESCAPE JUSTICE!

about. The *Ark Royal*'s CO, Captain Alan Massey, was absolutely confident his sailors would be able to do all that was required of them.

> *When the message came that, within forty-eight hours, we would be at war, we were completely ready for it.*

The frigate *Chatham* was in the middle of a refuelling at sea when she received the order to move up to her war station.

> *It was while we were refuelling with RFA* Orangeleaf *that we received news that the last diplomatic attempts to resolve the crisis had failed. We quickly filled up our tanks and then sped north to take up station just off the Iraqi coast, ready to be called upon when required.* [15]

The *Turbulent* had been back at sea for some time, still under national operational control, but given over to US tactical command. Although his submarine was submerged and on a war footing, Commander McKendrick felt it was important that some contact with the rapidly evolving situation in the world outside was maintained.

> *We listened to the BBC World Service on the radio but the best source of news was via a UK liaison officer in the 5th Fleet strike cell who e-mailed us web pages, including video clips of football matches back home. While we could concentrate on the task at hand, the massive amount of media coverage of all the opposition to war and preparations in the Gulf must have been difficult for our families to deal with. In the submarine, although we knew there was disagreement, we had no idea of the scale of disharmony going on in the international community, but we did worry about the impact on our families. We did get a lot of e-mails from back home, most of which said 'good luck...you are doing a good job... we are proud of you'. It was not easy to operate a boat submerged for that length of time, especially when the Gulf was so busy with Allied shipping that we had to keep an eye on. Ensuring the crew was busy enough during the waiting period to keep boredom at bay, while not getting them too hyperactive, was a challenge. But, as time wore on the notice to fire TLAM was being reduced, so we knew something was about to happen.*

CHAPTER TEN

KICKING DOWN THE DOOR

A lthough it was always notoriously difficult to pin down the exact location of Saddam Hussein, on the night of 19 March a well-placed spy, deep within the Iraqi regime, managed to inform the CIA that the dictator would be sleeping in a bunker beneath the Dora Farms compound, near Baghdad's university.

By the time CIA chief George Tenet was briefing President Bush about what looked like a golden opportunity to decapitate the Iraqi regime with a precision-strike, Special Forces troops, including the UK's SBS, America's SEALS and Poland's GROM, were already ashore in the al-Faw Peninsula. They were preparing to secure vital oil installations that might otherwise be destroyed by demolition charges when the main coalition attack was launched. In Washington DC the President gave the green light to the strike on Saddam, with two Nighthawk stealth fighters ordered to hit the Dora Farms with bunker-busting bombs. American warships and submarines in the Gulf and Red Sea were instructed to target the same area and important command and control facilities elsewhere in Baghdad. The Ticonderoga class cruiser USS *Cowpens*, part of the *Kitty Hawk* CBG in the Gulf, launched the first cruise missiles of Operation Iraqi Freedom just before dawn on 20 March, with TLAMs blasted out of her forward and after silos.

On short notice, the ship's strike team was directed to alert status and was on station when the mission orders were received. The crew executed the

As dawn breaks over the Gulf, the American cruiser Bunker Hill fires a cruise missile in an attempt to kill Saddam Hussein. US Navy.

197

orders within minutes of receipt...Commanding Officer Captain Charles B. Dixon gave the final permission to execute the missile salvo in accordance with the orders of the commander of the 5th Fleet. Much of the crew was uninformed prior to the launch, and some awoke to the sounds of missiles being fired. [1]

The cruiser's eleven TLAMs were the first batch within a total of forty cruise missiles on that first night, all launched by the US Navy. Others came from her sister ship *Bunker Hill*, the destroyers *Milius* and *Donald Cook*, plus the attack submarines *Montpelier* and *Cheyenne*.

As she prepared to fire, the *Bunker Hill* had been just twenty-five miles from the Iraqi coast, and the cruiser's CO, Captain Faris Farwell, told his crew over the PA:

We are in receipt of Tomahawk tasking...Following 9/11, gentlemen and ladies, you have not faltered, or tired, and we will not fail...God bless the USS Bunker Hill. *God bless America.* [2]

Whether or not Saddam was killed or injured by the first strike became the subject of much debate, but it was soon concluded that he had escaped unharmed.

The destroyer Donald Cook takes part in the same strike on Saddam. US Navy.

Later, on 20 March, with the invasion of Iraq just hours away, in his flagship, the aircraft carrier HMS *Ark Royal*, Commander UK Amphibious Task Group, Commodore Jamie Miller, was confident of success.

We are now on the point of committing our forces to action in Iraq. All options are available and, once 3 Commando Brigade is put ashore, we will sustain it and switch from war-fighting to humanitarian operations. Touch wood...it should all, hopefully, go very well indeed. [3]

Not far from Commodore Miller in the carrier, Royal Marines from 40 Commando's Delta Company were carrying out their last-minute checks on equipment, for it was *Ark*'s helicopters that would take them into action that night.

But, even before the invasion was launched, the sailors and marines poised in the northern Gulf got a taste of action, going to full chemical alert when the Iraqis fired retaliatory missiles at Kuwait. Some of those weapons actually turned out to be Silkworms and Seersuckers with

conventional warheads, able to evade detection and destruction by the Patriot anti-missile systems arrayed in Kuwait because of their low flight profile. Some of the other, battlefield ballistic, missiles were detected by the destroyer USS *Higgins*, using her AEGIS combat system, and prior warning of impact was passed on to Kuwait. It was the first time in history that a warship had been used in such a wartime role.

After night fell, the nuclear-powered attack submarine *Splendid* fired the first British TLAMs of the conflict. In total fifty TLAMs were launched in the second salvo against Baghdad, the US effort coming from the destroyer *John S. McCain* and the attack submarines *Columbia* and *Providence*. As the missiles sped to targets in Iraq, *Kitty Hawk* CBG commanding officer, Rear Admiral Matthew G. Moffit remarked:

The intention is to convince the regime that it is time to leave...if they don't we will try to take them out by force.

As the Iraqis retaliated with a shower of missiles, some potentially carrying chemical or biological warheads, the crews of the coalition warships in the Gulf were glad that they had prepared to combat the effects of NBC. British sailors are pictured undergoing NBC training as their ship heads into the Gulf.
McCaig Collection.

The British commando brigade's assault on the al-Faw Peninsula was a daring move that kicked down the door into Iraq for the rest of the coalition's front line combat force.

It was the biggest helicopter assault involving maritime forces, in the face of an enemy, since the 1956 Suez campaign. Another link to that earlier, equally controversial, military venture was the involvement of a carrier named *Ocean* and the participation of 40 and 42 Commandos.

Around 59,000 US Marines, 20,000 US Army and approximately 40,000 UK ground troops, including 4,000 from 3 Commando Brigade, would carry the war to the heart of Saddam's regime. To resist the coalition invasion, the Iraqis had an estimated 400,000 troops, but most of them were of questionable fighting efficiency and equipped with out-dated tanks and other weaponry that would be no match for the Coalition's overwhelming technological superiority and better-trained troops. The Iraqi Air Force had retained around 100 effective combat aircraft, but these were destined to not fly at all and, in fact, many of them were buried in the desert, the latest manifestation of Saddam's weapons concealment mania.

Half a dozen Republican Guard divisions were the only enemy units that could pose a serious threat, particularly if Saddam ordered them to use chemical and biological weapons.

Originally, the British contribution was to have been much smaller and would have come entirely from the sea, as 3 Commando Brigade's CO, Brigadier Jim Dutton, revealed in the immediate aftermath of the war.

> ... there was only going to be one commando unit involved and that was to have been 45 Commando. But then, for various reasons, the unit involved was switched to 40 Commando, but the scale of the operation got bigger and bigger. This was because of intelligence on enemy force levels in the south of Iraq, which were seen to be higher than originally expected. Also, as time went on, the UK wanted to play a bigger part in the overall operation. So, six months ago it was going to be a single unit operation and the whole thing was going to be launched from the sea because of the anticipated pressure on Kuwait ports.

In the final coalition war plan, 45 Commando still played its part, but covertly as the back-up force for Special Forces troops operating in the western desert of Iraq. Its objectives included the capture of key airfields and neutralization of mobile Scud launchers, to ensure Saddam could not attack Israel as he had done in the 1991 war.

There were factors other than force levels that ruled out a full-scale amphibious assault against the al-Faw, as Brigadier Dutton later explained:

> It was essentially a helicopter borne assault only, because the beach

Marines from Delta Company, 40 Commando, contemplate their flight into danger as they wait aboard HMS Ark Royal to embark in their helicopters.
Royal Navy.

gradients didn't allow the use of landing craft. There was also a threat to the RN ships from the offshore gas and oil platforms held by Iraqi troops. Until those had been taken down by the US Navy SEALS, it wasn't safe for the ships to get close inshore. In the event they were seized rapidly and the ships closed the coast early, but there was still less risk in having the bulk of the force actually ashore and then assaulting by helicopter from the west, rather than from the south.

While the majority of the commandos may have gone in from jumping off points in Kuwait, the support of the two carriers was still crucial, not only in putting 40 Commando's Delta Company ashore, from *Ark Royal*, using RAF Chinooks and Royal Navy Sea King helicopters, but also providing logistic support, without which the attack would have failed. In the first seventy-two hours of Telic, as the UK labelled the operation, the ground forces had to rely almost entirely on ammunition and other supplies coming from the British naval task force, as Brigadier Dutton acknowledged.

The ships were critical, not just for 3 Commando Brigade but for the whole of 1 UK Division. Unlike 1990, the deployment happened very quickly and it took some time for the land logistical system to catch up. So, in fact, during the entire build-up to the operation, and even when the assault had actually started, 1 UK Div were heavily dependent on the seaborne stocks originally designated for just one brigade, that is, for 3 Commando Brigade.

The workhorses of the resupply effort were the young sailors and marines in *Ark Royal* and *Ocean*. In the helicopter carrier, Lieutenant Colonel David Summerfield's 9 Assault Squadron Royal Marines (9 ASRM), having intensively rehearsed a traditional assault across the beach using landing craft, now found itself pivotal to the whole operation without even leaving the ship. Lieutenant Colonel Summerfield later recalled:

We carried out something like 355 air moves off Ocean's *deck in those first 72 hours, which was a huge amount of stores. It was crucial, for when the ammunition arrived ashore, a number of the marines were down to their last magazine of bullets.*

However, for superfit, highly trained Royal Marines who had expected to get their baptism of fire on D-Day, putting stores pallets together for helicopters was perhaps a bit of an anti-climax. Colour Sergeant Nev Nixon made sure the lads in 9 ASRM knew that they were making the difference between life and death for their fellow marines ashore.

Some of the young marines here were only eighteen or nineteen and you can imagine that, having seen their mates going ashore to do the fighting, they were very disappointed not to be in there with them. But, once it was explained how important their re-supply job was, they settled down and really gave it their all.

To ensure the helicopters had less transit time between the al-Faw and the ships, while carrying supplies and personnel, HMS *Roebuck* had carried out surveys right under the noses of the Iraqis. Twelve years on from *Herald* and *Hecla*'s experiences

201

off Kuwait, once again it was a ship from the Royal Navy's Hydrographic Survey Squadron that had often been most exposed to danger. The *Roebuck* charted two deeper stretches of water not recorded on existing charts, which were suitable for the two carriers to edge slowly into. Lieutenant Commander Andrew Swain, *Roebuck's* CO, and a veteran of the 1991 Gulf War, said that his young sailors rose to the challenge despite the risks.

> And it was very dangerous...but, by reducing the flight time for the helicopters by ten minutes, our surveys helped save lives, as the aircraft were less exposed in the air. As each piece of the jigsaw came together to make the charts, my sailors realized how important Roebuck's work was.

But, even with reliable charts, taking the two carriers in so close to the Iraqi coastline was a very risky thing to do, as *Ark Royal's* CO, Captain Alan Massey, later reflected:

> I think any commander would have a bunch of different things going through his mind. The principal one being, where do we stand in relation to risk versus gain in this sort of adventure? Are we finding ourselves in a situation where we're potentially putting big capital ships at excessive risk? I have to say, I always felt entirely comfortable about what we were doing, despite the fact that we were in very close proximity to the Iraqi coast, in very shallow water and with a considerable number of real threats against us: missiles; suicide boats; surface attack. We could have done something about all of those, but mines were a big worry and certainly that night, in the dark, after midnight, at action stations going right up into shallow waters that was probably the tensest moment. We worked hand in glove with Ocean. For most of the time we were within just a few miles of each other and sometimes even closer than that. When we launched the assault into southern Iraq she was about five miles on my starboard beam. Both of us were in the only tongues of deep water that exist that close to the Iraqi coast...

Lieutenant Rolf Kurth fully expected the *Ark Royal* to be targeted by the enemy's shore-based Seersuckers and Silkworms in the al-Faw Peninsula.

> ...there was certainly a feeling on board on that first night, when we steamed right up the assault lanes, to within about fifteen miles of the coast of Iraq, that those missiles would probably be fired at us...

For the UK marines, and the US Navy SEALS who joined them for the initial assault, flying into Iraq as the spearhead of the whole coalition attack involved considerable risk.

> A 20-minute low level helicopter flight beneath Iraqi radar made them targets for any enemy forces. And the Marines faced resistance from the moment the first helicopters landed... from Iraqis concealed in bunkers and dug outs... [4]

But the danger also came from the sheer volume of traffic in the air and complexity of modern warfare.

> Not only was it launched at night, but there was the threat of anti-aircraft fire and also the possible use of chemical and biological weapons by the

With a British Type 23 frigate visible in the distance, the Australian warship HMAS Anzac provides Naval Gunfire Support for Royal Marines fighting ashore. Royal Australian Navy.

enemy. Visibility was hampered by the few oil wells that the Iraqis did light. There were artillery shells in the air. Tomahawk missiles were on their way to targets. Helicopters and aircraft were sharing the same air space and warships were firing in support of the assault. There was a lot of stuff all in the air at the same time.[5]

Although the coalition's amphibious troops had to use air strikes and artillery to suppress enemy positions, there were Iraqi soldiers who preferred not to fight.

Iraqi conscripts shot their own officers in the chest yesterday to avoid a fruitless fight over the oil terminals at al-Faw. British soldiers from 40 Commando's Charlie Company found a bunker full of the dead officers, with spent shells from an AK47 rifle around them. Stuck between the US SEALS and the Royal Marines, whom they did not want to fight, and a regime that would kill them if they refused, it was the conscripts' only way out.[6]

Meanwhile, Rigid Raider boats and hovercraft from 539 ASRMs took in assault engineers to 'Red Beach' on the KAA, to assess if it could be used to bring across light tanks and supplies, including ammunition, from Bubiyan, in large US Marine Corps hovercraft. Unfortunately, due to difficult beach gradients, mines and other obstacles, this proved not to be possible in the opening hours of the attack, although an amphibious corridor was later established. However, 29 Commando Regiment Royal Artillery was still able to provide a covering bombardment, via its 105mm light guns, while land-based support for the assault also came from US Marine Corps 155mm artillery pieces and AS90 self-propelled heavy guns of the British

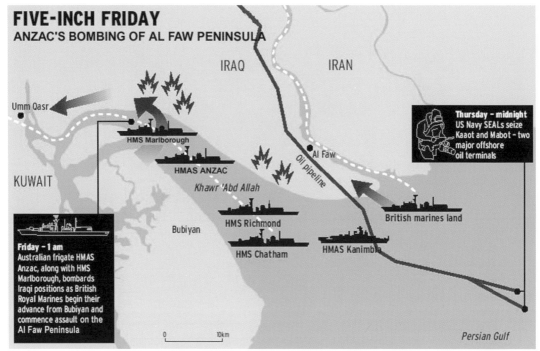

FIVE-INCH FRIDAY
ANZAC'S BOMBING OF AL FAW PENINSULA

IRAQ

IRAN

Umm Qasr

HMS Marlborough

HMAS ANZAC

Al Faw

Oil pipeline

Thursday – midnight
US Navy SEALs seize
Kaaot and Mabot – two
major offshore
oil terminals

KUWAIT

Khawr 'Abd Allah

HMS Richmond

British marines land

Bubiyan

HMS Chatham

HMAS Kanimbla

Friday – 1 am
Australian frigate HMAS
Anzac, along with HMS
Marlborough, bombards
Iraqi positions as British
Royal Marines begin their
advance from Bubiyan and
commence assault on the
Al Faw Peninsula

0   10km

Persian Gulf

A Royal Australian Navy map, showing the position of ships providing NGS for the Royal Marines' attack on the al-Faw, in the early hours of 21 March. It also depicts oil infrastructure secured by the US Navy SEALS. The Australians dubbed 21 March 'Five-Inch Friday' after the calibre of Anzac's gun. Royal Australian Navy.

Army. Basing supporting artillery pieces on Kuwait's Bubiyan Island had enabled them to fire across the KAA and reach most targets. The Royal Navy frigates *Chatham*, *Richmond* and *Marlborough* also provided Naval Gun Fire Support (NGS) with their 4.5-inch weapons. When *Marlborough* opened fire around 1 a.m. on 21 March, she was the first British ship since the Falklands campaign to bombard a land target in war. Joining the British warships was the frigate HMAS *Anzac*, herself the first Australian warship to fire on a land target since the Vietnam War. At around 5,000 tonnes displacement each, the bombarding ships had just enough water under their keels for safety, but sometimes it was 'less than six feet ...in rather badly charted waters'.[7]

Like the other ships on the gun line, the *Chatham* had been brought to action stations in the early hours of the morning, but didn't open fire until later on.

> *...we took up station close to the coast of Iraq. Just before 7a.m. we were given the order to open fire with our main gun. The whole ship shook as we began bombarding the Iraqi forces on the al-Faw. HM Ships* Marlborough, Richmond *and the Australian ship* Anzac *all fired alongside us as we bombarded enemy positions ashore all day. Guided by Royal Marine spotters, our gunfire was delivered with high accuracy and to great effect, allowing the Commandos to successfully sweep through the al-Faw encountering light resistance from the Iraqis.*[8]

204

The *Chatham*, together with *Marlborough*, *Richmond* and *Anzac*, would ultimately fire a total of 155 shells in seventeen fire missions.

Above the battlefield, 847 NAS's Gazelle reconnaissance helicopters played a key role in detecting emerging threats and calling in fire from artillery, strike jets or from the Lynx helicopters they were teamed with. Each of 847's Lynx AH-Mk7s was crewed by two pilots, with a door gunner operating a heavy machine-gun in the back. The pilot in the right-hand seat flew the aircraft while the one in the left-hand seat fought the aircraft, operating the weapon sight and firing the Tube-launched Optically-tracked Wire-guided (TOW) missiles. Each Gazelle AH-Mk1 also carried two pilots, with the one in the left-hand seat operating a lazer target designator to pinpoint targets. Four days before the coalition offensive began, the squadron had flown ashore from *Ocean*, to a Forward Operating Base (FOB) in Kuwait called Camp Viking. The carrier would still be used as a maintenance base for the aircraft and to provide aviators with a respite from the action, but 847 NAS would fight its war from ashore, moving the FOB into Iraq once the invasion got underway.

Early on the morning of 21 March a Gazelle, flown by Captain Dave Abbott, was the first 847 NAS aircraft over enemy territory, with a Lynx piloted by Captain Birty Cross close behind. As the crews of the two helicopters had prepared for the first patrol there was a real sense of a dangerous flight into the unknown. 'As we set off, everyone was shaking our hands and wishing us good luck, even people we didn't know,' recalled Captain Cross. The two helicopters flew over Bubiyan Island at around 100 feet and then, once they were over the sea, dropped to fifty feet, their approach to the enemy shore cloaked in mist. 'Because we were the first team in, we had decided to go low and slow,' said Captain Cross.

> I had my finger on the trigger because of observation towers the Iraqis had all the way along the coastline. We couldn't get info on whether or not they had been taken out. The door gunner was ready with his machine gun and I was ready with the missiles.

As Captain Abbott's Gazelle passed over the beach, down below some of the enemy had decided not to contest the territorial integrity of Iraq.

> There was about a dozen Iraqis trying to surrender to us, but we had to move on as we knew 40 Commando would need us.

The call for fire didn't, in fact, come until the afternoon when a US Marine Corps pilot on attachment with 847 NAS was asked to help 40 Commando prize open a bunker that was showing some unusually stubborn resistance. The marines on the ground told the Lynx that they were 'having trouble with opening the bunker's front door'. The helicopter pilot was happy to oblige, replying:

> 'Let me open it for you.'

The missile demolished the bunker and 40 Commando resumed its advance.

Strike jets from the *Constellation*, *Kitty Hawk* and *Abraham Lincoln*, in the Gulf, were among the 700 Allied aircraft providing support for the ground forces across Iraq on 20 and 21 March. The *Truman* and the *Roosevelt* were unable to contribute to the air assault due to the continuing lack of permission to use Turkish air space. On the first night of Operation Iraqi Freedom, as the Americans called the liberation of Iraq, the 15th MEU had burst through the border from Kuwait, aiming to take Umm Qasr within hours. It was immediately involved in combat with Iraqi forces. Marines managed to raise the Stars and Stripes over the city the following afternoon, but the flag was promptly pulled down again. It was seen as giving the wrong political signal to the Arab world - this was a liberation on behalf of the Iraqi people, not an occupation. To the West, the I MEF was pressing on with its advance into oil-fields south of Basra alongside the British Army's 1st Armoured Division. To the north of 40 Commando, by the morning of 21 March, after being heli-lifted in from Kuwait, were the marines of 42 Commando, providing a blocking force to halt any Iraqi counter-attack. The entry of 42 Commando had been delayed due to a tragic accident. At around 3.00 am on 21 March, a US Marine Corps Sea Knight helicopter crashed in Kuwait, claiming the lives of eight UK commandos aboard and four USMC aircrew. All the Sea Knights were withdrawn so they could be checked out and, after a delay of several hours, the Royal Marines were taken forward in RAF Chinooks.

> *Losing people in the helicopter crash on the first night was a blow. We were obviously hoping to have no casualties at all, but we also understood that we would take them and get on with it, as that is the nature of war.* [9]

By the late afternoon of 21 March it was being reported that the entire al Faw was secure in the hands of the Royal Marines. The primary objective had been to secure the oil production infrastructure so that it could not be destroyed to hinder the allied attack, by polluting the sea and the air, and to ensure it could be revived to produce revenue needed to rebuild Iraq after three decades of Saddam's corrupt rule. There was no doubt that the Iraqi dictator would far rather have laid waste to his oil fields, as he had done to Kuwait's more than a decade earlier, than let them be taken intact. His troops had still managed to set fire to thirty out of many hundreds of oil wells, but an ecological and economic disaster had been avoided.

> *By launching the attack slightly earlier than originally anticipated, we actually got control of the various parts of the oil infrastructure that were wired before they could be blown up.* [10]

The first casualty in fighting was a US marine belonging to the I MEF, killed during the initial advance. Another US Marine was killed within hours, during the battle for Umm Qasr. On the afternoon of 21 March, the head of the British armed forces, Chief of the Defence Staff, Admiral Sir Michael Boyce, gave a briefing in London. He revealed that the next step would be for the Royal Navy's mine-hunters to move forward and clear the KAA, to enable relief supplies to be brought in via Umm Qasr. Commenting on action in the al-Faw, Admiral Boyce said that the Royal Marines had faced some stiff resistance. He observed that 40 Commando was now taking the surrender of significant numbers of Iraqi troops. Turning to the wider picture, Sir Michael said elements of the UK's 7 Armoured Brigade were, in company with US troops, approaching the outskirts of Basra. He stated that other American formations were making good progress toward Baghdad, having covered 150km since the previous evening. On 21 March, both British submarines were in action, attempting to destroy the ability of the regime to repress the Iraqi people, with the hope that removing such shackles might encourage them to rise up in support of the coalition. This was the much heralded 'Shock and Awe' offensive that, in one night, expended thousands of precision-guided bombs and 300 cruise missiles. Its objective was the destruction of the regime's will to carry on fighting, as well as the infrastructure of terror that allowed it to continue to control Iraq. This was what US and UK military spokesmen described as 'effects-based warfare'.

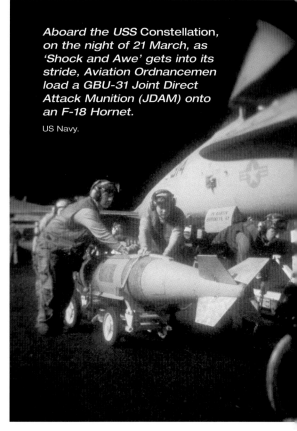

Aboard the USS Constellation, on the night of 21 March, as 'Shock and Awe' gets into its stride, Aviation Ordnancemen load a GBU-31 Joint Direct Attack Munition (JDAM) onto an F-18 Hornet.

US Navy.

> *The goal of effects-based warfare is to create specific effects on the enemy that lead to a rapid collapse of the enemy's willingness and ability to fight, without having to go through a time-consuming and potentially costly effort to destroy the bulk of the enemy's military forces through a gradual process of attrition.*[11]

However, it was so precise, that while 'Shock and Awe' hit all its targets, with minimal civilian casualties and achieved many of its objectives, it arguably did not cause the massive psychological damage needed to create an instant implosion of the regime. For example, the ability of Saddam and his acolytes to continue broadcasting propaganda via State television ensured the Iraqi people believed the regime had not loosened its grip and might even be winning. Meanwhile, during his own televised news briefing on 22 March, Defence Secretary Geoff Hoon said:

> *The main headquarters of the Iraqi intelligence service in Baghdad, a key part of the regime's intelligence and security network, was attacked last night by a United Kingdom tomahawk missile fired from a British submarine. This was a carefully targeted strike which will have had significant effect on the ability of the Iraqi intelligence service to contribute to the internal repression carried out by Saddam Hussein's regime. Attacks on this and other Iraqi intelligence service facilities will remove from the Iraqi regime a key source of its power, reducing the potential threat to coalition forces and reducing its ability to terrorise the people of Iraq.*

With the time between sensors (spies and special forces on the ground, or satellites and reconnaissance aircraft high in the sky) detecting a target and targeting information being relayed to the shooters (TLAM-armed submarines, surface warships and strike jets) reduced from the 1991 Gulf War's average of six hours to as little as forty-five minutes, the speed, flexibility and precision of cruise missiles could be fully exploited.

'The whole situation was very fluid, with changing targeting requirements and time lines,' recalled *Turbulent*'s Commander McKendrick.

Everything became more compressed and so, we just had to work faster, particularly on the 22nd. The targets and times of firing were continually switching between Turbulent *and* Splendid. *TLAM is an expensive precision weapon and targets would be assessed all the time, to make sure they were still viable. As the intelligence picture clarified so would the targets and the times. It is funny, you only reflect deeply on what you have been doing some weeks later. At the time, when you are in the middle of the Gulf, firing at a target hundreds of miles away, you are purely focussed on getting it right. You experience relief when the missiles are away...you have achieved what you set out to. Where did the missiles go, what did they land on? I knew the targets, as did some of the strike team. Knowing where the missiles went helped - they were regime targets of a strategic nature. In the rest of the crew there was no great desire to know. They didn't ask. We were told on the evening of 22 March that we could go when we had finished firing the final missile, which was slightly strange. There you were, experiencing the adrenalin of live operations and then they said 'you can go now', but the land war had only just started. But, you simply shifted mindset and changed your focus to thinking of that great day when you would get home.*

And for *Turbulent*, setting course for home was long overdue, for the Trafalgar class boat had completed a deployment lasting more than ten months, the longest ever by a Royal Navy nuclear submarine, in which she had clocked up around 50,000 miles.

Clearing the KAA leading to the container port and naval base at Umm Qasr was a significant maritime task, as the latter would be a major point of entry for humanitarian aid as well as military supplies. The challenges of working within the shallow waters were considerable and innovative thinking was necessary, as Australia's Captain Peter Jones later explained.

Fairly murky conditions made it difficult for ships to operate. A lot of it was in less than eight metres of water, which is very close to the limits of our ships and it was beyond the limits of a lot of the larger ships in the Coalition naval force. In such conditions it is also hard to make water and difficult to run ship systems. But it's something that we had got used to - for the previous eighteen months of MIF operations we'd always had ships operating within Iraqi territorial waters enforcing the sanctions. That not only meant we knew the area quite well, but also that we could identify any changes in the pattern of Iraqi activity.

The Australian assault ship *Kanimbla*, with her very shallow draught, was the command and control vessel for this important task, with Captain Jones' staff augmented by British naval officers. Captain Jones was in command of what was essentially a reinforced MIF, which aimed to achieve total domination of the KAA to ensure any attempts by the Iraqis to interfere with coalition operations were instantly snuffed out. Twenty boarding teams, drawn from 130 Australian, British and American forces personnel, worked from the *Kanimbla* and their principal task was to stop and search vessels that might be laying mines. Prior to the war there were estimated to be around 300 dhows and 150 merchant ships up the KAA, and while many of them could be legitimate, the Iraqis were bound to have concealed mine-laying and oil smuggling vessels among them. The Polish Navy, NATO's newest fleet, was determined to play its part in the coalition war effort, retaining the logistics support ship ORP *Kontradmiral Xawery Czernicki* in the northern Gulf as a base for Polish and US Navy special forces. Teams operated in small boats from the Polish ship, patrolling the coast of Iraq and the lower KAA. As a firm supporter of military action against Saddam, the Danish government deployed two of its warships to the Gulf - the frigate HDMS *Olfert Fisher* and submarine HDMS *Saelen*. When it came to the Gulf navies themselves, the Kuwaitis were to the fore, providing interdiction and surveillance patrols off the Iraqi coast while Bahrain sent its frigate, the BNS *Sabha* to take up station off the Shatt al-Arab. The *Chatham, Richmond* and *Marlborough* worked closely with the *Kanimbla* as did *Anzac*, in supporting clearance of the KAA. Two US Coast Guard and two US Navy patrol boats reinforced the force and were particularly useful in the shallow waters of the Gulf. However, on 17 March, thanks to the news media, things had nearly got out of hand before the coalition offensive had even started.

Two days before it commenced CNN announced that the war may start within five hours. The shipping owners and the smugglers got wind of that very quickly and we had ships coming out along with dhows, waving white flags, some throwing their contraband in the water. Because of this, some forty-eight hours before the war actually started, we started to clear the Waterway. In fact, in that time we cleared nearly fifty of the steel hulls and about the same number of the dhows. And that was pretty much it in terms of the shipping. It worked quite well in our favour that it was done really fairly quickly. But the fact was that we had a fairly well-orchestrated routine in place. And we had the extra capability to do it.[12]

On 21 March, the Iraqis discovered just how complete coalition control was, when one of their patrol craft made an unwise foray into the Gulf. It just happened to coincide with coalition troops securing an oil platform south of the al-Faw to make sure it wasn't about to be blown up. The Iraqi boat was detected by a US Navy P-3C Orion Maritime Patrol Aircraft flying surveillance cover for the special operations troops on the platform. A US Air Force AC-130 gunship was called in to eliminate the threat, using the overwhelming firepower at its disposal, including a 105mm howitzer and various cannons. Interrogation of some Iraqi Navy sailors who were pulled from the water further north revealed the strange story of the patrol boat's foolhardy mission.

They were suffering from varying degrees of hypothermia and they said basically that what happened to them was they were in Umm Qasr, alongside, and some people from the Republican Guard came along. They took most of the crew off, put on Republican Guard people who had orders to go out and to attack the Coalition ships. So, that patrol boat went down the KAA Waterway. However, these three warrant officers jumped over the side because they didn't want to be involved in what was essentially a pretty dangerous sort of mission. They'd just drifted down with the tide and were picked up by a US Coast Guard patrol boat. That sort of illustrates how the

Crew on four of HMAS Kanimbla's RHIBs keeps watch as a coalition boarding party continues its search of an Iraqi mine-laying tug.
Royal Australian Navy.

Iraqi regime felt it needed to put Republican Guard guys on Iraqi boats to provide a stiffening of resolve. [13]

As they moved up the KAA to secure the approaches to Umm Qasr on 21 March, Australian and American naval forces intercepted a barge and two tugs that were subsequently discovered to be covert mine-layers.

If those mines had been brought into the Gulf and released...there would have been mayhem. [14]

The Pentagon revealed that sixty-eight mines were discovered in one of the vessels, fifty in another and nineteen on the third. As with their WMD programmes, the Iraqis displayed remarkable ingenuity when it came to concealing their mines.

... we stopped them, did a very cursory inspection that didn't unearth anything but then sent Kanimbla's boarding party the next day to have a thorough search, because we had developed this suspicion about them...they'd developed this system of covert laying...even from a helicopter you couldn't actually see that the barge was laying mines. Luckily, one of the Petty Officers in Kanimbla's boarding party noticed two things. First off, he'd noticed on the barge that there was a construction hut similar to those that you see at building sites. Inside this hut was a little hole where

An Australian naval ordnance disposal expert inspects mines that were hidden inside oil barrels on the deck of an Iraqi barge. US Navy.

A Royal Navy Lynx helicopter acts as plane guard for an MH-53 Sea Dragon minesweeping helicopter, during operations near the mouth of the Khawr Abd Allah Waterway. US Navy.

a cable went down inside the barge and, when they unearthed and moved around a lot of the rubbish inside, they found the trapdoor through which the mines were laid. And then we went through a fairly thorough process of making sure the mines were in a safe condition...it's clear that, unencumbered, they would have sewn a minefield to prevent our ships getting in position to provide NGS. It would have added weeks to the actual clearance of the KAA Waterway and delayed quite considerably Umm Qasr being opened. On one tug we intercepted, the mines were very cleverly concealed indeed. One of our mine clearance officers went up there to have a look and he said to one of the Iraqi crew: 'Oh, what have we got here?' The man responded: 'A bomb, a bomb.' And our officer thought that he was actually meaning these 44-gallon oil drums, until the fellow moved them aside to show they hid mines.[15]

When it came to locating and destroying mines already in the water, the clearance effort was commanded by the Royal Navy, which, since the 1991 Gulf War, had maintained its world-renowned skills. The six British MCMVs, supported by the *Sir Bedivere* and *Roebuck*, worked closely with three American mine warfare ships - the *Ardent*, *Cardinal* and *Raven* - with the assault ship USS *Ponce* acting as a base for Sea Dragon mine-sweeping helicopters. Royal Navy Lynx attack helicopters armed with Sea Skua missiles acted as plane guards for the MH-53s, in case the Iraqis sent out a boat to interfere. Two American patrol craft, *Chinook* and *Firebolt*, also helped to locate mines while clearance divers from the US, UK and Australia had been hard at work in the waters of Umm Qasr itself within hours of the coalition attack starting.

Although casualties had been suffered in combat, they were to be expected and had, so far, been light, but, with the bitter blow of the Sea Knight crash still fresh, another air accident in the early hours of 22 March stunned the British naval task force.

At approximately 0430 local (0730 GMT) two Sea King Airborne Early Warning helicopters, from 849 Naval Air Squadron, were involved in a mid-

air collision over international waters...There are believed to be no survivors. Recovery operations continue. The incident was not the result of enemy action. [16]

The Sea King Mk7 was a crucial aircraft, operating around the clock, using its powerful radar to locate targets and potential threats over sea and land. One of the lost Mk7s was returning from a sortie while the other was just leaving the *Ark Royal* to begin one. A total of seven airmen died, three in one helicopter and four in the other, including a US Navy aviator. The sense of shock in the British fleet flagship, indeed throughout the whole UK task force, was profound. Recalled Captain Massey:

I'll remember it forever...I had a call to say that two of our Sea King helicopters had collided, had crashed into the sea and the likelihood of survivors was nil.

The whole ship's company were very inward looking and depressed...just for a moment. But, what really got us through, was the fact that we were only a day into the war. There was no way that we knew, at that stage, which way it was going to go. The sense of purpose and mission was overwhelming in terms of getting back on our feet and focussing on the issues at hand...and, indeed, the squadron had aircraft flying within two or three hours of the incident.

Leading Operating Maintainer Clare Farrar was on watch in the *Ark*'s Ops Room when the crash happened.

Accidents don't just happen in war of course, they happen all the time. So there's always somebody that needs rescuing. This time it was just...we couldn't rescue them and they were ours.

Seven members of the *Ark*'s family had been snatched away by the random cruelty of war. Even experienced senior ratings like Chief Petty Officer (Physical Training Instructor) David Randall would carry the sadness with them for a long time.

It still upsets me now... the guys used to come to PT circuits, we used to have fun and games with them. Have a laugh with them... They were there one minute, gone the next.

On 22 March the bombarding ships were informed that their services were no longer needed, as *Marlborough*'s war diary recorded.

...40 Commando confirmed that sufficient progress had been made to allow our ships to move from the very shallow and difficult waters occupied for nearly two days. As soon as the tide rose sufficiently, we picked our way back out of the estuary and into deeper water. As we left, we were given yet another good reason to pause for thought, as the minesweeping force entered the river to begin clearance operations in the water we had just occupied. To bring the situation home even more clearly, we learned of one of the American sweepers hitting a wreck, which caused some minor damage. This happened within 150 yards of the position we had held.

However, reaching the open waters did not mean an end to hazards, rather just a change in their nature.

Now back in more open, although very busy, waters, it was a return to more familiar surveillance and force protection duties for Marlborough, *watching all movement close to the Iraqi coast, particularly for suicide boats which, we had been told, were preparing to operate against coalition shipping. We were very conscious that there were still very many valuable assets, well forward and all possible targets for a small, fast boat. On a single occasion, we counted eighteen coalition units within ten miles of our position. The threat of suicide boats became very real when a Coalition patrol discovered a fast boat rigged with explosives, hidden beneath vegetation on the edge of one of the main Iraqi waterways. The boat was pre-positioned and no doubt its crew were just waiting their opportunity.* [17]

As the *Chatham* pulled back from her NGS mission, the Iraqis made a play and came off worse. A training frigate that had somehow avoided the depredations of Allied air power since 1991, edged down the Shatt al-Arab in company with two patrol craft. The Iraqi vessels were either going to try an attack run against coalition warships or they were carrying senior members of the regime, making an escape bid.

With the British frigate blocking their exit, a coalition strike jet was called down to attack the Iraqi vessels. The *Chatham*'s CO, Captain Michael Cochrane, gave his view of the incident to the embarked correspondent from the *Daily Mail*:

We had been tasked with moving up to the mouth of the Shatt al Arab to form a surface action group, with Chatham *in charge, assisted by the Australian frigate HMAS* Darwin *and Royal Navy helicopters. There was a fear that the Iraqi vessels could come out for some sort of do-or-die mission against Coalition warships. It was my job as the commander of the group to take whatever measures were necessary to ensure the safety of our ships in this area. A British Tornado was called in on a tactical air strike.*

At least one Iraqi vessel was destroyed and the others fled, to be picked off later. The *Chatham* maintained her position off the Shatt al-Arab, ready with her Harpoon anti-shipping missiles to fend off any further forays. In the meantime, the frigate's radio transmitters were being used to broadcast coalition propaganda into Iraq, via 'Radio Free Iraq'. A combination of 'modern Middle Eastern music interspersed with messages of peace, warnings of use of extreme force and how to surrender to the Allies' [18] was blasted at the local population. There continued to be great hopes that, with the right amount of pressure militarily and psychologically, and following more than a decade of economic restrictions, Saddam's regime would swiftly come tumbling down.

It was not quite so easy.

There was a view that we might be welcomed with open arms by the Iraqis, with very little fighting, but at the other end of the scale it was thought they would fight for the honour of the Iraqi Army if not for Saddam...Our aim was to overwhelm the enemy with the speed and violence of the assault, but we were not surprised by the resistance. You cannot go into a military operation assuming that the enemy will not fight. The Iraqis did fight strongly and bravely at a local level, but there was no joined up defence anywhere in Iraq. [19]

Nearly thirty years after it first entered service as an Anti-Submarine Warfare aircraft, the distinctly innocuous-looking S-3 Viking finally graduated to the modern era of combat. However, rather than dropping torpedoes or depth-charges, the Viking, which was designed to combat a growing Soviet submarine menace in the Cold War, found itself firing a laser-guided Maverick missile, another weapon of the early 1970s, originally devised to destroy Warsaw Pact tanks. On 25 March a number of Iraqi naval vessels were discovered lurking in the waterways around Basra and, to make sure they could not pose a threat to coalition troops or sneak down to the Gulf, strike aircraft from the USS *Constellation* were called in. While one Hornet destroyed two Iraqi craft, the other worked with a Viking to destroy a third. With the second Hornet painting the enemy vessel with its laser designator, the Viking fired its missile, which successfully rode the beam to target. It was the first time in naval history that a Viking had been tasked with destroying a target inland and also the first combat launch of a laser-designated missile by the aircraft type.

With the war approaching the end of its first week, the full might of the five US Navy carriers committed to the action was finally being felt on the battlefield.

Forty-eight hours after the start of Operation Iraqi Freedom, the Turks had relented, giving permission for strike jets and cruise missiles to use their airspace, enabling the *Roosevelt* and *Truman* CBGs in the eastern Mediterranean to enter the fray. Aboard the *Truman*, the CBG commander, Rear Admiral John D. Stufflebeem, told his sailors:

> We will strike with precision, we will strike with lethality, we will strike with persistence, and we will not fail.

But the admiral warned that American warships could also expect to be targets.

> To be sure, there are terrorists who would want to try to attack our ships...For this reason, we will stay at sea for the foreseeable future...

As the strike jets launched for combat missions, the mood in the *Truman* changed, with war videos being abandoned for news broadcasts. Sailors and marines witnessed some of the so-called 'Shock and Awe' being visited by their aviators on Iraq, broadcast from the scene of destruction as it happened. But the thunder of war was all around them.

> ...the USS Harry S. Truman's *flight deck was inundated with the unceasing roar of jet engines... Inside the ship, it was eerily silent. As HST entered Operation Iraqi Freedom in earnest, the crew seemed to hold their collective breath, their thoughts with those flying off the ship to liberate Iraq.* [20]

Then came a heart-stopping moment, when the call 'Full Bore' blared out on the carrier's PA. This was the code word for a possible attack on the ship, so suddenly sailors and marines were jostling past each other as they rushed to man weapons on the upper-decks. An SH-60 helicopter from the *Truman* was already in the air, flying fast and low towards the suspicious radar contact. The helicopter's aim was to destroy or chase away whatever appeared to be threatening the ship. Was Admiral Stufflebeem's warning about suicide boats about to come true? 'It took me by surprise at first,' said one of the helicopter's crew, Aviation Warfare Systems Operator Jeremy Burkart.

> The strikes were going on, so we were already pumped up, and, when we

An SH-60 Seahawk helicopter flies close protection on the USS Harry S. Truman, *in the eastern Mediterranean.* US Navy.

got the Full Bore call, it just added to the excitement. We protect the ship. That's our first priority. We're armed, so we're able to do that. Our goal is to put as much distance as possible between the ship and an aggressor.

Luckily the contact turned out to be what the US Navy terms a false radar hit. Aboard the *Roosevelt*, pilots returned with adrenalin-charged tales of their exploits. Commander Anthony Gaiani, CO of one of the carrier's squadrons exclaimed:

As we flew away, we could see the targets engulfed in flames...

Each mission demanded the utmost concentration and stamina from the aircrews, as time to and from target was in excess of seven hours, involving multiple refuelling from flying tankers. Turkey maintained its ban on coalition aircraft using its bases during the war, which forced tanker planes to fly from more distant locations in eastern Europe. This reduced their time over the war zone, and meant that 'sorties of Navy aircraft flying into Iraq from two carriers in the Eastern Mediterranean were reportedly reduced because Air Force tankers...could provide them with less on-station, in-flight re-fuelling capacity.' [21]

First strike targets for the *Roosevelt*'s squadrons included one of Saddam Hussein's palaces and a regime radio station. Cruise missiles were also being launched from the Mediterranean, the *Winston S. Churchill* among the ships tasked to hit targets deep within Iraq. Her baptism of fire made a lasting impression on the destroyer's Royal Navy navigator, Lieutenant Stuart Yates.

I witnessed the launch from the Bridge, where there was a charged, yet

The USS Winston S. Churchill *launches a Tomahawk missile.*
US Navy.

subdued, atmosphere. It was an impressive, awe-inspiring and intimidating sight. I had a whole mixture of feelings. I was extremely proud to have played a part in the action, knowing that each missile fired would aid the mission of the Coalition forces on the front line in Iraq. At the back of my mind, however, I knew that, for each missile to achieve its goal, human lives would be lost. This was cause for a short period of reflection and a quiet prayer.

As the cruise missiles and strike jets winged their way towards Iraq, nearby NATO's Standing Naval Force Atlantic was indirectly helping the war effort by conducting maritime surveillance in the shipping lanes of the eastern Mediterranean. It was under the command of the Royal Navy's Commodore Richard Ibbotson, who had been the boss of the British fleet's mine-hunters off Kuwait during the 1991 war and CO of the frigate *Boxer* during Desert Fox in 1998. Commodore Ibbotson had taken command of SNFL on 21 March, during a ceremony at Rota, Spain and he led the group to its operational station in HMS *Cornwall*, which had become SNFL flagship.

In the Gulf, the Harriers of the *Bataan* and the *Bonhomme Richard* were providing decisive air support to the US Marines in their drive to Baghdad. A sailor on the *Bataan* wrote:

With each roar of the engine and pressing of the throttle, the AV-8B Harrier thrusts itself off the flight deck...up until now, it has been for practice...Now, it's for real.[22]

Harrier pilots from the *Bonhomme Richard's* Marine Attack Squadrons 211 and 311 would drop more than 175,000 pounds of ordnance during the campaign. But, keeping the ships positioned correctly, to enable them to get enough wind over the deck during their many launches and recoveries, was not easy, as the carrier's CO, Captain Jon Berg-Johnsen explained:

Navigation was challenging and maneuvering the ship was difficult. We had limited space, and it was crowded with ships and potential navigational hazards - shallow water and oil wells, some unmarked.

With her more conventional air group of half a dozen Harriers, Sea Knight medium-lift and Sea Stallion heavy-lift helicopters, plus Cobra gunships, the *Tarawa* was providing direct air support to the marines of the 15th MEU and the UK's 3 Commando Brigade.

Since Operation Iraqi Freedom began, Tarawa's *flight deck has come to life at night. Under the glow of hazy moonlight...Sailors using florescent green and purple signal wands have maneuvered the Marine-piloted aircraft as they took-off and landed. Each night, the roar of a Harrier's 21,000 pound, thrust-vectored engine has announced the departure, or the successful return, of another mission.* [23]

Aboard *Abraham Lincoln*, the US Navy's combat aviation boss, Rear Admiral John Kelly, was up-beat enough by 24 March to declare that the Iraqi Army was 'on the run'.

..and we're going to keep them on the run. [24]

However, the CO of the *Lincoln*, Captain Kendall Card, warned his sailors that the unpredictable weather was going to be a problem, with sand storms and rain threatening to restrict flying operations.

We do not know exactly how much the weather will deteriorate over the next couple of days, but we do know that it's going to deteriorate significantly.

The Admiral, who was more blunt, declared that incoming weather conditions were likely to be 'a pain in the ass'. [25]

Already facing stiff resistance from the Fedayeen Saddam guerillas and foreign fighters, marines and soldiers in Iraq now experienced freezing rain and vicious sandstorms, which, combined with difficulties in getting supplies to the leading combat units, created the impression that the Allied offensive was stalled and going seriously awry. However, the reality was that the coalition had mounted an

The USS Bataan *up threat during combat operations, with an AV-8B Harrier hovering above her flight deck.* US Navy.

On the flight-deck of the USS Abraham Lincoln, as the US Navy's strike aircraft keep up a relentless pressure on Iraqi forces, an Aviation Ordnanceman checks over racks of precision guided bombs. US Navy.

astonishing blitzkrieg thrust that would soon take Baghdad. The measured encirclement of Basra by British troops would result in the city's fall with minimal civilian and coalition casualties. From the perspective of the UK's Gulf naval boss, Rear Admiral David Snelson, who was at the heart of maritime command and control in Bahrain, it was absurd to suggest that operations were bogged down.

There was quite a lot of talk from day three onwards, which lasted for about a week, about a pause, with people saying 'it's not going as well as it should be'. But that was partly because the press could only see one dimension - the ground dimension - they weren't seeing much of the maritime, or the air, dimension.

So, from the sea and the air, despite the weather, the relentless pressure was maintained and no objective was more pressing than getting humanitarian aid into Iraq via Umm Qasr. By 25 March, British forces had completed operations to secure the port that had been initiated by the 15th MEU before it moved north and out of 3 Commando Brigade's control. While no one in the coalition forces was under any illusions about the treacherous and brutal nature of the Saddam regime, the manner in which the diehards fought, or forced others to on their behalf, was still shocking. 'The fact that they used underhand tactics, such as using their own people as human shields, did tend to motivate you,' recalled 847 NAS Lynx pilot, Lieutenant Commander Jim Newton.

The Fedayeen Saddam were using taxis to go around and force the regular army troops to fight... We could see this happening and so those taxis were declared legitimate military targets, but we would still get close enough to see who was inside before firing on them to scare them off.

Later, the 847 NAS helicopters were called in to assist 40 Commando in demonstrating to the Iraqis that they could not get away with abusing the white flag of surrender.

There was this boat moving back and forth across this waterway south of Basra and it was really aggravating 40 Commando. The occupants of the boat were waving the white flag, but the marines could see the Iraqis were using it as cover to move ammunition and military equipment. The Royal Marines would fire on them, the white flag would go up and then this boat would carry on bringing the stuff across. Frustrated at not being able to see it off with their own firepower, they called us in and the offending boat was taken out by a TOW missile.[26]

On the long journey down to the Gulf in HMS *Ocean*, the 847 NAS aviators had devised their battle techniques, but, as Captain Abbott later revealed, the reality of combat soon saw a change in plan.

The commandos on the ground might have been able to get behind a bush or the occasional building, but up in the sky there is nowhere to hide. You couldn't hover over the desert either, because of the temperature, so we came up with this

A squad leader with the 15th MEU waits for orders to move north from Umm Qasr, after fighting alongside Royal Marines from the UK's 3 Commando Brigade. US Navy.

race track idea, which involved the pair of you - a Lynx and a Gazelle - circling over a potential target. Prior to combat we had decided that we would work at 30 - 50 ft high, which was okay, that was a normal height. But we discovered that, as the fighting got nearer to Basra, because we were so low, they could see us going past a landmark, which they ranged on. We decided it might be best in those circumstances to change tactics and go to 400ft up.

Whether low or high, the danger was always extreme, sometimes coming from multiple directions in the form of machine guns, RPGs, artillery shells and tanks that would suddenly lurch across the battlefield. Lieutenant Commander Newton and Captain Abbott often found themselves working as a pair, watching each other's

We wish only to liberate the people of Iraq from Saddam's tyranny.

OUR FIGHT IS AGAINST SADDAM AND HIS REGIME

NOT THE IRAQI PEOPLE

FOR YOUR SAFETY, RETURN TO YOUR HOMES AND LIVE IN PEACE.

IZD 7509

US Navy aircraft dropped Arabic versions of this leaflet, and others, to explain that coalition forces aimed to liberate the Iraqi people from Saddam. US DoD.

backs. 'If he was looking for a target, I would be trying to spot threats to him,' explained Captain Abbott.

> *The Rules of Engagement were very strict. For example, in the residential areas we sometimes had to pull our punches. There were a couple of times where we could see the target, but because of the risk to innocent civilians in homes nearby we decided against firing. We didn't underestimate the enemy, but we did underestimate the grip of fear that Saddam had. They were being pushed forward in their tanks. It was a combined effort - two to three tanks out at a time and, if they fired at you, you had to take them down, regardless of the coercion being used by the regime to make them fight.*

On one occasion Lieutenant Commander Newton found himself in a very tricky situation. Having fired a TOW missile at one Iraqi tank, he noticed another one turning its turret to fire an air burst shell at his Lynx. Keeping his nerve, he calmly took out the other tank as well.

> *I was worried, but the training keeps you calm and you have a high level of confidence in your own capabilities. And while you know that a lot of them are being forced to fight against their will, I am afraid when someone fires at you, you think 'hang-on a minute, I think I'll fire back'.*

It was a miracle that, despite all the metal hurled at them by the enemy, not a single 847 NAS helicopter was shot down nor were any of the squadron's aviators killed or wounded. There were many near misses, such as the air burst tank round that exploded close to Captain Abbott's Gazelle, but only buffeted it, or the artillery shell that landed between his helicopter and Jim Newton's Lynx. Lieutenant Commander Newton recalled:

> *It threw up a load of sand and stuff but, luckily, there was no physical damage to the Lynx. It was just like being in your car going past a gritter on a road back home. The tactics worked, but with a barrel full of luck too. A lucky shot by the enemy could have spoiled everything.*

The Lynx-Gazelle teamwork of 847 NAS racked up an impressive score sheet during the battle for southern Iraq.

A total of forty-seven TOWs were fired by the squadron's helicopters, which, in addition to blasting open various bunkers, destroyed eighteen T-55 tanks, twelve armoured personnel carriers, three artillery guns and one boat. Each missile that hit home helped save coalition lives and further loosened the regime's grip of terror. Overland surveillance by the Royal Navy's Sea King Mk7 made a major contribution to that tally, picking up likely targets that were then destroyed by 847 NAS aircraft.

The recent Hollywood movie *Black Hawk Down* had been watched by Saddam's military to glean lessons on how to destroy coalition helicopters. The movie was based on real-life mistakes made during combat in Somalia in 1993, where US Army helicopters established regular flight patterns low and slow over urban areas similar to those of southern Iraq. As their CO, Lieutenant Commander Jon Pentreath explained, the aircrews of the 845 NAS Sea Kings were determined to make sure they didn't make

One of the 847 NAS Lynx attack helicopters displays its kills: Two tanks, three armoured personnel carriers, a bunker and a sniper. Iain Ballantyne.

The main lines of coalition attack and Special Forces operating areas, as the campaign enters its second week. US DoD.

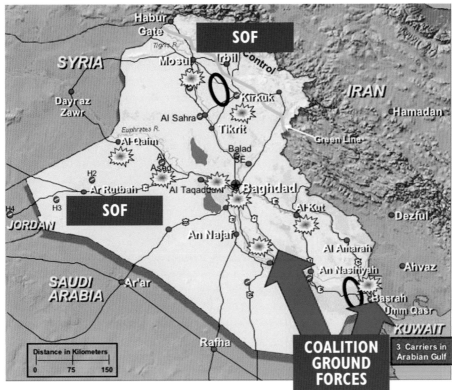

the same errors:

> When we flew over Iraq we tried not to set up a pattern, as the Iraqi irregular forces might have pitched up with RPGs and heavy machine guns to shoot us down.

Years of experience in Ulster, where 845 NAS was a veteran of 'Bandit Country', meant that *Black Hawk Down* had very little to teach the Royal Navy's aviators, but it was a useful reminder. At sea, the Lynx helicopters of the various British destroyers and frigates worked closely with the new Merlin helicopter, deployed in a combat environment for the first time. The Lynx, armed with the well-proven Sea Skua ASM, and recently fitted with night vision capability, was vectored in on suspicious surface contacts by the Merlin's formidable sensors.

On the afternoon of 25 March, 40 Commando, which was in a position south of Basra, was notified to stand by for a possible attack by an Iraqi armoured column. This duly emerged, with between seventy and 120 Iraqi tanks, armoured personnel carriers and other vehicles reportedly heading south. One thousand enemy troops were said to be in the column. However, before 40 Commando's marines were called upon to blunt the Iraqi advance with their anti-tank weapons, British Army artillery (including the light 105mm guns of 29 Commando), 847 NAS helicopters and Allied strike jets broke up the attack. In the 40 Commando battlefield operations centre, the movements of the Iraqis were monitored closely. 'Their intentions or motives are totally unclear, but they have adopted an offensive posture and do not want to surrender, so they have been attacked,' explained 40 Commando's Major Mick Green. 'For the Iraqis to move tanks around in daylight is suicide.'

Outgunned and outmanoeuvred by the Challengers of the Royal Scots Dragoon Guards, some of the Iraqis abandoned their vehicles and attempted to fight back with small arms and rocket-propelled grenades but, inevitably, their actions were futile. By the end of the action, fourteen Iraqi T55 and T62 tanks had been destroyed along with five armoured personnel carriers and a number of pick-up trucks manned by militia in civilian clothes. Up to 100 Iraqis were believed to have been killed. Although it represented a stunning success, coalition troops took little satisfaction in the slaughter. 'It was a devastating and incredibly effective assault,' said 29 Commando's Major Hugh Baker.

> But emotionally I think we all feel a little bit empty, a little bit numb. We know we have killed a lot of their soldiers and...another feeling I've got is anger - anger at their stupid officers and leaders for putting them in that appalling position.

The British landing ship RFA *Sir Galahad* was scheduled to be the first vessel into Umm Qasr, carrying much-needed humanitarian aid and, by 25 March, she had received her cargo, some of it a gift from Kuwait with the rest from the UK Government. It included bulk food such as rice, lentils, chick peas, milk powder, bottled water, flour, boxed rations, blankets, and World Health Organisation medical packs. However, the discovery of mine-like objects in the channel leading from Umm Qasr to the Gulf caused a delay. Royal Navy mine clearance ships,

The RFA Sir Galahad *makes her way up the channel to Umm Qasr, to deliver humanitarian aid from Coalition forces. Astern of her in this picture is a British Hunt class MCMV.* US Navy.

K-Dog, a bottle nose dolphin used by the US Navy to find and eliminate mines in the northern Gulf, leaps out of the water in front of his handlers while training. US Navy.

together with British, American and Australian ordnance disposal divers, set to work. The objects could have been munitions left over from the Iran-Iraq War, but may also have been mines laid in recent days by the Iraqis. In fact, a total of 100 suspicious objects that could easily have been mines were detected in the KAA.

At least three were confirmed as mines and destroyed by British divers and MCMVs.

The *Sir Galahad* finally docked on 27 March, the Royal Navy mine-hunter *Sandown* leading the way, with American and Kuwaiti patrol boats acting as out riders, to prevent suicide boat attacks and spot for mines. The *Kontradmiral Xawery Czernicki* had also helped provide cover for the British logistic ship in the early stages of her journey to Umm Qasr. To provide more visible support for the coalition, the Spanish sent the amphibious ship SPS *Galicia* to Umm Qasr carrying humanitarian aid supplies.

Two specially trained US Navy dolphins, belonging to Commander Task Unit 55.4.3, had assisted coalition divers with clearing the way for *Sir Galahad*.

Based in the assault ship USS *Gunston Hall*, CTU-55.4.3 was made up of ordnance disposal divers from the USA, UK and Australia plus US Navy personnel trained to handle the mammals. The dolphins used their own biological sonar to detect suspicious objects, which they captured on special cameras strapped to their bodies, with pictures transmitted back to their human handlers. During the war the Americans also used sea lions, to deter hostile frogmen from attacking coalition warships in Gulf naval bases.

As the war had entered its second week, Royal Marines boarded Rigid Raiders and hovercraft from 539 ASRM for a foray up the Shatt al-Basra Waterway, to seek out and destroy the remnants of Saddam's, already badly depleted, fleet. The British commandos discovered several gunboats and destroyed them with grenades.

Meanwhile, the success of British commandos in pacifying Umm Qasr was being put down to past experience in dealing with urban threats, such as the IRA in Northern Ireland. The Royal Marines, like most of the British Army units sent to the Gulf, learned, during many tours of duty in the troubled UK province, how to combine the need to pursue armed opponents while not causing deaths among the civilian population. In Umm Qasr the Royal Marines went from house-to-house, guided by Iraqis who wished to see the end of Saddam's rule, hunting down the dictator's agents and arresting them. One of Saddam's supporters tried to fire on Royal Marines manning a checkpoint, but a commando sniper on a nearby roof killed him before he could achieve his purpose.

On 30 March, a major offensive to secure the Basra suburb of Abu al-Khasib was launched by 3 Commando Brigade.

In what was the first full-blown land assault by the British commando brigade since the Falklands War of 1982, the Royal Marines were initiating what turned out to be the final phase of the battle for control of Basra.

Supported by Challenger 2 tanks, the artillery of 29 Commando and Royal Horse Artillery and 847 NAS, the Royal Marines were delighted to have the chance of emulating the heroics of their predecessors in the South Atlantic twenty years ago.

The offensive - codenamed Operation James - raged throughout the day and, by nightfall, about 600 men from 40 Commando had taken up consolidating positions close to the Shatt al-Arab Waterway. Operation James was named after Ian Fleming's fictional superspy, and naval Commander, James Bond, with objectives labelled Connery (as in Sean Connery), Moore (as in Roger Moore) and Pussy Galore (after one of the characters in *Goldfinger*). The nature of the close-quarter action made support fire difficult and some of the British forces were injured by artillery shells believed to have come from their own lines. However, about 300 enemy soldiers were captured, at least seventy were killed and a number of Iraqi armoured vehicles and bunkers destroyed.

> *There was thirty-six hours of fairly intense fighting and yet there were no casualties from enemy fire. The Iraqis did destroy four vehicles, which were empty at the time, with RPG 7 rockets. It obviously says something about the way that 40 Commando tackled the task, the standard of training, their capability. I'm sure it says something about the standard of the enemy and their will to fight at this stage. Quite what was motivating them to fight, I don't think that we are absolutely certain to this day. I think that a lot of them were being coerced into fighting. Either their families were being held, or they were being threatened with death if they didn't go forward and fight. So, some of them were fighting in a relatively half-hearted manner, perhaps firing their weapons and then dumping them and running.* [27]

Basra itself had previously only been subjected to fleeting raids by the British Army's Warrior armoured personnel carriers and Challenger 2s, but the Royal Marines' infantry assault won territory from the regime and sent a clear message to the city's defenders.

Among the casualties were some of Saddam's most loyal and competent fighters, the Fedayeen, dressed in black 'ninja-style' uniforms and red headscarves. While there had been no UK commandos killed in fighting ashore, a Royal Marine from *Ocean's* 9 ASRM, deployed forward for operations with 539 ASRM along waterways leading to Basra, was killed in action when his landing craft came under heavy fire. Several other commandos were injured in the incident. The death of Corporal Chris Maddison, a popular member of *Ocean's* complement, was made more traumatic for the sailors and marines in the ship because he was the only one who had sailed out of Plymouth in January who did not make it home. Lieutenant Colonel Summerfield put a brave face on it, but, like everyone else, he was pretty cut up.

In the Gulf, the destroyer USS Milius *launches a Tomahawk missile towards Iraq during the initial stages of Operation Iraqi Freedom. Only a limited number of cruise missiles were launched from the eastern Mediterranean.* US Navy.

War is our business and sometimes people get killed, but it was still a shock...we were very upset when we lost Chris, and of course some of our guys were wounded in the same incident and we felt for them too.

On 28 March CENTCOM briefers revealed that there had been some embarassing malfunctions with TLAMs launched from ships and submarines in the Red Sea and eastern Mediterranean.

...the failure of several Navy Tomahawk cruise missiles using certain flight paths over Turkey and Saudi Arabia prompted a decision by both countries to close down those flight paths...for the remainder of the conflict... [28]

But, the aircraft of the US Navy's carriers were able to provide support throughout the war for the US Marines during their drive on the Iraqi capital. As they had in the 1991 Gulf War and the recent campaign in Afghanistan, the carriers proved to have unrivalled reach and hitting power. For the Iraq War, the US Air Force managed to assemble a land-based strike force of 344 strike jets and bombers, whereas the US Navy and US Marines provided 362, most of them flying from carriers. US Navy and US Marine Corps strike planes flew 9,362 sorties, compared with 8,828 by the US Air Force. US Navy and Royal Navy warships launched a total of 802 cruise missiles, with an accuracy rate of approaching ninety-eight per cent claimed by the US Department of Defense. The sixty-six strike jets contributed by the UK's Royal Air Force flew 1,736 sorties. [29] Helping to protect the US Navy's strike aircraft from attack by what remained of Saddam's air defences, were the EA-6B Prowlers from the *Constellation*. On 27 March, for example, one of the carrier's Prowlers fired a High-speed Anti-Radiation Missile (HARM) at a SAM site just south of Baghdad. The Prowlers also packed electronic countermeasures equipment that was used to jam Iraqi air-defence radars. And, without the services of the flying tankers of the RAF, the US Air Force and US Marines, time over target and reach would have been severely restricted, making life immensely more difficult for ground troops relying on aerial firepower to make headway. Equally important to the naval strike packages were the E2-C Hawkeye early warning aircraft. In contrast to the forward-looking radar of strike aircraft, the E2-C is fitted with a revolving radar dish mounted on its fuselage, giving 360-degree coverage. Able to keep track of potential air threats, such as enemy fighters, the Hawkeye can also track targets on the ground and direct air strikes onto them. Despite being one of the most valuable aircraft in the coalition's naval air power inventory, the Hawkeye had no armament, but the Op Iraqi Freedom crews did carry their own weapons.

Lieutenant Sam Kesler, a Carrier Airborne Early Warning Squadron pilot, is sitting behind his duty desk passing out guns and bullets to a group of geared-up naval flight officers leaving on another mission. 'The guns,' one pilot said, 'are for our protection in case we get shot down'. [30]

During the war, naval air losses to enemy ground fire amounted to two Cobra helicopter gunships of the US Marine Corps, while a US Navy Hornet from the *Kitty Hawk* was shot down over Iraq by a coalition Patriot air-defence battery on 2 April, with its pilot killed. As the USS *Nimitz* steamed for the Gulf, to replace the *Abraham Lincoln*, her air group personnel had received a series of briefings. Although the ship

A Super Hornet takes off from USS Abraham Lincoln *during combat operations.* US Navy.

was no stranger to the Middle East, many of her aviators and sailors were first timers. Briefing topics included 'The War Against Iraq: Problems and Prospects', 'US Defense Strategy in the Persian Gulf', 'Deterring Asymmetric Attack' and 'The War on Terrorism: Past, Present and Future.' Theory changed to reality for the *Nimitz*, on 7 April, when she became part of the 5th Fleet, and for two days, until the *Lincoln* headed home, there were six US Navy carriers committed to action. The CO of the *Nimitz*, Captain Robert J. Gilman, told his sailors:

We trained like we fight, and now it's time to fight like we trained.

Four of the carrier's Super Hornets that had flown forward to operate from the *Lincoln*, at the end of March, returned to the *Nimitz* on 6 April and now their aircrews' experience helped ensure air strikes on the crumbling Iraqi forces were on the button.

Aboard the Abraham Lincoln, *a pilot inspects the exterior of an F -18E Super Hornet prior to launching for his next strike mission.* US Navy.

During the period 3-8 April, having pushed into the city with Operation James, the Royal Marines had subsequently been involved in operations to finally secure the city of Basra. Operation Sinbad was a three-pronged attack mounted by not only 3 Commando Brigade, but also the British Army's 7 Armoured Brigade, with support from its 16 Air Assault Brigade. The bootnecks of 42 Commando and 40 Commando led the push through the south-east of Basra, while the heavier forces of 7 Armoured came in from the south-west of the city. During Operation Sinbad, the men of 42 Commando stormed one of Saddam's many palaces and were astonished by the opulence they found within, which contrasted so greatly with the poverty beyond. The final crumbling of resistance in Basra came just before the Iraqi capital fell to the Americans.

Once we had the Palace, and once 7 Brigade had the main part of the town, then essentially the war was over and we switched to peace enforcement, peace-keeping and providing humanitarian aid. [31]

The fact that the defenders of Saddam's cruel regime were no longer able to persuade the people to fight - or even to use them as cannon fodder - became blatantly obvious when a Basra fisherman failed to carry out a suicide attack on 40 Commando's headquarters in Abu al-Khasib. Hand grenades were strapped to the fisherman's body and he was meant to detonate them as he got close to the entrance of the building. Instead, the fisherman warned Royal Marines on guard that he had been sent as a suicide bomber. 'When I walked up to the gate I thought "I cannot do this"', the fisherman revealed after the marines disarmed him successfully.

So I told the British soldiers I am their friend and I pulled up my shirt and showed them my weapons, and they didn't shoot me. There are other people like me, that the regime forces to do things they don't want. We just want freedom.

Having bulldozed aside Iraqi opposition, by 9 April the sea soldiers of the US Marines were involved in the fighting for Baghdad. Their opponents were the Fedayeen Saddam and foreign Arab fighters, for the Republican Guard had been destroyed by coalition air power before the final battle began. The most symbolic moment of the war came in the city centre that afternoon, where

The attack submarine HMS Turbulent was the first British naval vessel home from the war. Having been away for ten months, she returned to Plymouth on 16 April.

Tony Carney.

On her return, **Turbulent** *flew a skull-and-crossbones flag, with an* **appropriate symbol to indicate her** **successful completion of Tomahawk** **combat launches.** Tony Carney.

engineers of the Corps helped ecstatic Iraqis pull down a statue of Saddam Hussein. Like most American marines, Corporal Edward Chin was ambitious to equal the legendary moment during the Second World War when US Marines raised the Stars and Stripes at Iwo Jima. Egged on by the Iraqis, he covered Saddam's features with the American flag. However, it was soon taken off, and, to more loud cheers, the twenty-three year-old Corporal attached the old, pre-Saddam, Iraqi flag in its place. Having made sure there were no jubilant citizens to be squashed, the statue was pulled down by an assault vehicle. While dozens of delirious Iraqis celebrated their Liberation Day by clambering all over Saddam's statue, and giving it a good stomping, it was typically ironic that a British peace protestor, who had supported the regime as a 'human shield', yelled: 'Go home yankee bastards!'

A US Marines Corps tank commander, who had been at the Pentagon on 11 September 2001, where he saw several of his friends killed, yelled back: 'I don't give a F**k!'

It was the tank commander's flag, which he had recovered from the Pentagon rubble, that Corporal Chin had momentarily draped on Saddam. Among those watching the scenes of liberation in the centre of Baghdad, via a live television broadcast, was Captain Massey in *Ark Royal*.

> *I guess the most satisfying point was when we realized that Basra was going to fall and that coincided pretty much with that hugely iconic day when the statue of Saddam Hussein was pulled down in the centre of Baghdad. It came the day before the ship was told to re-deploy back to the UK, where she would convert into a fixed-wing carrier again and be ready to strike at the next crisis...We should avoid being triumphalist because I don't think it was that sort of mission. I think it was all about doing a job that was unpleasant but had to be done. It was done for the right reasons, which included liberation. We'd done that, so now we were sailing home, back to our families.*

As the sun set on the Pacific Ocean, President Bush gathered the sailors of the USS *Abraham Lincoln* around him.

'In this battle we have fought for the cause of liberty and for the peace of the world,' he told the crew of the carrier, which was on the final leg of her voyage home to the USA, after ten months on deployment. The President, a former Air National Guard fighter pilot, had just landed a S-3B Viking - dubbed 'Navy One' - and, emerging from the cockpit clad in a military flight suit, was mobbed by young men and women eager to press the flesh of their Commander-in-Chief. President Bush chose that day, 1 May, and the *Lincoln* as the location, to declare major combat operations in Iraq at an end.

With sailors cheering him on, and against a huge red, white and blue banner with the words 'Mission Accomplished' emblazoned on it, President Bush said:

> *Because of you, our nation is more secure. Because of you, the tyrant has fallen and Iraq is free.*

But the President did not forget those among the coalition forces who had given their lives and would not be returning home.

> *Every name, every life is a loss to our military, to our nation, and to our loved ones who grieve. There's no homecoming for these families, yet we pray, in God's time their reunion will come. Those we lost were last seen on duty. Their final act on Earth was to fight a great evil and to bring liberty to others.*

Just over a fortnight later, on the other side of the world, the British aircraft carrier HMS *Ark Royal* was, together with her escort ships, about to make her own return home. During the long voyage back to the UK, members of her ship's company were able, finally, to reflect on the war they had just fought.

Surgeon Commander David Campbell had seen the casualties of war from both sides.

At the controls of a Viking dubbed 'Navy One' President Bush successfully 'traps' aboard the USS Abraham Lincoln. US Navy.

President Bush poses with sailors for a photograph on the flight deck of the Abraham Lincoln on 1 May 2003. US Navy.

It really didn't matter what race, colour, creed or background they came from, everybody was treated with equanimity, in priority of medical need. Seeing the Iraqi people, particularly the children, actually getting good, immediate, treatment you could tell they had experienced a release. You could see it in their eyes. It brought great pleasure to me. I feel that I was very much a part of fighting something that was evil.

There was a regime, which was destroying peoples' lives and we removed it.

In HMS *Ocean*, as she made her passage along the English Channel, 847 NAS Lynx pilot Lieutenant Commander Jim Newton, who had been extremely lucky to come through intense combat without a scratch, felt that the cause had been just.

To see the relief in those people when finally it became apparent that it was going to stop and that they were going to be freed was wonderful. It was very rewarding to be part of liberating Iraq.

And so, the ships of the US Navy and Royal Navy returned from war, their crews

The Ark Royal *was greeted by a flotilla of small boats when she returned to Portsmouth.* Jonathan Eastland/AJAX News & Feature Service.

A sailor aboard the Ark Royal *cannot resist waving back to onlookers as the carrier enters her homeport.* Jonathan Eastland/AJAX News & Feature Service.

confident they had been part of a campaign that enabled the triumph of good over evil. Anyone who had, in any way, been touched by the malevolence of Saddam's regime had no doubt that it was a war worth fighting. At Stonehouse Barracks in Plymouth, the home of 3 Commando Brigade, the unit's CO gave the opinion that the final verdict on the war would be some time in coming. Brigadier Jim Dutton said:

> *I think the point is that none of us had a quarrel with the Iraqi people or, frankly, with the Iraqi military. Once they ceased to fight us, there was no personal animosity between the Royal Marines and the Iraqi soldier or civilian. The top villains of the piece are either being captured or giving themselves up on a regular basis. The regime has been overthrown. Iraq is a safer place...whether the world is a safer place we will find out in fifty years time when things have run their course. What is certain at the moment is that*

A Sea King helicopter from 845 NAS lands aboard HMS Ocean, *as the helicopter carrier comes in close to the Cornish coast the day before she reaches Plymouth.* Iain Ballantyne.

The helicopter carrier HMS Ocean, *during the final leg of her return home from war.* Iain Ballantyne.

we no longer have a regime that we knew owned, and was prepared to use, WMD.

By the end of May the USS *Harry S. Truman*, USS *Theodore Roosevelt* and USS *Nassau* and their accompanying strike groups had all returned home to the USA, part of a massive return flow of US Navy warships from the Gulf. The *Kitty Hawk* had made her passage back to Japan where she went into refit while the *Constellation* returned to the west coast of the USA, to prepare for decommissioning later in the summer, after a forty-two year career. The second oldest aircraft carrier in the US Navy, after the *Enterprise*, the *Connie* was one of only three remaining conventionally powered carriers in America's arsenal, the other two being *Kitty Hawk* and *John F. Kennedy*.

Commissioned at New York Naval Shipyard on 27 October 1961, some 120,000 sailors and marines served aboard the *Constellation* during a fighting life that spanned the Vietnam War, the Tanker War, the War on Terrorism and now the Iraq War. The first carrier to launch air strikes in support of Operation Iraqi Freedom, the *Connie*'s aircraft flew in excess of 1,500 sorties, dropping more than 1.7 million pounds of ordnance.

'Welcome home from the war, sir!' A ground crewman greets a Harry S. Truman *Hornet* pilot with a handshake, after the aircraft taxis to a halt at its home airbase. The *Hornet*'s strike mission tally is clearly visible on the plane's nose, above the slogan 'Give 'Em Hell!'.

Ray Bean/STILL MOTIONS.

As *Constellation* was preparing for her decommissioning ceremony, in Britain triumphalism was being scrupulously avoided by the UK Armed Forces, as they gave thanks for their good fortune in war. The presentation of a new Colour to the Fleet by the Queen was, in some ways, more important for what went unsaid, for what was implicit in the bond between Monarch and Navy, than what transpired on the surface. It was a day of reaffirmation for the most illustrious of all the world's fleets, held in the grand arena of Plymouth Sound, a mercurial expanse of water in the broad embrace of Devon to the east and Cornwall to the west. Across the same stretch of water, Sir Francis Drake sailed out in 1588, to help defeat the Spanish Armada that aimed to destroy Queen Elizabeth I, something that Queen Elizabeth II made reference to in her speech aboard the *Ocean*, where the ceremony took place. Looking on from the Hoe, like sentinels, were monuments that marked the other triumphs and tragedies of British naval history, including the towering Naval Memorial that lists the battles and casualties of two world wars. The new Colour symbolized that sacrifice - the true glory of the Royal Navy, which is prepared to pay the ultimate price to be the safeguard of the British nation. That price was paid in Iraq, as the Queen acknowledged aboard *Ocean*, in a speech that was deeply felt, and fully appreciated, by the sailors.

As Lord High Admiral, I take great pride in this link between the Sovereign and the Royal Navy. The special relationship stretches back in some respects to King Alfred, but more directly to the time of King Henry VIII. Every Sovereign since those days has recognized the great responsibility of the Royal Navy as protector of our island home. It is most appropriate that I should be presenting this Colour here in Plymouth Sound, with its long association with the services, and on the 415th anniversary of the defeat of the Spanish Armada. That decisive battle thwarted a potential invasion and secured the vital interests of the nation. Ever since then, our safety on the seas has continued to rest on the broad shoulders of the men and women of the Royal Navy. In recent years, their courage and dedication has been tested many times, and never found wanting. Yet success has its price, and I would like to express my sympathy once again to the families and friends of those who have recently given their lives on active service. As a daughter, wife and mother of naval officers, I want to pay tribute to the families for the support they give to those who serve far from home. I hope this Colour will be symbolic of the Fleet's enduring spirit and devotion to duty in times of stress and danger. I trust it will inspire you, as you face the challenges of an uncertain world. I give it into your care as a token of my admiration and trust in each and every one of you and the Fleet in which you serve.

The new Colour is paraded aboard HMS Ocean, **following its presentation by the Queen.**

Jonathan Eastland/AJAX News & Feature Service.

Taking part in a sailpast during the Colour Presentation were veterans of service in the Gulf - the destroyer *Newcastle*, which had escorted *Invincible* up threat in the northern Gulf in 1999; the minehunter *Walney* that had taken part in Saif Sareea in 2001; the frigate *Portland*, which had enforced the UN embargo on Iraq shortly before the war.

Immediately after the Colour Presentation, *Portland* left for a deployment in support of the war on terrorism, as part of NATO's Standing Naval Force Mediterranean. In command of the British frigate was Gulf veteran Commander

A veteran of service in the Gulf, HMS Newcastle, *turns in front of the new assault ship HMS* Albion, *before passing HMS* Ocean *to allow the destroyer's sailors to salute the Queen.* Nigel Andrews.

Richard Thomas, who said of his ship's mission, as she set sail:

> *Above all, my experience in the first Gulf War taught me what a powerful 'Force for Good' could achieve, when different Nations combined behind a common purpose. Therefore, deploying as part of a multi-national maritime force fighting the global War on Terror, in such a strategically important part of the world is a rare privilege. Even our youngest sailors are consummate professionals and now, knowing the very real threat posed by terrorism, they, together with their shipmates, are keen to make sure HMS* Portland *succeeds in her mission.*

Commenting on where the campaign in the Gulf stood in the history of the Royal Navy was something that was best left to the man who had coordinated its movements across the globe during the war, Commander-in-Chief Fleet, Admiral Sir Jonathon Band.

> *It's possible to look back at Operation Telic and say that it was inevitable, because of Saddam's history of defying the international community and miscalculation, but actually there was a great deal of uncertainty right up until the last moment. The only thing that was clear, was that, if committed to operations, the vast majority of the Royal Navy's capabilities, underpinned by its training, professionalism, and previous experience in the Gulf, would be needed. In the fullness of time history will deliver its final verdict on the overall achievements of Operation Telic by our armed forces and those of the Coalition. However, it is already clear that our exploits have further enhanced the Royal Navy's reputation. We were ready and we won.*

Meanwhile, the overall commander-in-chief of coalition naval forces in the Gulf, Vice Admiral Timothy Keating USN, warned that real and present dangers remained

Still safeguarding the Gulf, the USS Nimitz **turns into the wind for another launch cycle.** US Navy.

and that the story of conflict in the Gulf region was far from over.

...there are still bad guys out there.

As the Admiral spoke, from 5th Fleet Headquarters in Bahrain, the super-carrier USS *Nimitz* was on watch in the Gulf, ready for action as the ultimate sanction against those who sought to attack the USA and its Allies. The gigantic warship turned into the wind, to launch combat aircraft for another patrol high above the Gulf; the world appearing to revolve on her axis.

EPILOGUE

WAR WITHOUT END

Kuwait International Airport, 6 March 1991.

Black rain on my tongue. A cold hand squeezing my heart. The dull, thumping beat of Chinooks on the horizon, as they skim over the cluster bomb-laden runways, their rotors whisking lumpy, poisoned air against an obscene tapestry of flames vomited by an outraged Earth.

'Watch your step,' my US Marine guide advises. 'Guy kicked a coke can, lost a foot.'

'How careless,' I remark, as we skirt a car up on bricks, its wheels gone. The marine shakes his head and cracks a smile: 'Reminds me of the neighbourhood.'

He ever so gently pokes a crumpled computer keyboard lying on the ground, with the barrel of his M16.

'If it wasn't pinned down they took it.'

The background music rises in volume - throaty heavy machine gun fire, mingled with the pop-pop of rifles.

In the corner of the burned out room are shadows so black they ingest the dull, smoggy, light filtering pathetically through the shattered vertical blinds that flap despairingly in the wind.

I whisper: 'What is it?'

He is kneeling on the edge of the blackness and, when he glances up, his eyes are moist saucers. I edge forward and, as a shower of rain stings the blinds, I finally see what ripped his soldier's mask away.

The World that was.
The World this is.
The World that might have been
No more.
The tragic truth is that we blew it.
Threw it away. Lost it on the road to Basra.
An old man switched on his television and saw the gentleman from Baghdad who looked like he had an accident with a deep fat fryer, grinning at him from the bonnet of a blackened looters' charabanc.
Didn't look good.
Bad headlines.

Rein in the dogs of war.

Jesus George H. Bush...you were the one let them off the leash and then you let Saddam off the hook.

Where were the TV cameras when we entered the room of shadows, and found what remained of her?

...after they had done what we did to the Earth?

Raped, ripped apart and burned.

Bits and pieces of charcoal.

Her imagined screams are still whirling around and around inside my head, like a carrier bag full of napalmed souls.

But the old man in the White House saw the fried Iraqi soldier, and let The Beast live.

Me and my Leatherneck pal, we wept in the shadows and felt Satan kiss our brow. And we made our vow to kill him. [1]

Going to war in the Gulf to conclude the unfinished business of 1991 was not something anyone could support easily. War should always be a last resort, but the problem was that most of the international community, through ignorance of the full reality of Saddam's evil intent, or because certain nations had hidden agendas of national self-interest (lucrative oil and other commercial contracts), claimed not to believe it was yet necessary.

By late 2003 the fog of deliberate, or honest, confusion over the Iraq War was so thick that it was almost impossible to give a definitive verdict on one aspect of its justification - the weapons of mass destruction. That, beyond all else, had become so much the focus of the argument that it blinded everyone to the other valid reasons for removing Saddam from power. He had slaughtered his own people in their hundreds of thousands, on one occasion using chemical weapons; he ran an evil, brutal, Stalinist police state in which torture, rape and death were the routine instruments of rule (it was punishable by death to even tell a joke about the great leader); he had invaded two other countries since 1980, causing many more hundreds of thousands of deaths, again using chemical weapons; Saddam threatened to invade Kuwait again just three years after being evicted in 1991; he ran two on-going campaigns of ethnic cleansing (against the Kurds in the north of Iraq and Shia Arabs in the south); he diverted vast sums of money, intended to feed his people and provide medicines for them, into his own bank accounts (indeed medicines for Iraqi hospitals were sold by Saddam's sons on the black markets of the Middle East); he sponsored terrorism abroad by paying thousands of pounds to the families of suicide bombers and had allowed Iraq to be the host of many terrorist organizations; Saddam repeatedly ignored the solemn demands of the United Nations to abide by international law and instead harassed its representatives in Iraq. Of course, although Saddam sat at the centre of it all, his regime was run by many hundreds of thousands of loyal supporters in the extremist, Arab socialist-nationalist, Ba'ath Party, including his two equally evil sons, Uday and Qusay. To allow such a regime to continue in the twenty-first century would have been a crime against humanity and proof that the wider international community was gutless in the face of Evil. So, why should France, Russia and China work so hard to maintain the Saddam regime? The answer is easy: Oil, the control of which has also, of course, been a motivating factor behind the actions of the USA and UK.

Then, there has been the guilt of socialist-liberal society that dominates the West's political and social elites - they are still apologizing for what they perceive as the crimes of their nations' imperial past in the Middle East, and they also hate America for its uncompromising defeat of communism in the Cold War, and its pervasive cultural and economic influence. The self-interest of the nineteenth and twentieth centuries has been replaced with flagellation and an irrational hatred of the USA, which one would imagine had never fought two world wars for the good of mankind. It may be a clumsy giant, but it has a good heart.

At a deeper, more cynical, level Iraq was a potentially rich nation, that would reward its friends once the sanctions were lifted. And that is the whole point: The sanctions that had been initially imposed as part of the strategy to force Saddam out of Kuwait, had remained in place, enforced mainly by naval forces, to try and compel Iraq to honour the ceasefire conditions after the coalition victory in 1991. Any failure to honour UN resolutions since 1991 triggered a resumption of hostilities.

However, as time went on, the sanctions had been used by Saddam as a weapon against his own people - to increase their hatred of the West and decrease their determination, and ability, to fight his regime.

By 2002, it was clear sanctions were destined to be lifted soon and then the Iraqi dictator could have reactivated all of his WMD programmes, which had certainly been kept ticking over, and rebuilt his vast conventional arsenal. Anyone who thinks that the danger posed by Iraq could only be expressed in terms of actual shells and missiles possessing chemical, nuclear or biological capability seriously underestimates the skill of Iraq's formidable weapons scientists. The WMD did exist, but their mysterious disappearance was only the latest ploy by Saddam to hold onto his dream of eventually making Iraq a superpower, able to destroy Israel and control the world's oil. This was not fantasy - the facts spoke for themselves. Of course, Saddam's other great desire was revenge against both the USA and Iran, both of whom he had fought and failed to defeat. And, while there was no definite link between Saddam and Al-Qaeda, it was not beyond the bounds of possibility that the Iraqi leader might see it as worthwhile to assist his enemy's enemy, by providing bin Laden with anthrax or some other chemical, biological or nuclear weapon, for an assymmetric attack on the USA and its allies.

Once sanctions had been lifted, the genie would have been out of the bottle and that was the real reason the USA and UK had to go to war in 2003. It was a just war and history will judge it to have been so. Of course, it did not draw a line under the story of conflict in the Gulf, for there remained the problem of Iran's clerics pursuing nuclear weapons, Islamic extremism threatening to topple the rulers of the Gulf States and Saudi Arabia ripe for revolution. And the war in Iraq went on, with marines and sailors from Britain and the USA putting their lives on the line deep inland, and with coalition naval forces in the Gulf maintaining their watch, to prevent illegal oil smuggling by new profiteers, and contain the residual terrorist threat from those who refused to believe the Saddam regime was gone, or simply hated the West.

> *The only thing necessary for the triumph of evil*
> *is for good men to do nothing.* [2]

At Umm Qasr, Saddam's image is spattered with red paint - symbolizing the blood spilled by his deposed regime. USMC.

Appendix I:

Royal Navy and Royal Marines deaths while on operations
21 March - 30 March, 2003

At around midnight GMT on 21 March, a US Marine Corps CH-46 Sea Knight helicopter crashed south of the Kuwait border with US and UK personnel aboard; there were no survivors. Eight personnel from 3 Commando Brigade died in the accident, along with four US aircrew.

Colour Sergeant John Cecil - Royal Marines, from Plymouth.
Lance Bombardier Llywelyn Karl Evans - 29 Commando Regiment Royal Artillery, from Llandudno.
Captain Philip Stuart Guy - Royal Marines.
Marine Sholto Hedenskog - Royal Marines.
Sergeant Les Hehir - 29 Commando Regiment Royal Artillery.
Operator Mechanic (Communications) Second Class Ian Seymour RN - 148 Commando Battery Royal Artillery.
Warrant Officer Second Class Mark Stratford - Royal Marines.
Major Jason Ward - Royal Marines.

At around 01.30 GMT on 22 March, two Royal Navy Sea King Mk 7 Airborne Early Warning helicopters collided over the northern Arabian Gulf. There were no survivors from the six British and one US crew members aboard. The incident was not the result of enemy action.

Lieutenant Philip D. Green RN - 849 Squadron.
Lieutenant Antony King RN - 849 Squadron, from Helston, Cornwall.
Lieutenant Marc A. Lawrence RN - 849 Squadron.
Lieutenant Philip West RN - 849 Squadron, from Budock Water, Cornwall.
Lieutenant James Williams RN - 849 Squadron, from Falmouth, Cornwall.
Lieutenant Andrew S. Wilson RN - 849 Squadron.

On 30 March, a Royal Marine officer died of natural causes.
Major Steve Ballard - 3 Commando Brigade, Royal Marines.

A Royal Marine was killed in action during fighting in the area of Basra on 30 March.
Marine Christopher R. Maddison - 9 Assault Squadron Royal Marines.

Source: UK MOD

Appendix II:

US Navy deaths while on active service during
Operation Iraqi Freedom
As of 11/10/03

Lt. Thomas Mullen Adams, 27 - La Mesa, Calif., March 22, 2003, Over International Waters.
Petty Officer Third Class Doyle W. Bollinger, Jr., 21 - Poteau, Okla., June 6, 2003, Iraq.
Petty Officer 3rd Class Michael Vann Johnson, Jr., 25 - Little Rock, Ark., March 25, 2003, Iraq.
Lt. Kylan A. Jones-Huffman, 31 - Aptos, Calif., Aug. 21, 2003, Iraq.
Seaman Joshua McIntosh, 22 - Kingman, Ariz., June 26 , 2003, Iraq.
Petty Officer 3rd Class David J. Moreno, 26 - Gering, Neb., July 17, 2003, Iraq.
Lt. Nathan D. White, 30 - Mesa, Ariz., April 2, 2003, Iraq.

Source: US Department of Defense

In mid-September 2003, the decommissioned USS Constellation is towed past Fort Rosecrans National Cemetery in Point Loma, California, on her way to the US Navy's ship graveyard in Bremerton, Washington. US Navy.

Appendix III:

US Marine Corps deaths while on active service during Operation Iraqi Freedom.
As of 11/10/03

Lance Cpl. Brian E. Anderson, 26 - Durham, N.C., April 2, 2003, Iraq.

Chief Warrant Officer 2 Andrew Todd Arnold, 30 - Spring, Texas, April 22, 2003, Iraq.

Maj. Jay Thomas Aubin, 36 - Waterville, Maine, March 21, 2003, Kuwait.

Lance Cpl. Andrew Julian Aviles, 18 - Palm Beach, Fla., April 7, 2003, Iraq.

Pfc. Chad E. Bales, 21 - Coahoma, Texas, April 3, 2003, Iraq.

Capt. Ryan Anthony Beaupre, 30 - Bloomington, Ill., March 21, 2003, Kuwait.

Sgt. Michael E. Bitz, 31 - Oxnard, Calif., March 23, 2003, Iraq.

Lance Cpl. Thomas A. Blair, 24 - Broken Arrow, Okla., March 24, 2003, Iraq.

Gunnery Sgt. Jeffrey E. Bohr, Jr., 39 - Ossian, Iowa, April 10, 2003, Iraq.

Cpl. Travis J. Bradachnall, 21 - Multnomah County, Ore., July 2, 2003, Iraq.

Lance Cpl. Cedric E. Bruns, 22 - Vancouver, Wash., May 9, 2003, Kuwait.

Lance Cpl. Brian Rory Buesing, 20 - Cedar Key, Fla., March 23, 2003, Iraq.

Pfc. Tamario D. Burkett, 21 - Buffalo, N.Y., March 23, 2003, Iraq.

Staff Sgt. James W. Cawley, 41 - Roy, Utah, March 29, 2003, Iraq.

Cpl. Kemaphoom A. Chanawongse, 22 - Waterford, Conn., March 23, 2003, Iraq.

Chief Warrant Officer 2 Robert William Channell Jr., 36 - Tuscaloosa, Ala., April 22, 2003, Iraq.

2nd Lt. Therrel S. Childers, 30 - Harrison, Miss., March 21, 2003, Iraq.

Lance Cpl. Donald J. Cline, Jr., 21, - Sparks, Nev., March 23, 2003, Iraq.

Capt. Aaron J. Contreras, 31 - Sherwood, Ore., March 30, 2003, Iraq.

Pfc. Ryan R. Cox, 19 - Derby, Kan., June 15, 2003.

Cpl. Mark A. Evnin, 21 - Burlington, Vt., April 3, 2003, Iraq.

Capt. Travis A. Ford, 30 - Ogallala, Neb., April 4, 2003, Iraq.

Lance Cpl. David K. Fribley, 26 - Cape Coral, Fla., March 23, 2003, Iraq.

Cpl. Jose A. Garibay, 21 - Costa Mesa, Calif., March 23, 2003, Iraq.

Pfc. Juan Guadalupe Garza Jr., 20 - Temperance, Mich., April 8, 2003, Iraq.

Lance Cpl. Cory Ryan Geurin, 18 - Santee, Calif., July 15, 2003, Iraq.

Pvt. Jonathan L. Gifford, 30 - Macon, Ill., March 23, 2003, Iraq.

Cpl. Armando Ariel Gonzalez, 25 - Hileah, Fla., April 14, 2003, Iraq.

Cpl. Jesus A. Gonzalez, 22 - Indio, Calif., April 12, 2003, Iraq.

Cpl. Jorge A. Gonzalez, 20 - El Monte, Calif., March 23, 2003, Iraq.

Cpl. Bernard G. Gooden, 22 - Mt. Vernon, N.Y., April 4, 2003, Iraq.

Pfc. Christian D. Gurtner, 19 - Ohio City, Ohio, April 2, 2003, Iraq.

Lance Cpl. Jose Gutierrez, 22 - Los Angeles, Calif., March 21, 2003, Iraq.

Sgt. Nicholas M. Hodson, 22 - Smithville, Mo., March 22, 2003, Iraq.

Pvt. Nolen R. Hutchings, 19 - Boiling Springs, S.C., March 23, 2003, Iraq.

Cpl. Evan T. James, 20 - LaHarpe, Ill., March 24, 2003, Iraq.

Staff Sgt. Phillip A. Jordan, 42 - Brazoria, Texas, March 23, 2003, Iraq.

Cpl. Brian Matthew Kennedy, 25 - Houston, Texas, March 21, 2003, Kuwait.
Lance Cpl. Nicholas Brian Kleiboeker, 19 - Irvington, Ill., May 13, 2003, Iraq.
Sgt. Bradley S. Korthaus, 28 - Scott, Iowa, March 24, Iraq.
Lance Cpl. Jakub Henryk Kowalik, 21 - Schaumburg, Ill, May 12, 2003, Iraq.
Sgt. Michael V. Lalush, 23 - Troutville, Va., March 30, 2003, Iraq.
Lance Cpl. Alan Dinh Lam, 19 - Snow Camp, N.C., April 22, 2003, Iraq.
Sgt. Jonathan W. Lambert, 28 - Newsite, Miss., June 1, 2003, Landstuhl, Germany
(of injuries sustained in Iraq).
Capt. Andrew David LaMont, 31 - Eureka, Calif., May 19, 2003, Iraq.
Lance Cpl. Gregory E. MacDonald, 29 - Washington, D.C., June 25, 2003, Iraq.
Lance Cpl. Joseph B. Maglione, 22 - Lansdale, Pa., April 1, 2003, Kuwait.
Cpl. Douglas Jose Marencoreyes, 28 - Chino, Calif., May 18, 2003, Iraq.
Pfc. Francisco A. MartinezFlores, 21 - Los Angeles, Calif., March 25, 2003, Iraq.
Staff Sgt. Donald C. May, Jr., 31 - Richmond, Va., March 25, 2003, Iraq.
Sgt. Brian D. McGinnis, 23 - St. George, Del., March 30, 2003, Iraq.
1st Lt. Brian M. McPhillips, 25 - Pembroke, Mass., April 4, 2003, Iraq.
Cpl. Jesus Martin Antonio Medellin, 21 - Fort Worth, Texas, April 7, 2003, Iraq.
Gunnery Sgt. Joseph Menusa, 33 - San Jose, Calif., March 27, 2003, Iraq.
Cpl. Jason David Mileo, 20 - Centreville, Md., April 14, 2003, Iraq.
Lance Cpl. Jason William Moore, 21 - San Marcos, Calif., May 19, 2003, Iraq.
Major Kevin G. Nave, 36 - Union Lake, Mich., March 26, 2003, Iraq.
Cpl. Patrick R. Nixon, 21 - Nashville, Tenn., March 23, 2003, Iraq.

During a memorial ceremony on 10 October 2003, held at Camp Pendleton, California, thirty-nine inverted rifles, helmets and boots symbolize the marines and sailors of the 1st Marine Division who gave their lives during Operation Iraqi Freedom. USMC.

Lance Cpl. Patrick T. O'Day, 20 - Santa Rosa, Calif., March 25, 2003, Iraq.

Lance Cpl. Eric James Orlowski, 25 - Buffalo, N.Y., March 22, 2003, Iraq.

Lance Cpl. David Edward Owens Jr., 20 - Winchester, Va., April 12, 2003, Iraq.

Sgt. Fernando Padilla-Ramirez, 26 - Yuma, Ariz., March 28, 2003, Iraq.

1st Lt. Frederick E. Pokorney Jr., 31 - Tonopah, Nev., March 23, 2003, Iraq.

Sgt. Brendon C. Reiss, 23 - Casper, Wyo., March 23, 2003, Iraq.

Sgt. Duane R. Rios, 25 - Hammond, Ind., April 4, 2003, Iraq.

Pfc. Jose Franci Gonzalez Rodriguez, 19 - Norwalk, Calif., May 12, 2003, Iraq.

Cpl. Robert M. Rodriguez, 21 - Queens, N.Y., March 28, 2003, Iraq.

Cpl. Randal Kent Rosacker, 21 - San Diego, Calif., March 23, 2003, Iraq.

1st Lt. Timothy Louis Ryan, 30 - Aurora, Ill., May 19, 2003, Iraq.

Capt. Benjamin W. Sammis, 29 - Rehobeth, Mass., April 4, 2003, Iraq.

Cpl. Erik H. Silva, 22 - Chula Vista, Calif., April 3, 2003, Iraq.

Lance Cpl. Thomas J. Slocum, 22 - Thornton, Colo., March 23, 2003, Iraq.

1st Sgt. Edward Smith, 38 - Chicago, Ill., April 5, 2003, Qatar.

Lance Cpl. Matthew R. Smith, 20 - Anderson, Ind., May 10, 2003, Kuwait.

Sgt. Kirk Allen Straseskie, 23 - Beaver Dam, Wis., May 19, 2003, Iraq.

Lance Cpl. Jesus A. Suarez Del Solar, 20 - Escondido, Calif., March 27, 2003, Iraq.

Staff Sgt. Riayan A. Tejeda, 26 - New York, N.Y., April 11, 2003, Iraq.

Lance Cpl. Jason Andrew Tetrault, 20 - Moreno Valley, Calif., July 9, 2003, Kuwait.

Staff Sgt. Kendall Damon Waters-Bey, 29 - Baltimore, Md., March 21, 2003, Kuwait.

Staff Sgt. Aaron Dean White, 27 - of Shawnee, Okla., May 19, 2003, Iraq.

Lance Cpl. William W. White, 24 - Brooklyn, N.Y., March 29, 2003, Iraq.

Lance Cpl. Michael J. Williams, 31 - Yuma, Ariz., March 23, 2003, Iraq.

Source: US Department of Defense.

NOTES
'STRIKE FROM THE SEA'

PROLOGUE
IF NOT GADDAFI, THEN WHO?
1) Interview with the author, published *Somerset County Gazette*, 25 May 1990.
2) Stephen Howarth, *To Shining Sea*.
3) Jack Sweetman, *American Naval History*.
4) ibid.
5) Interview with the author, published *Somerset County Gazette*, 25 May 1990.
6) ibid.
7) ibid.

CHAPTER ONE
...THE HARDER THEY FALL
1) Robin Neillands, *A Fighting Retreat*.
2) Bruce W. Watson, *World's Navies*.
3) *Evening Herald*, Plymouth, 1 November 1956.
4) *HMS Ocean Commissioning Book*, 1998.
5) Julian Thompson, *The Royal Marines*.
6) H.P. Willmott, *War in Peace*.
7) Robin Neillands, op. cit.
8) Max Arthur, *The Royal Navy 1939 to the Present*.
9) John Winton, *Fly Navy*.
10) *Evening Herald*, Plymouth, 27 June 1951.
11) *Evening Herald*, Plymouth, 10 July 1951.
12) David Phillipson, *Roll on the Rodney!*
13) ibid.
14) ibid.
15) Dilip Hiro, *Desert Shield to Desert Storm*.
16) *Evening Herald*, Plymouth, 1 July 1961.
17) *Evening Herald*, Plymouth, 5 July 1961.
18) Anthony J. Watts, *The Royal Navy, An Illustrated History*.
19) Mike Dewar, *Brush Fire Wars*.
20) ibid.
21) *Evening Herald*, Plymouth, 5 July 1961.
22) *Evening Herald*, Plymouth, 14 July 1961.

CHAPTER TWO
PUTTING DOWN THE BURDEN
1) *Evening Herald*, Plymouth, 21 September 1965.

2) *The Navy*, Vol. 70, 1965.
3) *Oxford Illustrated History of the Royal Navy*.
4) ibid.
5) Kevin M. Pollack, *The Threatening Storm*.
6) Dan van der Vat, *Standard of Power*.
7) Dr. Edward J. Marolda, *The United States Navy and the Persian Gulf*, USNHC.

CHAPTER THREE
THE PRESSURE COOKER
1) Michael Orr, *War in Peace*.
2) Dr Edward J. Marolda, op. cit.
3) Lawrence Sondhaus, *Navies of Europe 1815 - 2002*.
4) Nathan Miller, *The U.S. Navy*.
5) James Cable, *Gunboat Diplomacy 1919 - 1979*.
6) Nathan Miller, op. cit.
7) Admiral Sandy Woodward, *One Hundred Days*.
8) US Department of Defense (US DoD).
9) Jack Sweetman, op. cit.
10) ibid.
11) Jeffrey L. Levinson and Randy L. Edwards, *Missile Inbound*.
12) Jack Sweetman, op. cit.
13) *Evening Herald*, Plymouth, 20 May 1987.
14) Jack Sweetman, op. cit.
15) Nathan Miller, op. cit.
16) *Evening Herald*, Plymouth, 22 July 1987.
17) *Evening Herald*, Plymouth, 21 July 1987.
18) *Evening Herald*, Plymouth, 24 July 1987.
19) ibid.
20) ibid.
21) *Evening Herald*, Plymouth, 3 August 1987.
22) *Evening Herald*, Plymouth, 4 August 1987.
23) *Evening Herald*, Plymouth, 8 August 1987.
24) *Evening Herald*, Plymouth, 11 August 1987.
25) *Evening Herald*, Plymouth, 12 August 1987.
26) *WARSHIPS IFR*, Dec 2000/Jan 2001.
27) Jack Sweetman, op. cit.
28) ibid.
29) *Evening Herald*, Plymouth,

18 April 1988.
30) Jack Sweetman, op. cit.
31) Nathan Miller, op. cit.
32) Charles Jaco, *The Gulf War*.
33) Captain Doug Littlejohns, interview with author.
34) Jack Sweetman, op. cit.
35) Mike Cox, *Warships Supplement 103, Winter 1990 - Armilla Patrol - The Gulf Patrol*, World Ship Society.
36) Lieutenant Commander Jeremy Stocker, interview with author.
37) Dr. Edward J. Marolda, op. cit.

CHAPTER FOUR
ARABIAN BLITZKRIEG
1) *Evening Herald*, Plymouth, 8 August 1990.
2) ibid.
3) ibid.
4) Dr Jeremy Stocker, *WARSHIPS IFR*, August/September 2001.
5) Charles Jaco, *The Gulf War*.
6) *TIME International*, 27 August 1990.
7) *The Middle East magazine*, October 1990.
8) US Department of Agriculture.
9) *The Middle East magazine*, October 1990.
10) A defence source in the USA, quoted in *NEWSWEEK*, 27 August 1990.
11) *New York Times*, 31 August 1990.
12) *NEWSWEEK*, 8 October 1990.
13) Captain Andrew Gordon Lennox, quoted in the *Evening Herald*, Plymouth 26 October 1990.
14) Edward J. Marolda and Robert J. Schneller Jr., *Shield And Sword*.
15) *Evening Herald*, Plymouth, 26 October 1990.
16) *NEWSWEEK*, 8 October 1990.
17) Interview with the author, *Evening Herald*, 20 October 1990.
18) *Gulf News*, 17 October 1990.
19) Edward J. Marolda and Robert J. Schneller Jr., op. cit.
20) ibid.
21) *NEWSWEEK*, 3 December 1990.

CHAPTER FIVE
MOVING IN HARM'S WAY
1) Interview with the author, *Evening Herald*, Plymouth, 7 January 1991.
2) Interview with the author, *Evening*

Herald, Plymouth, 8 January 1991.
3) Report by the author, *Evening Herald*, 10 January 1991.
4) Interview with the author, *Evening Herald*, Plymouth, 11 January 1991.
5) ibid.
6) ibid.
7) Captain Chris Craig, *Call For Fire*.
8) Max Arthur, *The Royal Navy 1939 to the Present Day*.
9) Interview with the author, *Evening Herald*, Plymouth, 11 January 1991.
10) *Evening Herald*, Plymouth, 10 January 1991.
11) Report by the author, *Evening Herald*, 10 January 1991.
12) Captain Chris Craig, op. cit.
13) Interview with the author, *Evening Herald*, Plymouth, 12 January 1991.
14) ibid.
15) *Gulf News*, 6 January 1991.
16) *Evening Herald*, Plymouth, 11 January 1991.
17) ibid.
18) Captain Chris Craig, op. cit.
19) Rick Atkinson, *Crusade*.

CHAPTER SIX
APOCALYPSE THEN
1) Colin Powell, *A Soldier's Way*.
2) Rick Atkinson, op. cit.
3) Edward J. Marolda and Robert J. Schneller Jr., op. cit.
4) Rick Atkinson, op. cit.
5) ibid.
6) *Evening Herald*, Plymouth, 17 January 1991.
7) Captain Chris Craig, op. cit.
8) *Evening Herald*, Plymouth, 17 January 1991.
9) *Newsweek*, 18 February 1991.
10) *Los Angeles Times*, 19 January 1991.
11) Edward J. Marolda and Robert J. Schneller Jr., op. cit.
12) *Newsweek*, 4 February 1991.
13) *Ark Royal - A Flagship for the 21st Century*.
14) ibid.
15) Edward J. Marolda and Robert J. Schneller Jr., op. cit.
16) ibid.
17) *TIME International*, 4 February 1991.
18) Edward J. Marolda and Robert J. Schneller Jr., op. cit.
19) *Evening Herald*, Plymouth, 18 January 1991.

20) Max Arthur, op. cit.
21) ibid.
22) ibid.
23) ibid.
24) ibid.
25) *The Independent*, 30 January 1991.
26) ibid
27) Edward J. Marolda and Robert J. Schneller Jr., op. cit.
28) In conversation with the author, June 2001.
29) *Sunday Telegraph*, 3 February 1991.
30) *Los Angeles Times*, 6 February 1991.
31) *Los Angeles Times*, 11 February 1991.
32) *Los Angeles Times*, Witness to War.
33) Edward J. Marolda and Robert J. Schneller Jr., op. cit.
34) ibid.
35) ibid.
36) Captain Chris Craig, op. cit.
37) Edward J. Marolda and Robert J. Schneller Jr., op. cit.
38) *Evening Herald*, Plymouth, 15 February 1991.
39) ibid.
40) ibid.
41) *Los Angeles Times*, 15 February 1991.
42) Edward J. Marolda and Robert J. Schneller Jr., op. cit.
43) ibid.
44) Captain Chris Craig, op. cit.
45) *Los Angeles Times*, 15 February 1991.
46) Edward J. Marolda and Robert J. Schneller Jr., op. cit.
47) *Los Angeles Times*, 21 February 1991.
48) Interview with the author, *Evening Herald*, Plymouth 15 July 1991.
49) Edward J. Marolda and Robert J. Schneller Jr., op. cit.
50) Interview with the author, *Evening Herald*, Plymouth 29 June 1991.
51) *Evening Herald*, Plymouth, 25 February 1991.
52) Edward J. Marolda and Robert J. Schneller Jr., op. cit.
53) Interview with the author, *Evening Herald*, Plymouth, 10 April 1991.
54) Max Arthur, op. cit.
55) Edward J. Marolda and Robert J. Schneller Jr., op. cit.
56) Interview with the author, *Evening Herald*, Plymouth, 10 April 1991.
57) Edward J. Marolda and Robert J.

Schneller Jr., op. cit.
58) Arnold Meisner, *Desert Storm Sea War*.
59) *Los Angeles Times*, 27 February 1991.
60) Edward J. Marolda and Robert J. Schneller Jr., op. cit.
61) General H. Norman Schwarzkopf, *It Doesn't Take a Hero*.
62) Interview with the author, *Evening Herald*, Plymouth, 29 June 1991.
63) Interview with the author, *Evening Herald*, Plymouth, 8 March 1991.
64) Article by the author, *Evening Herald*, Plymouth 7 March 1991.
65) Article by the author, *Evening Herald*, Plymouth, 20 March 1991.
66) Taken from an article by the author, *Evening Herald*, Plymouth, 7 March 1991.
67) ibid.
68) *Sunday Telegraph*, 24 March 1991.
69) ibid.
70) Norman Friedman, *Desert Victory*.
71) ibid.
72) Interview with the author, *Evening Herald*, Plymouth, 6 May 1991.
73) Interview with the author, *Evening Herald*, Plymouth, 10 April 1991.
74) Interview with the author, *Evening Herald*, Plymouth, 15 July 1991.
75) Interview with the author, *Evening Herald*, Plymouth, 29 June 1991.

CHAPTER SEVEN
KEEPING SADDAM CAGED
1) Interview with the author, *WARSHIPS IFR*, Spring 1999.
2) *Newsweek*, 20 January 1992.
3) ibid.
4) ibid.
5) Taken from a feature by the author, *Evening Herald*, Plymouth, 23 May 1992.
6) Interview with the author, *Evening Herald*, Plymouth, published 19 May 1992.
7) Anthony Tucker-Jones, *WARSHIPS IFR*, June 2003.
8) HMS *Southampton, A Deployment*.
9) *Navy News*, December 1997.
10) ibid.
11) *BROADSHEET* 1998/9.
12) ibid.
13) ibid.
14) ibid.
15) ibid.
16) *The Independent*, 21 December

1998.

17) Speaking on the BBC TV's *Breakfast With Frost,* 20 December 1998.

18) Interview with the author, *WARSHIPS IFR,* Spring 1999.

19) ibid.

20) Extract from article by author, *WARSHIPS IFR,* Spring 1999.

21) Interview with the author, *WARSHIPS IFR,* Spring 1999.

CHAPTER EIGHT
NO TOUGHER FIGHT

1) Sgt Matthew T. Olivolo, eyewitness account, published by US Marine Corps to mark second anniversary of 9-11 attacks on USA, Sept 2003.

2) Peter L. Bergen, Holy War, Inc.

3) ibid.

4) Quoted in 'Small Arms Protect Bigger Ships', article by Chief Petty Officer Bill Johnston-Miles, US Navy, published in *Surface Warfare* magazine.

5) US Navy admiral quoted in *WARSHIPS IFR,* Dec 2000/Jan 2001.

6) *WARSHIPS IFR,* Dec 2000/Jan 2001.

7) ibid.

8) ibid.

9) ibid.

10) Peter L. Bergen, op. cit.

11) BBC News correspondent Fergal Keane, *The Battle For Iraq.*

12) Bob Woodward, *Bush at War.*

13) Interviewed in *WARSHIPS IFR,* Oct/Nov 2001.

14) *WARSHIPS IFR,* Oct/Nov 2001.

15) Interviewed by the author, *WARSHIPS IFR,* Dec/Jan 2001/02.

16) ibid.

17) *Taken from the First Sea Lord's introduction, BROADSHEET 2001/2002.*

18) *The Times,* 20 September, 2001.

19) Interviewed by the author, *WARSHIPS IFR,* Dec/Jan 2001/02.

20) Interviewed by the author, *WARSHIPS IFR,* April/May 2002.

CHAPTER NINE
INTO THE GATHERING STORM

1) *The Age/Guardian,* web news report.

2) *WARSHIPS IFR,* February 2003.

3) Taken from press release by Chief Journalist William Polson, *USS*

Tarawa Public Affairs.

4) *WARSHIPS IFR,* March 2003.

5) Taken from an article by Lucy Halsall, of British Forces Cyprus, published *WARSHIPS IFR,* March 2003.

6) US Navy *News Stand.*

7) Commodore Richard Ibbotson RN, interview on SNFL with Guy Toremans, for *WARSHIPS IFR,* October 2003.

8) Anthony Tucker-Jones, writing in *WARSHIPS IFR,* June 2003.

9) *WARSHIPS IFR,* May 2003.

10) Writing in *WARSHIPS IFR,* December 02/January 03.

11) First Sea Lord in an interview with the author, published *WARSHIPS IFR,* March 2003.

12) Interview with Lucy Halsall, of British Forces Cyprus, published *WARSHIPS IFR* May 2003.

13) ibid.

14) Peter Hore, writing in *WARSHIPS IFR,* June 2003.

15) Account of HMS *Chatham's* part in Operation Telic, published on the ship's web site, 9 April 2003.

CHAPTER TEN
KICKING DOWN THE DOOR

1) Press release by Michael Brown, Carrier Group 5 Public Affairs, aboard USS *Cowpens,* 20 March 2003.

2) *The Daily Telegraph, War on Saddam.*

3) Interview with the author, via satellite phone, 20 March 2003.

4) *BBC News* web site report.

5) Brigadier Jim Dutton, in interview with the author.

6) Pooled dispatch from Tom Newton Dunn of the *Daily Mirror,* 22 March 2003.

7) First Sea Lord's post-war media briefing.

8) Account of HMS *Chatham's* part in Operation Telic, published on the ship's web site, 9 April 2003.

9) Brigadier Jim Dutton, in interview with the author.

10) First Sea Lord's post-war media briefing.

11) Report for US Congress, *Iraq War: Defense Program Implications for Congress,* 4 June 2003.

12) Post-war briefing by Captain Peter Jones, RAN.

13) ibid.

14) Australian Defence Ministry media briefing, 22 March 2003.

15) Post-war briefing by Captain Peter Jones, RAN.

16) Press release from UK Maritime Component Commander, 22 March 2003.

17) Account of HMS *Marlborough's* part in Operation Telic, published on the ship's web site, 9 April 2003.

18) Account of HMS *Chatham's* part in Operation Telic, published on the ship's web site, 9 April 2003.

19) Brigadier Jim Dutton, in interview with the author.

20) Press release by Journalist 1st Class April Gorenflo, USS *Harry S. Truman* Public Affairs, 26 March 2003.

21) Report for US Congress, *Iraq War: Defense Program Implications for Congress,* 4 June 2003.

22) Press release by Journalist 1st Class Sonya Ansarov, USS *Bataan* Public Affairs, 24 March 2003.

23) Press release by Chief Journalist William Polson, USS *Tarawa* Public Affairs, 24 March 2003.

24) Reuters web report, 24 March 2003.

25) ibid.

26) An 847 NAS aviator interviewed by the author, HMS *Ocean,* 27 May 2003.

27) Brigadier Jim Dutton.

28) Report for US Congress, *Iraq War: Defense Program Implications for Congress,* 4 June 2003.

29) Figures taken from *Operation IRAQI FREEDOM - By The Numbers,* USCENTAF, 30 April 2003.

30) Press release by Journalist 3rd Class Heather Stanley, USS *Abraham Lincoln* Public Affairs, 16 April 2003.

31) Brigadier Jim Dutton.

EPILOGUE
WAR WITHOUT END

1) Iain Ballantyne, *The World That Was.*

2) Edmund Burke, 1729 - 1797.

BIBLIOGRAPHY

al-Khalil, Samir, *Republic of Fear*, Hutchinson Radius, 1990

Arthur, Max, *The Royal Navy, 1939 To The Present Day*, Hodder & Stoughton, 1997

Ballantyne, Iain, H.M.S. *London*, Pen & Sword Books, 2003

- ed., Warships IFR Guide to the *Royal Navy* 2003, HPC Publishing, 2002

Barnett, Correlli, *The Lost Victory*, Pan 1996

Beck, Sara, and Downing, Malcolm, ed., *The Battle For Iraq*, BBC News, 2003

Bergen, Peter L., *Holy War Inc.*, Phoenix, 2002

Bishop, Chris, ed., *The Encyclopedia of World Sea Power*, Guild Publishing, 1988

Blackman, Raymond V.B.,*The World's Warships*, Macdonald & Co, 1969

Bonds, Ray, *The World's Elite Forces*, Salamander, 1987

The Modern US War Machine, Salamander, 1987

Bowman, Martin W., *Shades of Blue*, Airlife, 1999

Boyd, Jim, executed., *Saddam's Iraq*, Reuters Prentice Hall, 2003

Brown, Ben and Shukman, David, *All Necessary Means*, BBC Books, 1991

Brownstone, David and Franck, Irene, *Timelines of War*, Little, Brown, 1994

Butler, Richard, *Saddam Defiant*, Phoenix, 2000

Cable, James, *Gunboat Diplomacy 1919 - 1991*, Macmillan Press, 1994

Chant, Christopher, *Naval Forces of the World*, Collins Willow, 1984

Chesneau, Roger, *Aircraft Carriers of the World 1914 to the Present*, Brockhampton Press, 1998

- ed., Conway's *All the World's Fighting Ships 1922 - 1946*, Conway Maritime Press, 1995

Coughlin, Con, *Saddam, The Secret Life*, Pan, 2003

Craig, Captain Chris, *Call For Fire*, John Murray, 1995

David, Peter, *Triumph in the Desert*, 1991

de la Billiere, General Sir Peter, *Storm Command*, HarperCollins, 1992

Dewar, Michael, *Brush Fire Wars*, Robert Hale Limited, 1990

Dunn, Ralph, ed., *The Royal Navy Handbook*, Conway Maritime Press, 2003

Elliott, T.D., *A Gulf Record*, 1991

Faulkner, Keith, *Jane's Warship Recognition Guide*, HarperCollins, 1999

Friedman, Norman, *Desert Victory*, Naval Institute Press, 1992

Gardiner, Robert, ed., *Navies in the Nuclear Age*, Conway, 1993

- ed., Conway's *All the World's Fighting Ships 1947 - 1982, Part I - The Western Powers*, Conway Maritime Press, 1983

Hearn, Chester G., *An Illustrated History of the United States Marine Corps*, Salamander Books, 2002

Hill, Rear Admiral J.R., ed., *The Oxford Illustrated History of the Royal Navy*, Oxford University Press, 1995

Hindley, Geoffrey, *The Crusades*, Constable & Robinson, 2003

Hiro, Dilip, *Desert Shield to Desert Storm*, PALADIN, 1992

The Longest War, PALADIN, 1990

Holmes, Richard, ed., *The Oxford Companion to Military History*, Oxford University Press, 2001

Howarth, Stephen, *To Shining Sea - A History of the United States Navy 1775 - 1991*, Weidenfeld & Nicolson, 1991

Inskip, Ian, *Ordeal by Exocet*, Chatham, 2002

Ireland, Bernard and Grove, Eric, *Jane's War at Sea 1897 - 1997*, HarperCollins, 1997

Jaco, Charles, *The Complete Idiot's Guide To The Gulf War*, Alpha/Pearson Education, 2002

Keegan, John, and Thompson, Sir Robert, con eds., *War in Peace*, Harmony Books, 1985

Levinson, Jeffrey L. and Edwards, Randy L., *Missile Inbound*, United States Naval Institute Press, 1997

Ladd, James D., *By Land, By Sea*, HarperCollins, 1998

Li, Simon, text ed., *Witness to War*, Los Angeles Times, 1991

Manning, Charles, *Fly Navy*, Leo Cooper, 2000

Marolda, Edward J. and Schneller, Robert J. Jr., *Shield and Sword, The United States Navy and the Persian Gulf War*, Naval Institute Press, 2001

Marriott, Leo, *Royal Navy Frigates 1945 - 1983*, Ian Allan, 1983

- *Type 22*, Ian Allan, 1986

Meisner, Arnold, *Desert Storm Sea War*, Motorbooks, 1991

Mersky, Peter B., *US Marine Corps Aviation*, The Nautical & Aviation Publishing Company of America, 1997

Miller, David, ed., *Modern American Weapons*, Salamander, 2002

- *Conflict Iraq*, MBI, 2003.

Miller, Nathan, *The U.S. Navy*, Naval Institute Press, 1997

Moore, Edwin, *Dictionary of Modern Biography*, Geddes & Grosset, 1992

Moran, Daniel, *Wars of National Liberation*, Cassell, 2001

Neillands, Robin, *A Fighting Retreat*, Coronet, 1997

Parrack, Richard, text ed., *The Daily Telegraph War on Saddam*, Constable & Robinson, 2003

Phillipson, David, *Roll on the Rodney!*, Sutton, 1999

Pollack, Kenneth M., *The Threatening Storm*, Random House, 2002

Polmar, Norman, *The Naval Institute Guide to the Ships and Aircraft of the U.S. Fleet*, Naval Institute Press, 1993

Powell, Colin with Persico, Joseph E., *A Soldier's Way*, Hutchinson, 1995

Preston, Antony, *The Royal Navy Submarine Service*, Conway, 2001

Quarrie, Bruce, *The World's Elite Forces*, Octopus, 1985

Rayner, Caroline, ed., *Encyclopedic World Atlas*, George Philip, 1992

Schwarzkopf, General H. Norman with Peter Petre, *It Doesn't Take a Hero*, Bantam Press, 1992

Smith, Gordon, *The War at Sea - Royal & Dominion Navy Actions in World War Two*, Ian Allan, 1989

Sondhaus, Lawrence, *Navies of Europe*, Longman, 2002

Sweetman, Jack, *American Naval History*, Naval Institute Press, 2002

Thompson, Julian, *The Royal Marines*, Pan, 2001

Townson, Duncan, *Dictionary of Modern History 1789 - 1945*, Penguin, 1995

van der Vat, Dan, *Standard of Power*, Hutchinson, 2000

Walker, Martin, *The Cold War*, Vintage, 1994

Watson, Bruce W., *The Changing Face of the World's Navies 1945 to Present*, Brassey's (US), 1991

Watts, Anthony, J., *The Royal Navy, An Illustrated History*, Arms & Armour, 1994

Wheal, Elizabeth-Anne and Pope, Stephen, *The MacMillan Dictionary of the Second World War*, Macmillan, 1995

Witherow, John and Sullivan, Aidan, *War in the Gulf*, Sidgwick & Jackson 1991

Woodward, Bob, *Bush at War*, Pocket Books, 2003

Woodward, Admiral Sandy with Robinson, Patrick, *One Hundred Days*, HarperCollins, 1992

MISCELLANEOUS SOURCES

Ark Royal, A Flagship for the 21st Century.

BBC TV, *Breakfast With Frost*, 20 December 1998

Marolda, Dr Edward J., *The United States Navy and the Persian Gulf*, US Naval Historical Center

HMS *Ocean* Commissioning Book 1998.

Operation IRAQI FREEDOM - By The Numbers, USCENTAF, 30 April 2003.

Report for US Congress, *Iraq War: Defense Program Implications for Congress*, 4 June 2003.

Royal Navy BROADSHEET, 1998/1999, 2001/2002

HMS *Southampton*, A deployment 1996/1997

Newspapers

Daily Mirror, 14 August 1956

Evening Herald, Plymouth, 27 June 1951, 10 July 1951, 1 November 1956, 1 July 1961, 5 July 1961, 14 July 1961, 21 September 1965, 20 July 1967, 20 May 1987, 21 July 1987, 22 July 1987, 24 July 1987, 3 August 1987, 4 August 1987, 8 August 1987, 11 August 1987, 12 August 1987, 18 April 1988, 4 August 1990, 8 August 1990, 20 October 1990, 26 October 1990, 7 January 1991, 8 January 1991, 10 January 1991, 11 January 1991, 12 January 1991, 17 January, 1991, 18 January 1991, 15 February 1991, 25 February 1991, 7 March 1991, 8 March 1991,

20 March 1991, 10 April 1991, 6 May 1991, 29 June 1991, 15 July 1991, 7 May 1992, 11 May 1992, 19 May 1992, 23 May 1992, 28 May 1992, 27 July 1992, 8 October 1994, 10 October 1994, 6 January 1995

Gulf News, 16 October 1990, 17 October 1990, 6 January 1991, 11 January 1991

The Independent, 30 January 1991, 21 December 1998

Khalej Times, 19 October 1990, 9 January 1991

Los Angeles Times, 19 January 1991, 6 February 1991, 11 February 1991, 15 February 1991, 21 February 1991, 27 February 1991

New York Times, 31 August 1990

Somerset County Gazette, 25 May 1990

Sunday Telegraph, 3 February 1991, 24 March 1991

The Times, 20 September 2001

Western Morning News, 14 October 1994

Pooled News Reports

Taken from:
Daily Mail, Daily Mirror, Daily Telegraph.
Between 21 March - 9 April 2003

Agency Reports

Reuters, Sandstorms could be a big challenge, 24 March (web report).

Magazines & Other Publications

The Middle East, October 1990

The Navy, Vol. 70, 1965

Navy News, December 1997

Newsweek, 27 August 1990, 8 October 1990, 3 December 1990, 4 February 1991, 18 February 1991, 20 January 1992

Time International, 27 August 1990, 4 February 1991

WARSHIPS IFR, Spring 1999, Dec 2000/Jan 2001, Oct/Nov 2001, Dec 2001/Jan 2002, February 2003, March 2003, May 2003, June 2003

Unpublished Documents

Ballantyne, Iain, *The World That Was*, a novel.

World Ship Society

Warships Supplements, Autumn 1988, Winter 1990, Spring 1991

WEB SITES AND INTERNET SUBSCRIBER NEWS SERVICES

The Age
www.theage.com.au

BBC News
www.news.bbc.co.uk

CENTCOM
www.centcom.mil

Defend America
www.defendamerica.mil

Department of Defence, Australia
www.defence.gov.au/index.htm

GlobalSecurity.org
www.globalsecurity.org

Royal Navy
www.royal-navy.mod.uk

UK Ministry of Defence
www.operations.mod.uk

US Department of Agriculture
www.usda.gov

US Department of Defense
www.defenselink.mil

US Marine Corps
www.usmc.mil

US Naval Historical Center
www.history.navy.mil

USNAVCENT
www.cusnc.navy.mil

US Navy News Stand
www.news.navy.mil

US Department of State
www.state.gov

NATO Standing Naval Force Atlantic
www.eastlant.nato.int

INDEX